THE PENTAGON

AND THE CITIES

THE PENTAGON

AND THE CITIES

Edited by

Andrew Kirby

Volume 40, URBAN AFFAIRS ANNUAL REVIEWS

SAGE PUBLICATIONS
The International Professional Publishers
Newbury Park   London   New Delhi

For information address:

SAGE Publications, Inc.
2455 Teller Road
Newbury Park, California 91320

SAGE Publications Ltd.
6 Bonhill Street
London EC2A 4PU
United Kingdom

SAGE Publications India Pvt. Ltd.
M-32 Market
Greater Kailash I
New Delhi 110 048 India

Printed in the United States of America

Library of Congress Cataloging-in-Publication Data

Main entry under title:

The Pentagon and the cities / edited by Andrew Martin Kirby.
  p. cm.—(Urban affairs annual reviews; v. 40.)
 Includes bibliographical references and index.
 ISBN 0-8039-3845-4. —ISBN 0-8039-3846-2 (pbk.)
 1. United States—Defenses—Economic aspects. 2. United States—Economic conditions—1981—Regional disparities. 3. Economic conversion—United States. I. Kirby, Andrew. II. Series.
HT108.U7vol. 40
[HC110.D4]
307.76 s—dc20   91-31796
[330.973′0928]   CIP

FIRST PRINTING, 1992

Sage Production Editor: Judith L. Hunter

Contents

Preface

THIS BOOK DEALS WITH important phenomena—the impacts of military spending on local economies. This is a complex issue, as is indicated by this volume's own history. When a publication was first suggested by Susan Clarke in 1988, the "evil empire" was still a strategic reality for most Americans. Then, as researchers were approached to contribute to the volume and as they worked on their chapters, peace broke out between East and West and unprecedented political changes took place throughout Eastern Europe. For a while, during the editing of the manuscripts, it appeared that the volume would be a recollection of the role of heavy military spending in urban development during the Cold War.

Instead, peace was again replaced by war. As I write this introduction in February 1991, allied service personnel and a full array of complex weaponry are engaged in the Middle East. Once again, there is an emphasis upon military investment; already, the evaluation of planes, tanks, and missiles has begun, with an eye to the replacement of used ordnance and the production of new weapons. This in turn has implications for local economies. For instance, plans to phase out the ungainly A-10 aircraft—normally based in Arizona—may be delayed by its success in the Gulf; this development was not lost on a local newspaper, which noted on only the fourth day of the war, "Tucson may share in A-10's success."

The events of the last two years emphasize two important issues. The first is that the military continues to be of great fiscal importance within the United States and is likely to remain so for years to come. It still employs large numbers of women and men and continues to offer the main route out of educational disadvantage and unemployment for many. It also continues to consume vast amounts of materiel. Moreover, this equipment is continually upgraded and changed to meet new strategic circumstances. The war machine tested in the

Middle East employed weapons designed for use within a limited theater of operations; their use, and the lessons learned there, will define many technological priorities for the next two decades.

The second issue relates more explicitly to the concerns of this book, namely, how these cycles of military spending have enormous implications for local economies. The threat of peace between 1988 and 1990 caused much consternation in cities where military bases and/or contractors are located. In contrast, a new round of technological development—with respect to antimissile missiles, for instance—will guarantee employment for tens of thousands of workers for years to come.

In many ways, the relation between the Pentagon and the residents and corporations of local economies is similar to that existing between the global economy and any locality. Broad tendencies (say, the shift to offshore assembly) have repercussions within the local economy; moreover, those involved in such changes (as workers, residents, employers, or political representatives) have only limited control over these economic developments. While there have been varied studies of the recent impact of economic restructuring on cities (see Beauregard, 1989; Cooke, 1989), these have rarely explored the role of defense spending. Yet, as the work of individuals such as Ann Markusen has indicated, along with chapters in this volume, military expenditures can play a significant role in both regional and urban development. Broad strategic shifts in the last 50 years have moved both bases and contractors away from older industrial centers; more recent changes in production methods may usher in a new period of retrenchment and relocation, as will planned base closures (both are already taking place in Southern California, for example). The sheer scale of military expenditure underscores the fact that it has a crucial role in the health—or demise—of many urban economies. Furthermore, national, rather than local, priorities will dictate that defense spending will continue to contribute directly to the complex processes of uneven capitalist development.

Yet we should be wary of totalizing statements. The ways in which military spending influences the local economy vary from city to city. In consequence, any changes within the system resolve themselves in different ways from location to location. Straightforward economic shifts are worked through as complex alterations within the social relations that exist within the locality, which are in turn linked to changes in the built environment and the local political environment.

While these factors are understood in a general sense, they have not been explored systematically. The literature that deals with the military has remained at a level of generality that permits broad argument (about macroeconomic performance, for instance) but necessarily overlooks the incorporation of defense spending into particular urban areas (Yudken & Black, 1990; for an exception, see Breheny, 1988). Conversely, the rich literature that explores the development of urban places has made little systematic mention of the role of the state (military spending included). This body of work, which can be subsumed under the *growth machine* label, has explored the connections between economic development and local political regimes, but has not paid any particular attention to the exogenous role of the state apparatus (Logan & Molotch, 1987).

The contributions to this volume are to be seen, then, as defining some of the issues to be developed in this field. For the most part, the chapters are among the first statements being made in their respective areas. They lay out basic perspectives on the influence of military activity on local economies, the ways in which urban elites have linked development to defense spending, and the growth of political coalitions that resist such expenditures.

The book is informally organized into three parts. The first two chapters lay out the basic premises: the relations between the state apparatus and the localities with regard to defense, and the specific roles of military spending in regional growth. The second part provides some different empirical examples of the relations between the Pentagon and the cities, beginning with the complex historical-geographical development of military-industrial cities throughout the United States, and moving on to examine the cycles of growth and decline of New England's local economies and the examples of the free enterprise cities of Houston and Las Vegas. The last trio of chapters deals with the processes of change and the future. The focus ranges from the spillover effects of military activity and the possibility of political response, to the long-term and costly cleanups that will haunt the American economy for decades to come, to the potential for economic conversion and its implications for a local economy. An epilogue offers far-reaching discussion of the long-term future of the military within our nation and our cities.

From these chapters, it will be clear that all of us working in urban studies need to address these issues of warmaking and peacemaking, and the contributors to this volume have provided plenty of material, from the positions of anthropology, geography, and sociology, to make such conjectures possible. Differences—in methodologies, scales of analysis, regional definitions, and historical perspectives—may mean that the interpretations vary; Peter Hall and Ann Markusen (Chapter 3) are much more sanguine about the prospects for New England than is Richard Barff (Chapter 4), for example, but he is also evaluating a rather different entity. Throughout the chapters, authors have wrestled with the difficult issue of measuring just what military spending is, exactly where it goes, and what its impacts really are. Consequently, the blueprints are all valuable.

My thanks go to all those who have been timely enough to see the project through to the end. In addition, I need to acknowledge Blaise Donnelly, who agreed to publish the book, and various people who have commented on parts of the manuscript, including Dennis Judd, Marvin Waterstone, and Susan Clarke. The responsibility for any errors of fact or interpretation remain, as usual, with the editor.

—Andrew Kirby

REFERENCES

Beauregard, R. (Ed.). (1989). *Economic restructuring and political response.* Newbury Park, CA: Sage.

Breheny, M. J. (Ed.). (1988). *Defence expenditure and regional development.* London: Mansell.

Cooke, P. (Ed.). (1989). *Localities: The changing face of urban Britain.* London: Unwin Hyman.

Logan, J. R., & Molotch, H. (1987). *Urban fortunes: The political economy of place.* Berkeley: University of California Press.

Yudken, J. S., & Black, M. (1990, Spring). Targeting national needs. *World Policy Journal*, pp. 251-288.

The Pentagon *Versus* the Cities?

ANDREW KIRBY

PUBLIC EXPENDITURE ON DEFENSE was of political interest throughout the 1980s for three well-rehearsed reasons: its sheer size, the assertion of a negative impact on industrial productivity, and its urban and regional development implications. Of these issues, only the first is straightforward. As Figure 1.1 shows, military spending constitutes a significant proportion of the federal budget (25% in 1991, a proposed total of $308 billion).

Such high rates of expenditure have been linked to the country's poor macroeconomic performance, and in turn to a nagging concern, namely, the relative decline of the United States and subsequent weakness in the international arena (Kennedy, 1987; Melman, 1988). Both debates coalesced in 1990, as the global geopolitical map was

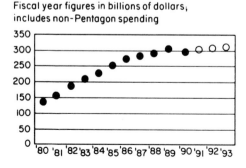

Fiscal year figures in billions of dollars; includes non-Pentagon spending

Figure 1.1. Changes in Military Spending, 1980-1993
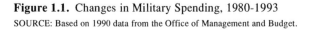
SOURCE: Based on 1990 data from the Office of Management and Budget.

redrawn and long-standing tensions within Europe shrank. Without the imperative of acknowledging Soviet forces, it became feasible to question seriously the negative social, economic, and political implications of a large defense budget here in the United States.

The narrow defense debate extant until the demolition of the Berlin Wall was thus overtaken by a new set of concerns. However, these are not beginning *de novo*. The legacy of the last five decades is a rooted one, and repays careful examination.

DEFENSE SPENDING
IN THE ERA OF THE BERLIN WALL

This book focuses upon a dimension of defense expenditure that has received scholarly attention but less political scrutiny: the ways in which military spending has profound impacts on urban and regional development. The disbursement of the military budget has a number of repercussions, both for local economies with close ties to the Pentagon and for those that are excluded from the relationship. Collectively, this book explores both these impacts and a number of consequent policy proposals.

THE SPATIAL STRUCTURE OF FEDERAL EXPENDITURE

Virtually all components of the federal budget have spatial impacts; that is, the funds display clear geographical concentrations when recipients are mapped (Johnston, 1980). This occurs for different reasons. Some categories of expenditure have explicit locational targets: The Department of Energy's Waste Isolation Pilot Project (WIPP), in Carlsbad, New Mexico, is a simple example, in which the state of New Mexico receives federal funds in return for "hosting" the facility (Downey, 1985). Other forms of funding become concentrated in specific regions or localities: Expenditure on the Forest Service and Urban Development Action Grants both appear in predictable places.

Beyond this, there are other instances where the concentration of expenditure depends upon more complex, contingent factors. Although many funding instruments are targeted to groups, differentiated by age or income, they may nonetheless become concentrated spatially. For example, AFDC funding has gone primarily to states with low aggregate incomes and to older metropolitan areas; in short, the dollar distribution has followed the spatial organization of poverty, which is in turn a product of the economic history and economic geography of the country (Wohlenberg, 1976). Pensions to former military personnel need show no spatial component, except that many retirees remain in states with military facilities. Colorado, for example, retains many of its Air Force personnel, and their pensions contribute approximately $500 million per month to the state's economy.

The consequences of these different types of federal expenditure can be summarized as follows. First, visualize a simple map of the United States, on which there are "problems" at key locations: say, several hundred toxic waste sites in need of cleanup; several dozen metropolitan areas experiencing economic restructuring, hosting large, welfare-dependent populations; the danger of a catastrophe as a result of a major earthquake in California, or a hurricane striking the Texas coast. On top of this, we can overlay a second map, which portrays the distribution of federal expenditure with explicit spatial targets. So, the net of Superfund spending has followed, in large measure, the net of the worst waste sites. HUD activity takes place (scandals notwithstanding) where poverty and homelessness problems are at their worst. Federal Emergency Management Agency funding is directed to mitigating the results of an earthquake in the western states or storm damage close to the Gulf of Mexico. The fit between the two maps cannot be perfect: The political process (in the guise of pork barreling) ensures some slippage.[1] Moreover, there is another factor, and in order to include this we need to overlay a third map, again of federal expenditure; this one, however, is restricted to military spending.

The complexity of the defense budget, and its magnitude, makes it impossible to determine exactly where all the funds are spent. This is especially the case when manufacturers' contracts are included, as subcontracts can be dispatched around the country (Malecki & Stark, 1988). Putting this problem aside, however, we can still make some informed comments. First, at the regional scale, we can assert that there are broad patterns of spending, for reasons that will be explored below. Figure 1.2 shows the overall military expenditure for each state, corrected for population as of 1980.

Within the individual states, we should not be surprised to find that the urban counties have a preponderance of the defense pie. Figure 1.3 illustrates this for California, showing 1987 Department of Defense contracts concentrated in the San Francisco Bay Area, Los Angeles, and San Diego; extremes range from $104,000 in Sutter County

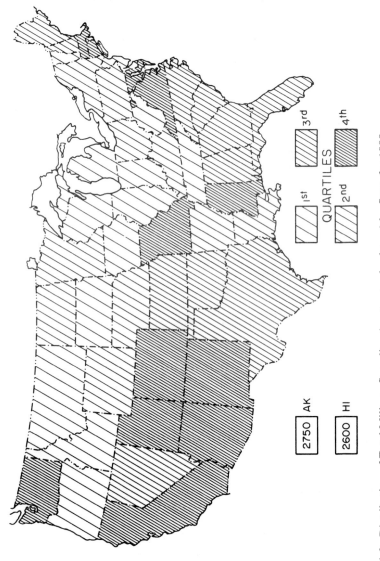

Figure 1.2. Distribution of Total Military Spending (contracts plus bases) by State for 1988

NOTE: Data corrected for 1980 population totals. Ranges are from $205 per capita in West Virginia to $3,679 per capita in Virginia.

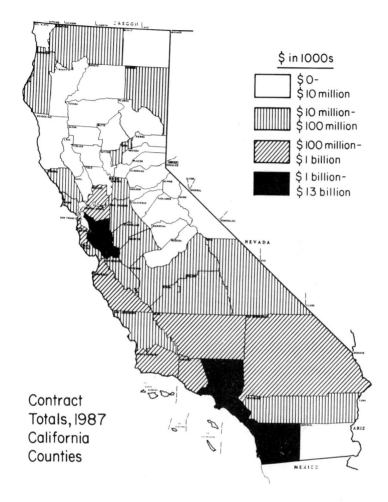

Figure 1.3. Distribution of Defense Contracts in California, by County, 1987

to $12.9 billion in Los Angeles County. Of course, not all cities fare as well as others. As far as a military presence is concerned, this occurs typically in medium-sized and middle-aged cities such as Omaha, Jacksonville, Tucson, and Salt Lake City (Noyelle & Stanback, 1983). As far as defense contracting is concerned, a number of localities have R&D reputations, and these are places, in the main, of recent and spectacular growth: Colorado Springs; San Jose,

San Diego, and Orange County in California; Route 128 in Massachusetts. Further, there are the manufacturing sites, such as Tampa, Amarillo, and Albuquerque.

This map of the military is a palimpsest of numerous decisions. Some of these have had an explicit geographical component—for example, the distribution of military facilities rests upon a number of strategic locational premises, many of which were developed during the last world war (Bernard & Rice, 1983; see also Hall & Markusen, Chapter 3, this volume). Others are less complex, if not less contentious, such as the current home-port decisions made for major warships. And yet others are now incremental, insofar as defense contracts are awarded to a finite group of research and manufacturing establishments that are concentrated in a relatively limited number of locations.

Of crucial importance here is the degree of overlap among the three maps—that is, problems, civilian expenditure, and the defense budget. Naturally enough, there is no intentional overlap between the first and third maps: Defense expenditure is not targeted to the solution of civilian problems such as urban poverty. However, we can go further and argue the existence of an *inverse* relationship—military expenditure actually *reinforcing* some of the country's community problems. In certain cases, this is because the military acts exactly as other major employers do; a large number of the nation's worst hazardous waste dumps are on military sites or are run by defense contractors, and reports suggest that cleanup of 17 major weapons facilities alone may cost in excess of $100 billion (see Jacob, Chapter 7, this volume).

On a broader level, the whole structure of Pentagon funding has been tilted toward local economies that exhibit research and industrial entrepreneurship, rather than those associated with obsolete technologies and marginalized work forces. As Ettlinger argues in Chapter 2 of this volume, this has contributed to the migration of skilled labor in the country and has compounded the cumulative disadvantage facing some communities. And, because much of this expenditure is made incrementally to individual corporations, the overall effects upon urban and regional economies are not taken into account by the Department of Defense (DOD). We have seen urban and regional growth that is not subject to direction and limitation, in contrast to the experience of many European countries with regional disparities (Lovering, 1985). The net result is that production stagnation and declining aggregate incomes in some labor markets exist alongside economic overheating, corporate overcrowding, and infrastructural strain in others. In addition, much of the resultant population growth occurs in locations where the incidental costs of growth are high, due to episodic events such as earthquakes or hurricanes, or long-term problems such as the pollution of the atmosphere by hydrocarbons, or water table depletion and poor sewage management (Kirby & Lynch, 1987; Russell, 1988).[2]

THE SPATIAL DISTRIBUTION OF DEFENSE EXPENDITURE

There are at least three imperatives that have determined this distribution of military expenditure. First, there is the relatively inert pattern of many kinds of military bases—inert insofar as no base was closed between 1977 and 1989.[3] This distribution represents several prior periods of decision making, although many of the facilities have been constructed since the 1940s, at which time areas with low-density populations were sought. The Second World War and its successors in the Pacific have provided a strategic focus on deployment away from the traditional eastern seaboard (Hall & Markusen, Chapter 3, this volume).

Second, we can factor in the 20,000 civilian prime contractors and 150,000 subcontractors that receive DOD funds. Econometric studies have shown that this pipeline of funds did much to account for the shift of the nation's economic center of gravity away from a relatively narrow Northeast-Midwest axis to incorporate the South and West in the 1960s and 1970s. To understand this shift, we need to examine in turn two additional factors. The first is the structure of the contemporary defense budget, which has focused very strongly on new technologies such as electronics and computer engineering. This, for instance, has militated against producers in the Midwest, suppliers of traditional hardware to the armed forces. Vehicle manufacturers or those producing machine tools can expect to sell less than 10% of their output to the DOD (Markusen & McCurdy, 1989).

The third factor is the history of innovation in new technologies in this country since the 1950s. New military communities have emerged in a peripheral belt that runs from Boston through to Tampa in the East, from Huntsville to Tucson in the South, and from San Diego to Washington in the West (with important outliers in the Rocky Mountain states). These "upstart" cities (as Hall & Markusen term them in Chapter 3) and their managers have sought growth in competition with longer-established local economies. As the work of

Markusen, Hall, and their colleagues emphasizes, the search for a single explanation for this pattern is probably a chimera (Markusen, Hall, Campbell, & Deitrick, 1991): It makes little sense to try to force the growth of Silicon Valley in California and Route 128 developments in Massachusetts into the same mold of product development and locational decision making. Once more, it is much simpler to note the failure of the midwestern states, despite their excellent universities, to generate significant high-tech industrial parks crammed with DOD contractors (Ettlinger, Chapter 2, this volume). Michigan and Illinois, for instance, ranked second and sixth nationally in terms of the receipt of DOD contracts during World War II; they are now ranked sixteenth and twenty-first, respectively (Markusen, 1988). One point of departure for an explanation of this failure lies in the structure of the labor force in such states, where union membership is still relatively high; as Ettlinger points out in Chapter 2, however, military industrial firms frequently recruit nationally and search for specific skills. Others have suggested that defense industries have an added incentive to avoid putative disruptions to their production schedules, which points more explicitly away from traditional manufacturing locales. The relative importance of these issues is summarized by Markusen (n.d.):

> Manufacturing plants . . . associated with military procurement have led to new, spatially concentrated industrial complexes . . . disproportionately located outside the older manufacturing cities, because of the attraction of large parcels of undeveloped land, the proximity of existing military bases, and the presence of an un-unionized workforce. (p. 26)

IMPACTS ON LOCALITIES

Whatever different locational decisions are made, there is a common paradox that connects the behavior of defense-oriented corporations. As Ettlinger notes in Chapter 2, the military industrial firm is an explicit public-private relationship, yet little attention has been paid—by government, corporations, or policy analysts—to the ways in which this works and to the impacts that are experienced by local economies. Further, because spending within the military itself is distributed overwhelmingly in terms of goals defined by the armed forces and the executive, tensions emerge automatically between civilian priorities and military institutions (Lovering, 1987; President's Economic Adjustment Committee, 1989).

Lovering's argument is provocative in that he emphasizes the way that militarism is historically situated within capitalism. This has important implications for arguments raised in this book concerning the possibility of reduced weapons production, which will be developed further in the next section. Here, it reminds us that military ordnance has long been a crucial part of the state apparatus, and cannot be understood in any other way (Tilly, 1990). The construction, organization, and deployment of this hardware take place without particular reference to broader social goals or to the preferences of individual communities. Social conflicts will inevitably appear at the local level as broad structural imperatives—"the national interest"—come into conflict with the varied norms and standards of everyday life. We need to examine in greater depth the kinds of situations in which political conflict occurs between civilian and military goals; the following examples are grouped, somewhat arbitrarily, into four categories.

(1) Local resources and land-use issues. In this situation, we find conflicts arising over how broad categories of "resources" are to be used within a locality. A prototypical example is the case of the MX missile: In 1982, a grandiose scheme was proposed by the U.S. Air Force that would have involved the construction of complex underground silos beneath a 10,000-square-mile area straddling Nevada and Utah (Holland, 1984). Traditional patriotic support for the military from ranchers and mining interests was replaced by opposition as these groups perceived threats to their economic potential (Logan & Molotch, 1987). A coalition of civilian interests, including the Mormon church, succeeded in replacing the proposal with a much more modest net of stationary silos.

These instances involve not only land uses, but the definition of the locality itself. The MX case would have constituted a major expansion of the traditional defense activity in the area. As Armitage shows in Chapter 6 of this volume, such spillovers from urban to nonurban areas are virtually inevitable, with the result that both development and the externalities associated with military use spread further and further into nonmilitary communities.

(2) Levels and forms of local economic development. While it would be unusual for a locality to blame the Department of Defense for its level of unemployment (when Southeast Asian economies and numerous other symbolic scapegoats can be found), there are opposite instances in which the sheer weight of defense-related investment in a locality may cause community opposition. A rapidly expanding electronics-based or similarly based local economy is likely to experience se-

vere internal disruption: Housing price inflation, strains placed upon schools, and infrastructural congestion can all lead to a precipitate drop in the quality of life. In Huntsville, Alabama, for example, in excess of $850 million was directed to four corporations in possession of Strategic Defense Initiative contracts in the last four years of the decade, while NASA spent $600 million during 1987 alone. Amid the affluence of the white, working population (many in-migrants) there remains a large black community in which the rate of unemployment has not been eased, and for whom the cost of living is rising while basic social services, such as public housing, are disappearing in order to improve the "image" of the city (Charles, 1987; Hall & Markusen, Chapter 3, this volume). In San Diego County, a growth rate that has added at times 1,000 new persons per week has produced an even larger manifestation of economic overheating (see also Figure 1.3). Four separate initiatives were placed on the November 1988 ballot to propose slower growth within the metropolitan area, 15% of which is estimated to be military related.

(3) Risk, environmental degradation, and pollution. One of the most obvious manifestations of overrapid growth is some form of pollution: of the air, of water, of open space. By definition, this is rarely enough to limit the rate of in-migration. There are, however, many instances in which military bases and/or defense contractors have engendered serious threats to personal health and community livelihood.[4] Plants generating large quantities of toxic or radioactive material can lead to community health problems, and various studies suggest that long-term etiologies may result (Edelstein, 1988; Jacob, Chapter 7, this volume; Johnson, 1981, 1988).

One crucial policy problem is the way in which the process of risk analysis is undertaken by corporate or public institutions, with emphasis being placed upon the *probabilities* of accidents occurring, rather than the *outcomes* of possible accidents. Such a risk calculus can become a basis for minimizing the urgency of any problem; a poignant example of this is given by Hohenemser (1987), who was able to employ a complex analysis of the Rocky Flats nuclear weapons plant in Colorado to argue that the facility represented a "hazard management success," despite a number of serious fires and community litigation over pollution levels. Within months of publication of Hohenemser's article, the plant was closed by the Department of Energy due to an apparent collapse of safety standards (Kirby, 1990a).

Wherever large corporate investments and substantial numbers of jobs intersect, there will be pressure from growth interests, unions, and even residents to downplay any risks and to minimize the possibility of disinvestment. These pressures to depreciate the threats within the locality have also manifested themselves in other settings in which risks must be judged to be high—such as the transport of military hardware through residential communities. Despite the secrecy that surrounds this issue, there is evidence that the levels of technical and personnel safety that are usual in civilian contexts are not applied to DOD transport, which may carry anything from rocket fuel to nuclear weapons (Jacob & Kirby, 1991).

(4) Attitudes and political mores. The interpretation of risk is more than a scientific exercise, and may rest upon community standards and norms—what has been called a *common* sense (Kirby, 1988). The MX missile silo proposal cited above roused the powerful opposition of the Mormon church, which argued that the region in question should not be a military establishment, but rather "a base from which to carry the gospel of peace" (Logan & Molotch, 1987, p. 212). This is not to imply that only metaphysical arguments may be employed in such instances. A legal case in the state of Washington, opposing the construction of a home-port site for the USS *Nimitz*, was based on the assertion that the dumping of 4 million cubic yards of dredged mud into Puget Sound would constitute an ecological hazard, insofar as it transgressed state standards; construction was halted by the Ninth Circuit Court of Appeals in March 1988. Similar arguments were employed in San Francisco, where the proposed construction of a home port for the USS *Missouri* has produced a complex set of intralocality tensions, with gay organizations, environmentalists, and peace groups opposing organized labor and commercial lobbies ("Night of the Living Missouri," 1988). In such cases, opposition results from a real mismatch between national standards and local definitions of "normal" economic development.

ASSESSMENT

These cases give a glimpse of the tensions within localities that can result from the trajectory of military-related growth, defined in terms of national interests. The examples appear to be consistent with the arguments of Logan and Molotch (1987) in their study of growth machines, in which they demonstrate the clash between the rhetoric of growth—generated by those who stand to gain from an increase in exchange values—and the quality of life, which is seen as a use value and a separate dimension within the community. These defense-related tensions have tended to receive only limited attention, however, for a number of reasons. In the first instance, the peace movement has been easily sidelined as a fringe social movement, or castigated as a threat to national security (despite the inherent contradictions between the two assessments; see also Armitage, Chapter 6, this volume). Second, the nonclass basis of these political struggles has allowed them to be marginalized by specific readings of the urban political process. The most obvious example of this tendency is the work of Gottdiener (1987), who has identified "the death of local politics" in this country. The error of this insight depends much more on his own theoretical constructs than on an empirical reading of the American city, however (Clarke & Kirby, 1990).

Local politics is far from dead, but any assessment of the social movements contesting militarism and military spending prior to 1990 would have to distinguish carefully between the symbolic successes and the practical failures. More than 150 nuclear-free zones existed at the end of the decade, spread across 24 states. A far larger number of sister-city projects connected citizens in the United States with communities in numerous countries, including the Soviet Union. In terms of specific impacts, it would be hard to point to changes in federal activity caused by such "municipal foreign policies" (for a fuller discussion, see Alger, 1990; Alger & Mendlovitz, 1984). The gravity of the threat perceived by the state to its monopoly of control over foreign policy and sensitive domestic issues should not be ignored, however. Legal rulings have placed nuclear-free zones in the same intergovernmental struggle that now encompasses land-use and handgun control laws (Kirby, 1990b).

The situation at the end of the decade was thus one in which the basic terrain of opposition to high levels of military spending was developing; it would, however, be a very bold commentator who would assert that the apparent collapse of the Cold War was to any significant degree ushered in by a locality-based peace movement in the United States. The dismantling of the Berlin Wall owes everything to significant changes in the global economy and the ostensible collapse of the political economy within the Warsaw Pact. This search for relative causes notwithstanding, the 1990s began with the prospect of a new political debate, although the long-term implications of the Gulf War remain to be seen.

DEFENSE SPENDING AFTER
THE COLLAPSE OF THE BERLIN WALL

In April 1990, Mayor Dinkins of New York City argued in congressional testimony that plans to construct a home port for warships on Staten Island were now obsolete, as "the strategic rationale has collapsed." Dinkins went on to say that he was redirecting more than $30 million away from projects linked to the proposed home port, and that, in his opinion, New York would be better served if federal disbursement was "redirected away from unnecessary military expenditures" ("Can NY Sink," 1990).

In a relatively short period of time—dating from the outbreak of peace between the superpowers, so to speak—the debate over military spending shifted dramatically. It was possible to conjecture about a reordering of priorities within public spending, and the phrase "the peace dividend" entered the lexicon of sound bites. Yet this did not occur without complications. As much as some communities see this as an opportunity to return federal spending to the priorities of the 1960s, for others this is a development of threatening proportions. Many jobs depend on the production of weapons and their storage; many localities see the disappearance of bases as akin to the disappearance of oil or gold reserves, leaving behind nothing but a massive environmental liability (see Jacob, Chapter 7, this volume). Already, competition has begun between localities for the privilege of keeping some bases open and closing others, as Parker and Feagin indicate in their study of facilities in Nevada (Chapter 5, this volume).

This section examines the current developments within the defense budget, the implications for local economies—including the possibilities of economic conversion—and the long-term issues of political development within localities.

THE CURRENT PROPOSALS: WHAT CHANGES?

Defense spending at the beginning of the 1990s is projected to run between $290 and $300 billion annually. However, there have been rumblings of change for some time, and defense contractors have complained of tight funding and falling profits for several years (Scott, 1989). Most important has been the recognition that large-ticket items—such as the Stealth bomber (cost to date, $22 billion), Strategic Defense Initiative (so far, $23 billion), Midgetman and Trident missiles (likely cost, $30 and $18 billion, respectively), and MX deployment (calculated at $10 billion)—are simply too costly to develop.

The apparent change in the geostrategic map offers a way out of this cycle of extravagant hardware; the U.S. Navy's A-12 Avenger bomber, designed to penetrate the Soviet Union from carriers, was scrapped early in 1991, saving a possible $57 billion. In addition, military leaders identify new roles for combat forces that involve very different types of weapons. Drug trafficking, terrorism, and insurgency are all identified as important issues for the U.S. Army and Marine Corps in coming years, and expensive materiel would not be effective in any of these theaters (Stone & Vuono, 1990). The active duty rosters of the services are also scheduled to be cut back from 2.1 million by 250,000 persons.

Initial discussions of service reorganization have centered on cuts rather than restructuring. The Air Force still emphasizes the need for B-1, B-2, and B-52 bombers, and the Navy accentuates the importance of maintaining its carrier fleet. In the longer term, however, different organizational structures will appear. The Army, for example, is discussing the replacement of its divisional structure with smaller units, such as the cavalry regiment armed with new antitank hardware. These changes will in turn have important implications for the types of materiel used by the services. The switch to lighter ground forces has already dictated that there will be little demand for tank production in the United States (although export orders to nations such as Saudi Arabia should not be forgotten). A new emphasis upon ready-to-intervene forces will necessitate the creation of a fast, sealift fleet, very different from current ships. Cargo planes, too, will be smaller and more maneuverable.

SPATIAL ORGANIZATION OF THE MILITARY

Smaller armed services require fewer bases, and changed strategic roles also make some facilities obsolete. At the end of 1988, 86 bases were proposed for closure; plans in 1990 marked another 72 bases as candidates for investigation and possible closure. These lists leave intact the American forces in Japan, Guam, and the Philippines, but involve closures in South Korea, Greece, the United Kingdom, Germany, and Turkey. Domestic sites considered for possible closure are scattered throughout the United States, although there are 10 bases concentrated in California alone. (More than 90% of the bases chosen by the secretary of defense are in House Democratic districts, with 41,000 civilian jobs at stake. Only 499 jobs are threatened at bases in House Republican districts.)[5] These calculations do not, however, address the jobs that will be created in the process of cleaning up old base sites; as Jacob indicates in Chapter 7 of this volume, this will be a long and extremely costly process, and it is frequently argued that it is cheaper to keep bases open than to prepare them for civilian use.

CORPORATE IMPLICATIONS

The new military will bring forth a new military-industrial complex. Falling profitability throughout the American economy has already pushed many smaller contractors out of business, while larger corporations have on occasion been pressured into accepting highly unpopular fixed-price contracts (in contrast to the cost-plus contracts of an earlier era, which allowed contractors to make significant profits from their research and development work). This has led to a round of corporate restructuring, including mergers and acquisitions. Some corporations (e.g., Fairchild) have been sold to foreign arms producers, and others have opted to move out of defense work; Honeywell announced plans in 1990 to limit its links to the Pentagon and to diversify its product lines to include civilian commodities.

The history of the Bell Boeing V-22 Osprey is a good metaphor for likely changes in the defense contracting world. This plane has the "vertical takeoff and landing" capabilities necessary for counterinsurgency operations in areas without sophisticated landing facilities. Unlike former generations of hardware, this aircraft has been designed to appeal to all four services, in order to maximize the possibility of profit, and the risk has been shared between two corporations, Bell Textron and Boeing. The risk is not inconsiderable. The Osprey was canceled (after $2 billion in research expenditure) in April 1989 by incoming Defense Secretary Cheney. A major lobbying effort by the makers and the Marine Corps was successful in restoring funding, although the debate took on a new twist when the manufacturers began to emphasize too the *civilian* applications of the plane, including its ability to fly rooftop to rooftop between major cities—as yet, an unidentified market. In June 1990, Bell Boeing began an extensive advertising campaign in periodicals such as the *National Journal* to emphasize again the military applications of the aircraft; interestingly, the phrase *cost-effective* is given more prominence in these ads than is *operationally effective*.

CIVILIAN CONVERSION

The mention of civilian uses is an unusual innovation for defense contractors. In the past, corporations who work on DOD contracts—such as IBM, Boeing, and General Electric—have kept their military production entirely separate from their civilian divisions. In part this is dictated by federal accounting and secrecy restrictions, and in part by sensitivity about corporate image. The net result, however, is that the civilian applications of technologies or products have rarely been developed. Standard stories of abject failure have arisen to describe those occasions when this has been attempted: Corporations used to long cost-plus contracts have often proved unable to produce to deadline or to cost, and have manufactured overdesigned products more applicable in space than on city streets or in homes (Dumas, 1986; Waterstone & Kirby, Chapter 8, this volume).[6]

These stories notwithstanding, there is a growing activism that presses for federal action to support the conversion of military production lines to civilian purposes. The literature on economic conversion is also growing and argues optimistically for the ability of defense contractors and workers to redirect their activities. Advocates of the process envisage a progressive decline of military production, coupled with worker retraining, that avoids the ravages of corporate layoffs in producer localities and contributes to an ongoing commitment to disarmament (*Questions and Answers*, 1987).

While there is a persuasive logic to the conversion argument, it has failed in both intellectual and practical terms to deal with two serious types of critique. The first has to do with the close historical connections among militarism, capitalism, and the rise of the capitalist state system (Enloe, 1987; Lovering, 1987). Simply put, it is implausible to expect that a powerful state apparatus will voluntarily dismantle its legitimate forces of coercion, for to do so would threaten its very legitimacy (a point developed further in Chapter 8). Second, there is the feminist critique, which goes a stage further in linking the violence of male-dominated society to militarism and personal oppression. As Enloe (1987) notes, the states of war and peace are similar in their implications for women, for neither disturbs the oppression and male violence that are centered in many households. This perspective draws a straight line between the implicit violence of militarism and the personal oppression of women in everyday life—the way, for instance, that women who live close to military bases are drawn into employment as barmaids or prostitutes, gender-specific examples of the links between the dominant culture of masculinity and the particulars of militarization (Armitage, Chapter 6, this volume; Enloe, 1989). Enloe (1987) concludes that it is the "patriarchal structure of privilege and control that must be dismantled if we are to be rid, once and for all, of militarism" (p. 544).

Both of these perspectives reveal that economic conversion is by no means a force for automatic social change. As much as individual citizens may press for the so-called peace dividend, this ignores the structural ties that bind the power of the state to the means of violence and the production of military hardware. Nor does it take into account the mutual reinforcement that links violence in the public sphere with violence and control in the home. In consequence, any hope for a significant restructuring of the military foundations of the American economy must be based on explicit strategies of social and political change, and these must be designed and implemented, in the first instance, in sympathetic localities.

SOCIAL CHANGE WITHIN THE LOCALITY

All the contributions to this volume deal explicitly with change: the restructuring of the defense sector over the last 50 years, the strategic shifts to the Sunbelt, the contractions of the federal budget, and the precipitate redrawing of the geopolitical map. Predicting the next round of changes—economic, social, political, geographic—is not at all easy. Some localities are trying to diminish the impacts of militarism within their borders; others remain closely tied to their bases and the dollars generated. For the future, both strategies will depend upon a change in the relations between the state and the local state.

ATTRACTING MILITARY ACTIVITY

Some localities are already struggling to keep their connections to the Pentagon. A nonpartisan coalition in Tucson has worked hard to get public support for the local Air Force base to remain open, arguing that the Air Force believes community support to be an important factor in closure decisions. In an extension of typical corporate strategies, we see the military pitting one locality against another, thereby extracting the maximum concessions from local authorities.[7]

Some local economies are already feeling the winds of change and have seen bases dwindle and/or contractors diminish in number. In these cases, there is pressure on state government to provide assistance for retraining (as has happened in the state of Washington), although for the long term some recognition of regional priorities at the federal level is necessary. It would be possible to place defense expenditures within the legislative framework established during the New Deal, which has grown to include Title V Commissions, Interstate Compacts, River Basin Commissions, and so on. These structures have, however, been superseded by the political realities of the New Federalism of the 1980s, and a reconstitution of regional planning is without effective precedent in recent U.S. history.

CONTROLLING MILITARY ACTIVITY

The most interesting developments remain in those localities attempting to gain greater control of external institutions, corporate or military. The goal is frequently the imposition of *conformity* upon military activities, ensuring that the presence of military establishments, or the scale of defense contracting, is consistent with local views on economic and community development. The 1969 National Environmental Policy Act (NEPA) has been invoked in several situations where citizen opposition to federal plans has existed, including the MX siting case noted above. Indeed, it has been suggested that "in essence, NEPA institutionalizes the public's right to be part of the process on such major defense decisions as the deployment of nuclear weapons systems" (Holland, 1984, p. 58). In reality, the potential seems quite limited. The collapse of the MX proposal resulted from the delays that stemmed from legal discussions related to the environmental impact documents, delays that undermined the Air Force's strategic timetable (Holland, 1984, p. 53). In situations where punctuality is of no importance, NEPA has proved to be ineffective.[8]

In contrast, a number of modest legal cases that test the ability of the local jurisdiction to impose more limited strictures on actions already covered by federal law are currently working their way through state and federal courts. Examples include the rights of communities to direct military transport via the building of street signs (in Columbus, Ohio) and the requirement that the Fernald weapons installation observe the environmental regulations laid down by the state of Ohio (Schierholz, 1988). These cases are particularly interesting because they dovetail with other legal struggles taking place currently at the community scale over abortion, pollution control, gun control, and land-use ordinances. At stake is the ability of residents to recapture control of their quality of life, rather than their ability to determine the broad contours of military spending (see Kirby, 1990b, for a review).

Long-term changes in the relations between the state apparatus and its components will depend in large part upon a prolonged reinterpretation of the notion of sovereignty (Walker & Mendlovitz, 1990). Such struggles are about the ability of the local state to determine particular forms of economic development and certain styles of social organization—which may, in some localities, be closely tied to the military in its many guises.

This question of choice is beginning to appear with much greater frequency in the context of intergovernmental relations. The nation's mayors, faced with problems proliferating faster than they can be identified, are demanding federal support *for programs of their choosing* in a way that has not been heard since the urban riots of the 1960s. The ever-present deficit problems dictate that Great Society largess is unlikely to reappear. However, the dramatically different dimensions of foreign policy have given local politicians the ability to address the redirection of existing funds from the military to social programs without being branded as hopelessly naive or unpatriotic. The next decade promises to be an exciting one, both for students of the Pentagon and for America's cities.

NOTES

1. Although most quantitative studies of public spending fail to yield statistically clear results, there is a mass of anecdotal evidence (and the plural of *anecdote* is *data*; see, for example, *Congressional Quarterly*, October 24, 1987, pp. 2581-2594).

2. The costs involved in replacing infrastructure and homes following natural hazard events should not be discounted. The immediate costs of the Bay Area earthquake and Hurricane Hugo in 1989 alone exceeded $10 billion. Longer-run issues, such as tropospheric ozone buildup in cities, are even more costly; EPA studies suggest that in order to bring Los Angeles into compliance with the Clean Air Act, draconian regulations would have to be introduced immediately. Tripling the costs of gasoline and parking fees, a $1,000 second-car tax, mandatory no-drive days, and four-day workweeks would in 20 years reduce the hydrocarbon level in L.A. by a grand total of 8% from the 1983 base (Russell, 1988).

3. Proposals to begin trimming the defense budget produced plans in 1990 to scrutinize 72 bases for closure. Environmental cleanup costs mean that it is cheaper in the short term to keep bases open than to close them.

4. In Tucson, for instance, the major defense contractor, Hughes Aircraft, is responsible for more than two-thirds of all toxic air pollution, in excess of 600,000 pounds of materials such as Freon 113 and TCA ("Tucson Firms Emitting Less," 1990).

5. Secretary of Defense Cheney replied that the charge was "not a valid one" when asked if there was a concentration of base closures in the districts of liberal Democrats

("Cheney Seeks," 1990). The contradictory data on pork barreling are from *USA Today* (May 7, 1990, p. A1).

6. Corporations—such as computer manufacturers—who deal with the military *inter alia* seem to perform much better than those that develop close ties; see the comments of Gold (1991).

7. Such concessions would include extensions to overflight times and routes and zoning changes near bases.

8. Base closures, to take one example, were subjected to the processes dictated by NEPA as a result of a 1976 amendment. In consequence, each closure required an Environmental Impact Statement, and would have been open to legal challenge by environmentalists, historians, and so on. As a result, DOD scheduled no bases for closure between 1977 and 1988. The 1988 Defense Savings Act, which promised savings of $2-5 billion per year, received Defense Department support because it scraps this level of EPA control over military actions and allows the armed forces to close bases as they choose.

REFERENCES

Alger, C. (1990). The world relations of cities: The gap between social science paradigms and everyday human experience. *International Studies Quarterly, 34*, 493-518.

Alger, C., & Mendlovitz, S. (1984). Grass roots activism in the United States: Global implications? *Alternatives, 9*, 447-474.

Bernard, R. M., & Rice, B. R. (1983). *Sunbelt cities.* Austin: University of Texas Press.

Can NY sink the Staten Island homeport? (1990). *Bulletin of Municipal Foreign Policy, 4*(3), 28.

Charles, C. (1987, December 19). Star Wars fell on Alabama. *Nation*, pp. 748-750.

Cheney seeks to shut, realign 72 U.S. bases. (1990, January 30). *Arizona Daily Star*, p. A1.

Clarke, S. E., & Kirby, A. M. (1990). In search of the corpse: The mysterious case of local politics. *Urban Affairs Quarterly, 25*, 389-412.

Downey, G. L. (1985). Politics and technology in repository siting: Military versus commercial nuclear wastes. *Technology and Society, 7*, 47-76.

Dumas, L. J. (1986). *The overburdened economy: Uncovering the causes of chronic unemployment, inflation and national decline.* Berkeley: University of California Press.

Edelstein, M. (1988). *Contaminated communities.* Boulder, CO: Westview.

Enloe, C. H. (1987). Feminists thinking about war, militarism, and peace. In B. B. Hess & M. M. Ferree (Eds.), *Analyzing gender* (pp. 526-547). Newbury Park, CA: Sage.

Enloe, C. H. (1989). *Bananas, beaches and bases.* London: Pandora.

Gold, D. (1991, January/February). Military R&D a poor scapegoat for flagging economy. *Bulletin of Atomic Scientists*, pp. 38-43.

Gottdiener, M. (1987). *The decline of urban politics.* Newbury Park, CA: Sage.

Hohenemser, C. (1987). Public distrust and hazard management success: The Rocky Flats nuclear weapons plant. *Risk Analysis, 7*, 243-259.

Holland, L. (1984). The use of NEPA in defense policy politics: Public and state involvement in the MX missile project. *Social Science Journal, 21*(3), 53-72.

Jacob, G. R., & Kirby, A. M. (1991). On the road to ruin: The transport of military cargoes. In A. Ehrlich & J. Birks (Eds.), *Hidden dangers.* San Francisco: Sierra.

Johnson, C. (1981). Cancer incidence in an area contaminated with radionuclides near a nuclear installation. *Ambio, 10*, 176-182.

Johnson, C. (1988). Mortality among plutonium and other radiation workers at a plutonium weapons plant. *American Journal of Epidemiology, 127*, 1321-1323.

Johnston, R. J. (1980). *The geography of federal spending*. Chichester: John Wiley.

Kennedy, P. (1987). *The rise and fall of the great powers*. New Haven, CT: Yale University Press.

Kirby, A. M. (1988). Context, *common* sense and the reality of place. *Journal for the Theory of Social Behavior, 18*, 239-250.

Kirby, A. M. (1990a). Epilogue: Towards a new risk analysis. In A. M. Kirby (Ed.), *Nothing to fear: Risks and hazards in American society* (pp. 281-298). Tucson: University of Arizona Press.

Kirby, A. M. (1990b). Law and disorder: Morton Grove and the community control of handguns. *Urban Geography, 11*, 474-487.

Kirby, A. M., & Lynch, K. A. (1987). A ghost in the growth machine: The aftermath of rapid population growth in Houston. *Urban Studies, 24*, 587-596.

Logan, J. R., & Molotch, H. (1987). *Urban fortunes: The political economy of place*. Berkeley: University of California Press.

Lovering, J. (1985). Regional intervention, defence industries, and the structuring of space in Britain. *Environment and Planning D: Society and Space, 3*, 85-107.

Lovering, J. (1987). Militarism, capitalism, and the nation state: Towards a realist synthesis. *Environment and Planning D: Society and Space, 5*, 283-302.

Malecki, E. J., & Stark, L. M. (1988). Regional and industrial variation in defence spending: Some American evidence. In M. J. Breheny (Ed.), *Defence expenditure and regional development* (pp. 67-101). London: Mansell.

Markusen, A. (1988). The military remapping of the United States. In M. J. Breheny (Ed.), *Defence expenditure and regional development* (pp. 17-28). London: Mansell.

Markusen, A. (n.d.). *The economic development implications of defence led innovation in the United States*. Discussion paper, Korea-U.S. Seminar on Science and Technology Policy.

Markusen, A., Hall, P. G., Campbell S., & Deitrick S. (1991). *The rise of the gunbelt: The military remapping of industrial America*. New York: Oxford University Press.

Markusen, A., & McCurdy, K. (1989). Chicago's defense-based high technology: A case study of the seedbeds of innovation hypothesis. *Economic Development Quarterly, 3*(1), 15-31.

Melman, S. (1988). Economic consequences of the arms race: The second rate economy. *Papers and Proceedings of the American Economics Association, 78*(2), 55-59.

Night of the living Missouri. (1988). *Bulletin of Municipal Foreign Policy, 2*(3), 30-32.

Noyelle, T. J., & Stanback, T. M. (1983). *The economic transformation of American cities*. Totowa, NJ: Rowman & Allenheld.

President's Economic Adjustment Committee. (1989). *Diversifying defense dependent communities*. Washington, DC: Pentagon, Office of Economic Adjustment.

Questions and answers about economic conversion. (1987). New York: Columbia University, Corliss Lamont Program in Economic Conversion.

Russell, M. (1988). *Tropospheric ozone and vehicular emissions* (Paper ORNL/TM-10908). Oak Ridge, TN: Oak Ridge National Laboratory.

Schierholz, T. (1988, December 13). U.S. wrestles with nuclear-weapons plant problems. *Christian Science Monitor*, p. 3.

Scott, W. B. (1989, March 20). Contractors must adapt to survive under new U.S. acquisition policies. *Aviation Week and Space Technology*, pp. 76-79.

Stone, M. P. W., & Vuono, C. E. (1990). *Trained and ready in an era of change*. Washington, DC: Department of the Army.

Tilly, C. (1990). *Coercion, capital and European states*. Oxford: Basil Blackwell.

Tucson firms emitting less toxins in air. (1990, September 3). *Arizona Daily Star*, p. B1.

Walker, R. B. J., & Mendlovitz, S. H. (1990). *Contending sovereignties*. Boulder, CO: Lynn Rienner.

Wohlenberg, E. H. (1976). Interstate variations in AFDC programs. *Economic Geography, 52*, 254-266.

2

Development Theory and the Military Industrial Firm

NANCY ETTLINGER

THIS CHAPTER FOCUSES on the role of military industrial firms (MIFs) in economic development, emphasizing both production processes and effects on local economies and workers. A second and related purpose is to situate MIFs in development theory, specifically theory that concerns the behavior and performance of firms, for, with few exceptions, defense-related production is conspicuously absent from the rather voluminous development literature. Finally, this chapter represents an effort to anticipate theoretically some of the changes in MIF production and related social processes that we may expect in the post-Cold War era.

THE GENERAL PROBLEM OF DEVELOPMENT IN THE CURRENT PERIOD

Since the mid-1970s, two pillars of American society have been shaken. First, U.S. economic hegemony in the global economy has dissolved. In terms of productivity, the United States has lagged behind other advanced economies (Borrus, 1988; Cohen & Zysman, 1987; Dertouzos, Lester, Solow, & the MIT Commission on Industrial Productivity, 1989; Johnson, Tyson, & Zysman, 1989; Zysman & Tyson, 1983). Over a seven-year period, the productivity of U.S. businesses increased 0.6% annually, compared with gains of 2.8% in Japan, 2.4% in France, 2% in West Germany, and 1.9% in Britain (Clark & Malabre, 1990). For the United States, economic development hinges on savings and appropriate investment in a general sense, and operationally on technological and organizational change in firms, the agents of production, and change in the modern capitalist economy. Second, employment in the relatively high-wage, middle-income manufacturing sector has declined precipitously, while at the same time employment has increased significantly in the low-wage consumer-services sector. These concurrent processes call into question the traditionally large size and continued expansion of the American middle class (Harrison & Bluestone, 1988).

Declining corporate productivity and threats to the well-being of the American populace have received a great deal of attention and have been subjects of controversy, yet they typically are treated as discrete subjects. Actually, these two sets of problems, representing the production and consumption dimensions of political economy, are integrally related and are mediated by firms. They are the agents that produce and contribute directly to the position of a nation in the global political economy; at the same time, firms are the agents that provide the means (wages) by which people earn their livelihoods and consume what is produced in a capitalist society. Firms operate within local contexts and thereby affect and are affected by their immediate social, economic, and political environments. Accordingly, the types of firms in a community and their propensity to develop innovative and constructive adaptive strategies will condition the socioeconomic prospects for the people of that community, who represent labor for production as well as consumers whose standard of living depicts the community.

Patterns of development and positive/negative socioeconomic change vary across locales within a nation for two reasons. First, variation in the mixes of industries and types of economic activities (e.g., headquarters and administration, branch plants, entrepreneurial ventures, consumer services, business services) among locales affects spatial variation in local industrial and business cycles. Second, increasingly restrictive allocations of funds from the federal government (due to the budget deficit) have prompted state and local governments and community organizations to pursue grass-roots development strategies.

THE RELEVANCE OF MIFs
TO ECONOMIC DEVELOPMENT

MIFs are of special interest from a development point of view for several reasons. First, from the perspective of *local* development, they represent a special case of corporate culture because of the network of local as well as local-national political and social alliances that support and nurture the continued existence of these firms. These alliances, which link labor with local and national politicians, often have the effect of creating employment stability (with respect to local MIFs) and community solidarity (Ettlinger & Crump, 1989). Second, although MIFs represent a small percentage of firms, they nevertheless employ a disproportionate share of the highly skilled American labor force. Employment in high-tech, defense-related manufacturing in the United States increased from 37.8% to 41.3% between 1977 and 1984; with respect to "white-collar" defense labor, as much as 60.2% of aerospace engineers and 35% of electrical engineers worked on defense-related research by the end of the 1970s (National Science Foundation, 1979). Third, research and development expenditures are high in MIFs, and federal investment in R&D always has been substantially higher in MIFs than in civilian-oriented firms (CFs). By 1960, defense research constituted upward of 80% of federal R&D funds, declining thereafter until the early 1980s, when it again increased dramatically (Mowery & Rosenberg, 1989, p. 130); the Department of Defense, the Department of Energy, and NASA combined accounted for 97% of all federal R&D funds to industrial firms in 1982 (Mowery & Rosenberg, 1989, p. 132).

The strong emphasis on product development and innovation in MIFs after World War II had indirect positive effects on commercially oriented R&D, especially the electronics industry (Mowery & Rosenberg, 1989, pp. 137-147). Indeed, the technological edge that the United States enjoyed through the mid-1970s may not have been forthcoming without the lead role of defense production. However, as other nations have developed competitive production strategies oriented toward the international private market, the relative absence of U.S. government policy to convert defense to commercial investments has prompted concern that MIFs are inefficient engines of development, and actually drain the civilian economy of both skilled labor and investment funds (DeGrasse, 1984; Dumas, 1982b; Melman, 1986; Mowery & Rosenberg, 1989; Reich, 1982).

Traditionally, military industry has occupied an unusually secure position, characterized by a guaranteed market and substantial financial backing from the government for uncertain ventures (Gellen, 1971). However, the long-term burden of the budget deficit and the savings and loan crisis, combined with increased international competition and a post-Cold War climate, threaten to reduce the government's traditional support of MIFs. As they suffer, so too do communities that house these firms, as MIFs lay off workers and pursue strategies to reduce labor costs, such as canceling overtime options. Further, we might wonder if MIFs can maintain a lead role in basic research in the long run, and whether they can convert effectively to production for commercial markets.

Development theory should instruct us in assessing current problems, and should guide appropriate policy formulation with respect to the role of MIFs in the economy in general and the well-being of the communities that host these firms in particular. Curiously, it does not. Below I consider why development theory is unable to account for a segment of the economy that has figured prominently in development processes. First, I address regional development theory in the United States as it evolved specifically in relation to CFs; subsequently, I consider the relation of MIFs to the existing body of development literature. The special case of MIFs provides an interesting window on development thinking.

MIFs AND DEVELOPMENT THEORY

REGIONAL DEVELOPMENT AND
CF ORGANIZATION AFTER WORLD WAR II

The American economy was dominated by small firms until the second half of this century. After 1945, as the United States rose to a position of hegemony in the global economy, firms grew substantially in size as well as in scope of operations (Chandler, 1962; Watts, 1980; Williamson, 1981). In the aftermath of the war, large multinational corporations (MNCs) became significant features of the world capitalist system, ushering in a "new international division of labor" (NIDL; Frobel, Heinrichs, & Kreye, 1980). Qualitative differences in the activities of large and diversified MNCs (e.g., high-skilled R&D, low-skilled production) were expressed in terms of the production cycle, which instructed MNC managements to locate different activities in different types of countries, consistent with existing wage and skill comparative advantages (Vernon, 1966). High-skilled and high-wage R&D and administrative activities were located in advanced economies, and low-skilled production activities were located in low-skilled and low-wage Third World countries (Aydalot, 1981; Hymer, 1977). While manufacturing output and productivity increased in the Third World, illiteracy and severe poverty remained prominent there

(Griffin, 1978; Kinzer, 1979). Accordingly, Third World scholars reacted against optimistic readings of productivity growth by Anglo-Americans; they cited the problem of growth without development in technoeconomically dependent regions, formerly the colonial territories of countries that became economic rulers under the aegis of MNCs (Amin, 1974; Anell & Nygren, 1980; Frank, 1967; Sauvant, 1980).

The paradigm of motivational behavior after World War II in the United States was growth, such that small firms would strive to become larger in size, scope, and markets, eventually reaching the status of MNCs (Hakanson, 1979). Product cycle theory originally was intended as a prescriptive framework, but eventually became a general, descriptive model of the locational behavior of large and diversified manufacturers that operated with distinct and rigid divisions of labor according to Taylorist principles of management.[1] As the multi-establishment, multilocational MNCs effected an international division of labor, large domestic firms effected an intranational, interregional division of labor. In the United States, this became clearly visible in the 1960s and 1970s, most popularly in terms of Frostbelt/Sunbelt differences, as well as more refined, disaggregated differences within regions.[2] Core regions (such as the Frostbelt, in the aggregate, or major metropolitan growth pockets in other regions) housed R&D activities, headquarters, and high-skilled manufacturing; the periphery (e.g., the Sunbelt or nonmetropolitan areas of any region) housed the low-skilled, low-wage branch plants, owned and controlled from Frostbelt centers of corporate activity (Cohen, 1977; Erickson, 1976). The branch plant industrialization of peripheral areas in the United States was likened to the dependent economies of Third World countries, characterized by economic leakage, few local spin-offs, unstable or insecure employment, and negligible programs for upgrading skills (Gray, 1969; Klimasewski, 1978; McGranahan, 1982; Pred, 1976). The development implications of external control were pejorative.

Product cycle theory (originally prescriptive and later descriptive) was an important foundation for recognizing the urban and regional development implications of corporate locational behavior (Malecki, 1981). Marxist literature emerged that sought to explain and account for the evolution of spatial divisions of labor (Clark, 1981; Massey, 1979, 1984). According to this framework, any significant and positive developmental change in one region represents the spatial displacement of problems. Change could occur with respect to the regional location of different activities, but, fundamentally, the same system prevailed that fostered and maintained inequality across space.

MIFs AFTER WORLD WAR II AND DEVELOPMENT THEORY

As large, multilocational firms began to dominate the U.S. economy after World War II, qualitatively different corporations emerged: the MIFs. Especially after the Soviet challenge to American science with the launching of *Sputnik* in 1957, and in the wake of the Cold War, MIFs in the United States became seedbeds of scientific innovation and targets of federal investment.[3]

MIFs have behaved quite differently from the large CFs. Whereas the latter expanded to penetrate new, international markets, MIFs catered principally to one guaranteed market. MIFs depended on the U.S. government, which in turn depended on MIFs for basic research that was too costly and risky for CFs without a federal cushion of support (Gellen, 1971; Marfels, 1978; Mowery & Rosenberg, 1981, 1989; Peck & Scherer, 1962). Federal monopsony and dependence on MIFs has had consequences for government permissiveness, and has opened the door to cost overruns and production inefficiency (Dorfer, 1983). In part, these problems are predictable, since prime contractors as a group are oligopolistically structured and confront virtually no competition from CFs. Indeed, the industry is remarkably concentrated: In 1984, the top 5 MIFs accounted for 20% of the monetary value of defense procurement contracts, the top 25 accounted for 50%, and the top 100 accounted for 70% (Markusen, 1986).

Although MIFs have competed with one another, the competition has been more political than economic, because obtaining a contract often hinges on the efforts of political representatives of communities that house MIF establishments. Whereas corporate strategies in CFs have centered generally on efficient production and marketing methods (Miller & Vollmann, 1985; Williamson, 1981), MIF strategies have involved lobbying congressional and Pentagon officials, information gathering, and substantive efforts to influence government proposals for new or modified weaponry (Adams, 1981).

The symbiotic relationship between MIFs and the government distinguishes MIF behavior from that of CFs and renders product cycle theory irrelevant. MIFs focus mostly on product innovation and produce small quantities of goods. A significant portion of the overall effort in an MIF is involved with R&D. In contrast, large CFs traditionally have been dedicated to large-volume production, catering to large markets. Product innovation in CFs has been typically more a matter of minor product modification, and much of the R&D is focused on process innovations that will permit more efficient production.[4] Accordingly, CF production has located commonly in regions or countries where production costs are low and/or new markets are located. MIF emphasis on R&D and low-volume production in general and product innovation in particular has meant that (a) the MIF labor force typically is highly skilled and (b) the spatial segmentation of labor pools, which has characterized CFs and is described by product cycle theory, does not apply to MIFs.

The different organizational principles and emphases of MIFs and CFs have clear spatial implications. MIFs have not had to locate establishments in a wide range of places for market reasons, because the government has provided a guaranteed market. In addition, the distinctive character of the production system has negated spatial divisions of labor within MIFs, across territories. Although prime contractors may be multilocational, the distinction among facilities is typically a matter of specific product line, as opposed to an entirely different set of activities, as is the case with CFs (e.g., R&D in one locale, different aspects or stages of manufacturing in vertically integrated production programs elsewhere). Moreover, even though subcontracting activity has occurred on a limited interregional basis, divisions of labor are more a matter of product line and interfirm relations (e.g., small subcontractors acting as suppliers to large prime contractors) than a reflection of fundamental differences in skills and other qualitative features of the labor force (Malecki, 1984).[5]

Principal MIFs have become spatially concentrated in a few regional locations, notably the Southwest, the Pacific Coast, and New England (Malecki, 1984; Malecki & Stark, 1988; Markusen, 1987, 1988). Although the particular mix of locational determinants for specific military industrial establishments is complex, the availability of high-skilled labor and research institutions has figured prominently, especially with respect to East and West Coast locations of defense-related research. Still, professional labor tends to be highly mobile, and large pools of scientists and engineers frequently are brought to a locale from other regions when locational factors other than the local labor force are salient (Markusen & Bloch, 1985, pp. 112-113). Los Alamos, New Mexico, is a case in point: A large defense-related scientific community was created and persists, with minimal labor input from the local area. After World War II, the Sunbelt (and especially the Southwest) became a logical location for R&D facilities that involved great secrecy or testing and required sparsely settled and relatively isolated areas. In addition to the wide-open spaces of the South and West, population shifts in the United States and related congressional geopolitics have fostered federal spending in the Sunbelt (Krumme, 1981; Markusen, 1988; Rundquist, 1978).

The regionally specific locational tendencies of MIFs eventually prompted a revision of the product cycle view of regional economic change and differentiation in the United States. Indeed, development theory as related to the firm and industrial behavior became centered on the peculiarities of MIFs and their locational tendencies for the first time. Markusen (1987) argues that the location of high-tech production, which has been dominated by defense-related activity, has resulted in a shift in the hierarchical status of regions in the United States (see also Bolton, 1966). Accordingly, the Frostbelt—the traditional manufacturing belt—has been superseded by regions of the "defense perimeter" as the economic core and technological seedbed of this country. Markusen (1985) states this view of regional economic change in the United States in terms of *profit* cycle theory. Unlike the product cycle, which conceptualizes stages in the life of a product and the locational requirements of those stages within a firm, the profit cycle conceptualizes stages in the life of an industry, with respect to regional industrial specialization. Accordingly, the traditional low-tech and mature manufacturing of the Frostbelt has been eclipsed by the high-growth, high-tech, and defense-related production of the Sunbelt.

As in the case of product cycle theory, power and control in profit cycle theory are functions of the location of growth-oriented and innovative production, much in the spirit of Schumpeterian thought. However, from the perspective of regional economic change in the United States, the substantive outcomes of the product and profit cycle theory are antithetical: The regional development implications of product cycle theory, framed within the context of CF behavior, are that the traditional core regions (the Northeast or Frostbelt) maintain economic dominance; profit cycle theory, framed within the context of MIF behavior, embraces the view of a power shift from core to periphery, as old industries in the Frostbelt core reach maturity and new high-tech and defense-related industries emerge in the Sunbelt.

MIFs and CFs possess other divergent locational tendencies. For example, the pejorative connotations of external control in CF branch plants may not pertain to MIF establishments. Ettlinger and Crump

(1989) argue that external control in the case of an MIF establishment may nurture local solidarity through alliances among local political representatives, the MIF labor force (also a political constituency), and national-level officials in Congress and the Pentagon. Another relevant difference is that the CF *intra*firm division of labor across locales does not tend to characterize MIFs, largely as a function of the relatively high-skill and high-wage profile of MIF employment in most locations.

Note, however, that the scope of local solidarity varies with city size. The alliances that form around MIFs penetrate most aspects of small cities that are dominated by such employment. Alternatively, the effects of MIFs may be positive but limited to a relatively small percentage of the population in large cities that encompass a wide range of communities, some or only one of which may be dominated by MIF employment. The location of MIF establishments in large cities produces an enclaved effect, which culturally, politically, and socioeconomically distinguishes military-dependent communities within a metropolitan area (Markusen & Bloch, 1985). These communities, despite external ownership and control of facilities, often have histories of relatively stable employment because of the alliances that support MIFs (Ettlinger & Crump, 1989).[6] Defense-employed enclaves also commonly exhibit locally specific behaviors. Enclaves of "military culture" may help to explain some anomalies, such as the strong tradition of Republican or "hawk" voting on Long Island (a traditional host to MIFs, notably Grumman) despite a blue-collar heritage that is associated with the Democratic or "dove" party.

Conceptualizing MIFs as sociopolitical, economic, and cultural enclaves is, ironically, consistent with some of their less positive development effects. While beneficial for their labor forces and local communities, MIFs have tended to operate in relative isolation from the outside community. In part, this enclaved character may be related to the high level of secrecy, as well as red tape, associated with MIF production.[7] Accordingly, MIFs have substantially fewer local spin-offs and linkages with other local firms than is the case with CFs (Cooper, 1971; Erickson, 1977; Malecki, 1982). Small defense-dependent cities and communities within larger metropolitan areas tend to be characterized by local economies dominated by one or only a few sectors, and spread effects into other sectors are minimal. In small defense-dependent cities, this specialization may be devastating if MIF facilities are shut down or cannot rebound from the loss of a contract. During the Cold War era, however, community- or citywide disasters associated with MIFs have rarely compared with CF shutdowns in places such as Youngstown, Ohio.

From a long-run perspective on urban development—beyond immediate problems of employment—the apparent lack of multipliers and spread effects of MIF activity suggests that they are far from catalysts of development beyond the enclave itself. Moreover, the typically high level of skill required in MIF establishments sidesteps the increasingly severe problem of a swelling uneducated underclass in urban America (Markusen & Bloch, 1985).

RECAPITULATION

MIFs have made a mixed contribution to development since World War II. *Positive effects* include spin-offs in the civilian electronics industry, as well as tendencies toward employment stability and community solidarity in defense-dependent communities. *Negative effects* include inefficiency, cost overruns, and other signposts of monopsony and economically noncompetitive production, plus a brain drain on the domestic civilian labor force, nationally and locally. The negligible spread effects of MIFs to other firms and sectors create an elite enclave characterized by employment stability, high skills, and high wages. This enclavement of privilege, in turn, is nurtured and reinforced by virtue of political alliances and the social reproduction of defense culture.

Interestingly, these development effects of MIFs have largely escaped the post-World War II literature on corporate organization and regional/local development, with the exception of profit cycle theory and some studies of spin-off potential and spread effects. The firm-related development literature has been dominated, at least until the mid- to late 1970s, by product cycle theory, which focuses on large, multilocational CFs that operate in accordance with Taylorist principles, resulting in the separation of tasks and associated labor pools. The empirical context for this theoretical framework has been economic growth. Not surprisingly, product cycle theory evolved in the United States after 1945, when the country emerged as an undisputed superpower. This conjunction of economic growth and hegemony was founded essentially on the private sector, and was possible in a country that avoided the devastation of war at home and the consequent burden of rebuilding. It is only against this empirical backdrop that the nonpublic character of traditional, U.S.-centered development theory is intelligible.

THE CHANGING CONTEXT
FOR DEVELOPMENT THEORY:
MID-1970s TO THE PRESENT

In the mid-1970s, Japan effectively challenged U.S. hegemony; moreover, by the early 1980s, the "Four Tigers" of East Asia (Hong Kong, Singapore, South Korea, Taiwan) were also defying Western supremacy. It was in reaction to these changing realities that the non-public and non-policy-conscious character of traditional neoclassical analysis were attacked by the "new institutional economics" (Langlois, 1986) rooted in institutional theory of the firm (Chandler, 1962, 1977; Coase, 1937; Williamson, 1975, 1981, 1985). This holds that different modes of corporate organization and types of transactions occur as the costs of internal organization are weighed against the costs of contracting and pursuing transactions with other firms. The micro- and macroeconomic environments affect the relative benefits of externalizing or internalizing costs, and it is through legal, social, political, economic, and technological institutions that firms adapt to changing circumstances through the restructuring of their activities. To be effective, this restructuring must be consistent with the state's policies, precisely because corporate behavior occurs within the context of institutions. Unsurprisingly, in the current period of relative American decline, the institutionalist literature has become quite policy conscious (e.g., Freeman, 1989; Johnson et al., 1989; Jorde & Teece, 1989; Lodge & Walton, 1989; Mowery & Rosenberg, 1989; Reich, 1989; Zysman & Tyson, 1983).[8]

In addition to criticisms of neoclassical thinking by revisionist institutionalists, the mainstream Marxist literature that had focused on irreconcilable problems of dependency—largely in Latin America, but with applications in advanced economies—became increasingly limited in the 1980s (Browett, 1985; Evans, 1987). Explanations of how and why formerly peripheral countries of East Asia emerged as potent challengers to traditional core countries were wanting (Deyo, 1987b). Wallerstein's (1974, 1979, 1980) world-system analysis had accounted for historic shifts in the international regional hierarchy, but did not offer a systematic and parsimonious explanation of how a nation's status could change. Nor could this framework prescribe paths to development for lagging regions.

Neoclassical and Marxist research has been decidedly nonactivist, in that policy recommendations have occupied little more space than notes at the end of analyses. Neoclassical work has excluded the public sector conceptually because it is irrelevant in an efficient, free market economy. Policy is considered to be important in developing regions, yet principally in opening the way for the evolution of free market forces and the diffusion of modern thinking and consumption.[9] Marxist analysis has provided a provocative and highly competent foil to the conventional wisdom of the West, resulting in a wealth of insights into problems posed by the capitalist system. Change would have to be fundamental, structural, and long term, and at issue, then, was not how to resolve problems in the immediate environment, but how to understand and explain empirical realities.

Yet, the realities of East Asia escaped much of this literature, due in part to the Latin American roots of much contemporary Marxist thinking on development. Whereas advanced Latin American countries—Brazil, Mexico, Argentina—remained saddled with poverty despite productivity gains, the Four Tigers were experiencing income convergence, entrepreneurial success, and greater advances in manufacturing production than their Latin American counterparts (Barrett & Chin, 1987; Haggard, 1989; James, Naya, & Meier, 1989). Traditional development theory, entrenched within Western thinking (whether the advanced market economies or the developing countries of the Western Hemisphere), could neither explain dramatic change nor prescribe solutions to problems resulting from economic shifts.

BOTTOM-UP DEVELOPMENT STRATEGIES, AMERICAN LOCAL PUBLIC SECTOR INVOLVEMENT, AND MIFs

Fundamental changes in the international economy and within nations in the mid-1970s prompted reactions in development theory. Persistent socioeconomic problems, especially in developing regions, have cast doubt on the traditional notion that modernization, the diffusion of production processes, and consumer welfare are inevitable features of development. Moreover, the persistence of poverty, illiteracy, and lack of skills in a knowledge-intensive world economy dictate change, which the political economy literature neglected. Conventional strategies of development that assume, but do not operationalize, appropriate national policies to diffuse modern production and consumption from the most developed to the least developed regions have been superseded by a vision of bottom-up, territorial, endogenous development and local planning (Stohr, 1982; Stohr & Taylor, 1981; Stohr & Todtling, 1977).

Parallel, though independent, changes have recently occurred within the United States. Nationally, the repercussions of change in the international economy have included a budget deficit and a reduced federal budget for allocations to states and local economies; more locally, these have included severe economic decline in areas where regionally/locally specific industries have unsuccessfully faced international competition (Glickman & Wilson, 1986). In response to these changes, two relatively dramatic changes in development theory emerged by the end of the 1980s: local action to effect change, and recognition of the strategic role of the state in planning for local and regional development. Community organizations and local public-private partnerships have become explicit means to achieve change. Such partnerships have existed throughout U.S. history, but it was in reaction to recession conditions during the Carter administration that this policy figured prominently in local development (Lyall, 1986), and the Reagan administration subsequently popularized partnerships as part of a New Federalism (Berger, 1986).[10] While the notion of industrial policy in the United States has persisted at the national level as a taboo, local public involvement in private development has become necessary, acceptable, and even popular. Public-private partnerships assume many forms, with different degrees of public contribution. Common are government-sponsored incubators for new, especially high-tech, firms; cooperation between firms and applied research programs at universities; government support of not-for-profit organizations, and of small business and fledgling neighborhood/community cooperative organizations (Allen & Levine, 1986; Bradford & Temali, 1986; Gupta, 1989; Smilor & Gill, 1986; Wiewel & Mier, 1986).[11]

Ironically, the MIF—the one institutional form in the United States based explicitly on public-private sector interaction—remains outside the purview of the local planning and development literature. In part, its neglect is a function of timing. CFs and MIFs have reacted to changing realities with rudimentary differences in behavior and operation. For example, American CFs initiated a period of relatively dramatic production reorganization in the wake of oil shocks and increasing international competition during the mid-1970s and 1980s; these included increasing subcontracting arrangements among firms and decreasing internalization of activities within the firm, increasing rates of product innovation to compete, and streamlining management, consolidating operations, and eliminating redundant labor (see Ettlinger, 1990, for a review and appraisal of employment effects and policy).

While CFs and CF workers experienced stressful conditions in the late 1970s and the 1980s, MIFs were comparatively unaffected, because their guaranteed market and steady flow of funding protected them from increasing competition, especially during the Reagan administration. MIFs are now undergoing radical changes, principally because of political, not economic, changes in the world system. MIFs are confronted with a competitive market in which government funding and guarantees are greatly reduced.

Restructuring within the top-tier MIFs echoes the restructuring that continues among CFs. Accordingly, large contractors are reorganizing production, using a host of adaptive strategies that by now are commonplace among CFs. These strategies include spatial rationalization and consolidation of production (Naj, 1990; Wartzman, 1990a, 1990c), subcontracting routine activities that were previously internal while maintaining in-house performance of nonroutine activity (Naj, 1990), joint ventures between primes (Asinof, 1990a), streamlining management (Wartzman, 1990c), and job rotation (Fuchsberg, 1990). Most of these tactics involve laying off workers. In addition, MIFs are pursuing a strategy of "defense conversion," or the transfer of military to commercial production, which involves the development of aggressive marketing strategies (Wartzman, 1990b).

The economic restructuring of defense activity is not, however, a unilateral process, largely because political support for different divisions of the military and different types of activities is uneven. The Pentagon's current interest in maintaining maritime superiority has more negative consequences for firms producing for the Army than for the Navy (Pasztor & Wartzman, 1990). Furthermore, the emphasis on electronics, computer-related equipment, and communications suggests that MIFs in or developing into these sectors will fare better than others (Pasztor & Wartzman, 1990). These growth industries of the military are also the growth industries of the world economy, and strides in these sectors could be converted to civilian applications.

A POST-COLD WAR SCENARIO FOR MIFs

MIF activity stands to be reduced in the post-Cold War climate, but it will continue. Despite great strides in East-West relations, instability in geopolitically significant and volatile areas such as the Middle East ensure the persistence of a military complex in the United States. At issue, then, are the possible consequences—both negative and positive—of industry contraction. The contention here is that changes in MIF activity will extend far beyond obvious immediate impacts, such as plant closures and layoffs. Furthermore, a scenario for defense conversion requires more than recognizing the potential for a transfer of military to civilian-oriented research programs. Aside from the supply-side need to develop appropriate policies to ease occupational transfers (Dumas, 1982a), we need to consider how change will occur, within and among firms, from the perspective of production.

INDUSTRY STRUCTURE, DIVISIONS OF LABOR, AND POSSIBILITIES FOR DEFENSE CONVERSION

Prime contractors focusing on activities that currently receive support from the Pentagon and Congress (particularly maritime and electronic products) should gain an initial advantage at the outset of the restructuring period. Small MIF supplier firms are likely to be the most immediate and numerous casualties, in part because typical subcontractors are highly specialized and are vulnerable if orders are reduced (Selz, 1989).

The experience of CF restructuring carries an important message relevant to MIFs, notably, that uncertain markets require that firms either (a) become internally diversified with respect to product lines (i.e., achieve internal economies of scope), or (b) specialize flexibly so that they can change rapidly from one specialized product line to another to meet changing demand. Larger, prime contractors, which have not had to rely on efficient production processes for survival, will most likely find flexible specialization a more difficult option than expanding internal economies of scope, at least in the short run. Moreover, maintaining in-house activity may ensure cash flow during stressful times (Asinof, 1990b). Accordingly, the survival strategies of primes may have negative and perhaps fatal impacts on smaller subcontractors.

Subcontractors that survive are likely to be medium-sized firms with sufficient internal economies of scale to produce routine, standardized parts regularly. Presumably, such parts (e.g., valves) could be marketed to CFs or to prime MIFs, thereby providing a relatively immediate, operational, and short-run avenue to defense conversion. This role of subcontractors may represent a division of labor that would enable the primes to focus on basic research, while the subcontractors pursue routine production of standard parts. In this regard, the MIF sector may achieve a division of labor on an *interfirm* basis somewhat similar to what evolved among large CFs on an *intra-firm* basis after World War II. In addition, we may expect a further articulation of existing divisions of labor within the top-tier MIFs, whereby branch or subsidiary establishments produce routine parts for military as well as civilian uses. Although such segmentation of tasks and labor already exists within the prime contractors, increasing segmentation in the future—through consolidation combined with allocation of exclusively routine activities to branches or subsidiaries—may provide an in-house cushion of support for relatively limited and risky basic research.

Although the concept of routine and nonroutine operations in different establishments and regions appears similar to the hierarchical structure of CF activity, CF divisions of labor in the post-World War II growth period, and MIF divisions of labor in the post-Cold War period, are likely to differ qualitatively. Isomorphism between the *spatial* divisions of labor of these two is unlikely, because the footloose nature of CF production, requiring neither skilled labor nor specialized services, will not prevail in the case of MIFs. Routine or standardized production in MIFs typically involves skilled blue-collar labor, such as machinists and welders, who are neither ubiquitous nor numerous. Skilled blue-collar workers historically have been situated in particular regions, especially the Great Lakes states and the Northeast, where generations have worked within a regional industrial specialization (Browne, 1983). These workers are in short supply for MIFs, as well as for CFs that are reducing the scale of their operations and require higher-skilled workers in smaller, craft-oriented operations (Mitchell, 1987).

The limited supply of skilled blue-collar workers suggests one of three locational possibilities for MIFs and/or CFs requiring such labor: (a) Locate near this source of labor, as CFs and MIFs traditionally have done; (b) locate in an area without an experienced and skilled blue-collar labor force and import workers, as often occurs with respect to the MIF white-collar labor force; and (c) train a local, inexperienced work force. The third option, although desirable from the perspective of endogenous development in lagging regions, is most unlikely due to the high costs of training, especially in light of short-run problems of production. The second option implies some degree of footlooseness, and carries the potential to affect and alter existing regional economic differentiation in the United States. However, in the absence of a local employment crisis creating a significant push factor, blue-collar labor is typically less mobile than its white-collar counterpart, especially over long distances.[12]

The possibility of interregional migration would represent a post-Cold War version of the early Frostbelt to Sunbelt migration. The critical difference between the migration streams of the Cold War and post-Cold War eras is one of skill: Frostbelt-Sunbelt population shifts of the early 1980s largely entailed movements of relatively unskilled workers; population shifts of the 1990s would entail a much more skilled population, fewer than in the early 1980s but a more powerful shift of human resources. Most likely, a combination of the first and second locational options will ensue, suggesting that although traditional areas of military activity will continue to dominate, an increased dispersion of medium-sized subcontractors producing standard products is possible, especially in the Great Lakes states, with their history of blue-collar skills.[13]

Reduced financial support of MIFs from the federal government is leading to an uncertain market and dwindling Wall Street support (Asinof, 1990b), which suggests that MIF basic research will increase its dependency on routine production of subsidiaries/branches and/or subcontractors, located both in the defense perimeter and in such regions as the Midwest. This carries important implications for both management and spatial divisions of labor. Interdependence between primes and subcontractors or between units/divisions within an MIF suggests a relatively high degree of managerial interaction, in contrast to the hierarchical separation of tasks associated with Taylorism.

Reliance of nonroutine activity on routine yet skilled operations is provocative, and prompts revision of the traditional dominance-dependence model of (spatial) divisions of labor in the United States (Clark, 1981; Cohen, 1977). In the years of CF growth after 1945, branch plants (notably in the Sunbelt and later in the Third World) were characterized by unskilled work, economic leakage, and dependent linkages; the headquarters and R&D (notably in the Northeast) exhibited high-skilled work, high profits, and dominant linkages (Ettlinger, 1984). The spatial manifestation of these intrafirm links was dominance of one regional economy and dependence elsewhere. In the case of future MIF activity, divisions of labor may be characterized more by interdependence. Units engaged in routine production, which can provide a critical cushion of commercial support for nonroutine basic research, may depend more on CFs than MIFs for their forward (market) linkages. At the same time, basic research programs of large MIFs may offer routine defense-related production units a competitive edge, because these programs may be channeled into process changes and increased efficiency, notably in electronics. Prime contractors and their satellites have an edge over their exclusively civilian counterparts, as MIF research will continue to receive federal support, provided that productivity is apparent.

Surviving MIFs may then represent an embryonic form of mixed economy at the scale of the firm, and possibly an effective firm-scale model of public-private sector interaction. Accordingly, MIFs that persist may well be more engaged in the civilian economy than in the production of weaponry alone. To recapitulate, modifications in the relations of production among divisions of labor—specifically, the changing relationship between routine and nonroutine operations—may foster collaborative public-private sector interaction on an inter-firm basis (through prime-subcontractor linkages) as well as on an intrafirm basis (through linkages between routine and nonroutine operations within MIFs). The critical factor here is the necessity of routine production establishments, whether units of prime MIFs or subcontractors, to establish nonmilitary markets.

From the perspective of changes in the world political economy, the development of new strategic industries poses interesting possibilities for MIFs. The last two decades have seen the evolution of the electronics industry as a strategic element of world economic and political power (Borrus, 1988; Prestowitz, 1988). In the future, strategic industries may be linked to environmental concerns, along with the increasing political expedience of avoiding oil as a principal energy source. These elements of environmental and energy research may translate into new foci of federal R&D expenditures in the United States.

Strides in the development of civilian applications in alternative energy research (e.g., in production systems and transportation industries) are theoretically likely to involve government support and may well occur through MIFs, largely because CFs are constrained to maintain short-run profits in a competitive world economy. These CFs cannot reasonably venture into major basic and applied R&D programs, which entail high risk and are inherently long run. The United States has long held the capability for shifting from oil to ethanol or methanol, but such changes have not been lucrative for CFs (Ettlinger, 1984). American taboos on explicit national industrial policy suggest that short-run government support of basic research with clear civilian applications is more likely to be directed at MIFs than at CFs. The catalyst for such imminent changes will be political, not economic, as the U.S. government may view different energy sources as an alternative to long-term military engagement in the Middle East. In this regard, the development of new research foci and different bodies of scientific knowledge within MIFs appears likely, although hardly an immediate process. Ironically, it may be through federal R&D funding of the military complex that civilian-oriented, economically efficient production eventually supports—and even overshadows—the production of weaponry as a means to achieve political ends.

From the perspective of general development theory, this juncture in world history and the possibility of public-private sector coordination at the scale of the firm in the United States have interesting implications. If some version of the above scenario should transpire, then we may anticipate an unprecedented involvement of the government in the private sector in the long run. In the past, such involvement often has been considered meddlesome, even coercive. The character of public-private sector interaction envisioned here is collaborative and constructive. Accordingly, U.S. economic development theory will be related inextricably to government policy, much as it has been in East Asian countries. In light of the ethnocentric character of development theory, an appreciation of the role of the state apparatus in U.S. economic development is not likely to evolve from an appreciation of different processes around the world and the inherently non-American developmental trajectories of the countries of East Asia; rather, the recognition of the critical role of the U.S. government in the domestic economy will have to come from observation and anticipation of endogenous production processes, in response to and in the context of global changes.

COMMUNITY IMPACTS AND CONSUMER WELFARE

Apart from the dimension of production processes, the prospects for consumer well-being in defense communities are mixed. Most negative and immediate consequences of post-Cold War restructuring will involve citywide and communitywide disasters akin to what befell Youngstown in the 1970s. Small and highly specialized subcontractors may face closure, with ensuing negative multiplier effects in the local economy. Lima, Ohio, exemplifies the type of defense-dependent community that most likely will be a casualty of restructuring at the outset of the post-Cold War era. This city has been dominated by a General Dynamics tank plant since 1980. The establishment of this facility effectively saved Lima's struggling blue-collar economy, reducing local unemployment from around 18% to 8% (Yocum, 1990). Cutbacks, especially in MIFs producing for the army, and an uncertain market threaten a shutdown in 1993. As 75-80% of the employees are local, closure would have a devastating effect on local employment, consumer spending, and, indirectly, the local tax base and the city government. Whereas at the national level MIFs may be considered a drain on tax dollars, at the local level they contribute significantly to community financing. Furthermore, indirect effects in this defense-dependent community will be felt by other firms that supply the tank plant; overall, goods and services sold to the plant from local vendors currently total around $26 million (Yocum, 1990).

In contrast to the highly specialized economy of Lima, localities that are characterized by a diverse industry and activity mix are likely to survive plant closures and associated decline. The California defense-related economy is a likely example of one in which communities will not be affected negatively in the long run. In the short term, the shrinkage of the MIF sector in the Los Angeles area has displaced about 360,000 civilian aerospace jobs, with negative multiplier effects on construction activity and the temporary help industry (Ferguson, 1990). However, whereas military spending in Lima, Ohio, has encompassed the local economy, the military share of California's gross income has been declining since the 1960s (Esparza, 1989; Ferguson, 1990). This situation reinforces the findings of a number of case studies that suggest that the mix of industries and economic activities in a region prior to defense spending conditions the degree to which a local economy becomes dependent on external resources such as public sector support (Barff & Knight, 1988; Browne, 1988; Clayton, 1967; Henderson, 1990). Plant shutdowns will not affect host communities unilaterally.

Whereas defense-dependent cities will most likely experience extensive out-migration, diversified urban economies, such as Los Angeles, hold the potential for localized occupational transfers of MIF workers. Lima and Los Angeles, as two environmental types, represent pronounced cases of specialization and diversification: Most areas housing displaced MIF workers will experience a mix of out-migration, occupational transfer from MIF to CF positions, and entrepreneurial ventures of laid-off workers pursuing their skills in their own businesses, in addition to a wide range of employment problems.

At the aggregate level, concerns regarding a squeezing effect on an already packed labor market (Karr, 1990) may be overstated, because the crowding of the U.S. labor market has occurred perhaps most dramatically in the services sector and unskilled segments of the labor force.[14] As noted, both blue- and white-collar MIF labor forces tend to be skilled, an attribute that remains in short supply. This highlights a possible negative dimension of occupational transfer from MIF to CF positions. The need for a restructuring of the American educational and training system may be delayed, as displaced MIF workers satisfy CF demands for more skilled labor—a potent echo of the relatively privileged status of MIF workers in this society.

Despite the skill profile of MIF workers and increasing corporate demand for those skills, the employment prospects for MIF workers remain mixed, and vary from one locale to another. In relatively large metropolitan areas, where agglomeration economies are present and skilled workers tend to cluster, further pressure on an already-crowded skilled labor market is quite likely.[15] The consequence of this crowding may be more a matter of increased underemployment (less than full-time and intermittent work) than unemployment. Accordingly, we may expect employment problems to differ both regionally and across the urban hierarchy. For example, we might expect increased problems of underemployment in large cities of the defense perimeter; initial unemployment and, later, out-migration to larger cities may characterize problems of worker displacement in smaller cities. As suggested, it is an open question whether migration occurs on an interregional basis. The retention of defense workers within regions may depend upon whether state-governed support services are developed for occupational transfers within such states.[16]

In addition to issues of city size and agglomeration economies, the mix of defense establishments in a local or regional economy may critically affect the employment impacts of reduced defense activity. For example, whereas defense manufacturing has had positive impacts on the New York economy with respect to blue-collar jobs (Warf, 1989), its contribution to the California economy has been slight (Esparza, 1989). Thus the effects of pressure on an urban labor market may differ substantially, depending upon the salient segment of defense-related workers (e.g., blue-collar, white-collar) in a community. Overcrowding of a white-collar urban labor market may result mostly in problems of underemployment, whereas overcrowding of a blue-collar counterpart may entail underemployment as well as the development of local tensions between industrial unions and defense workers (Dumas, 1982a, p. 33). Indeed, imminent occupational transfers from MIFs to CFs in the post-Cold War era provide fertile ground for studying the differential effects of organized and unorganized labor on (a) spatial movements within the labor market and

(b) local politics and community factionalism in cities with different mixes of labor and industry.

The possibility of intracommunity tensions in relation to a skilled, politically enfranchised segment of local communities may be the critical factor that will stimulate city and state governments to develop support services and policies regarding occupational transfers. Effective policies to help displaced MIF workers are likely to originate at the local rather than the national level, for many of the same reasons that other development strategies have evolved there. First, the federal budget deficit restricts the direction of government resources to social problems. Second, the local employment effects of reduced MIF activity will vary considerably across regions and cities, posing problems for unilateral policy. Quite possibly, the political economy of MIFs and their impacts on local employment—traditionally an enclave unconnected to the larger local or state community—may become enmeshed in existing public-private sector interactions and grass-roots plans for local change, as restructuring in the MIF and CF sectors coincide.

CONCLUDING REMARKS

Conversion of MIF to CF labor hinges in part on local, supply-side policy that is sensitive to a city's needs with respect to local industrial and activity mix and types of displaced MIF workers. Conversion also hinges on the range of employment possibilities that are forthcoming in light of changes in production processes and consequent changes in corporate demand for labor. Following the logic of the scenarios developed above, explicit policy regarding people is likely to develop at the local level while industrial policy regarding MIFs as organizations is likely to develop at the national level. Such federal policy would evolve in the context of new, environmentally conscious growth industries of the world economy and the potential political requirement for developing and funding alternative energy resources. What are currently MIFs may become much more of a hybrid of the public and private sectors at the scale of the firm, and be the agents that most potently affect the domestic economy through the development of new industries and energy sources. In this regard, future MIFs may become operational intermediaries between the public and private sectors. MIFs would occupy a position that is commonly filled by specific institutions in the rapidly developing countries of

East Asia, but has been absent to date in the United States (Johnson, 1987).

Finally, from the perspective of the articulation of production and consumption, the issue remains as to how to spread the positive effects of public-private sector interaction to the growing population of unskilled U.S. workers. Until this final issue is resolved, the enclaved character of MIFs, manifested in the Cold War era in terms of discrete communities, may persist as an intensification or negative enhancement of existing polarities in the U.S. labor market.

NOTES

1. Product cycle theory has been criticized on several grounds. First, it did not account for cycles characteristic of many high-tech firms, which neither standardize nor operate with skilled labor through the final stages of production (Aydalot, 1984; Oakey, 1985). This is characteristic of high-tech CFs and MIFs (Markusen, 1986). Second, the theory, especially as developed by geographers, tended to overemphasize labor-intensive production and neglect capital-intensive establishments in less developed regions (Sayer, 1985). Third, it overlooked substantial foreign investment in advanced economies (Sayer, 1985). Fourth, product cycle theory had no predictive value (Auty, 1984), and could not explain many circumstances and the trajectories of many firms (Storper & Walker, 1989). These last criticisms are somewhat misconstrued because product cycle theory was never intended to describe or predict the behavior of all firms. Theory develops within an empirical context, and many criticisms may be more appropriately conceptualized as observations of changing empirical realities and the inability of context-specific theory (such as product cycle theory) to describe, explain, or predict behavior during such changes.

2. The translation of core/periphery in the United States into the Frostbelt/Sunbelt dichotomy has been criticized for inappropriate regional delineations (Browning & Gesler, 1979) and negligible consideration of the wide range of production processes, each of which has different locational implications (Storper & Walker, 1984).

3. The Cold War and *Sputnik* represented especially significant exogenous stimuli to federal investment in defense-related R&D. Other external events included the Soviet nuclear explosion in 1948 and thermonuclear explosion in 1951, the Korean War in 1950, strategic nuclear missiles in the mid-1950s, the Vietnam War, and energy research (Mowery & Rosenberg, 1989, p. 128).

4. There is a differential focus on product and process change in high-tech firms with substantial R&D components (of which MIFs are a subset) and other, less innovative firms with much smaller R&D components (Malecki, 1986). Some implications of this for MIFs are indicated in Malecki and Stark (1988, p. 73).

5. Workers in ammunition production tend to be relatively unskilled, suggesting an interesting exception to the general portrayal of MIF employees as high-skilled blue- or white-collar workers (Malecki & Stark, 1988, p. 95). Malecki and Stark also indicate that ammunitions plants occur mostly in southern states, notably in Tennessee and Virginia. Indeed, if there is to be an exception to the qualitative differences in CF and MIF spatial divisions of labor, we might expect a southern, possibly Appalachian, location of unskilled MIF workers. Malecki and Stark suggest that MANTECH programs, oriented

toward automating standardized processes and possibly displacing labor, may be targeted toward these ammunition plants.

6. Alternatively, Markusen (1989, pp. 124-125) notes that the development of new defense establishments in a boom period may create conflict between the established civilian community and the new defense community over issues such as skyrocketing housing costs.

7. Hayes (1989, pp. 33-34) provides an interesting "quasi-cultural" account of the implications of secrecy in defense enclaves.

8. In other social sciences, notably geography, formal analyses from economics' institutionalist paradigm have been employed with respect to changes in corporate organization from prevalence of internalized to externalized transactions (Scott, 1985). However, the field's larger context and its policy consciousness have been eschewed.

9. Deyo (1987a, pp. 11-12) aptly conceptualizes modernization theory as the institutional complement to traditional neoclassical theory.

10. Interestingly, Bahl and Duncombe (1988) found little structural break between the Carter and Reagan administrations with respect to state and local government finances.

11. Urban enterprise zones also have been considered a form of public-private partnership. Although they have failed from the perspective of both social well-being (Goldsmith, 1984) and locational principles (Blackley, 1985), they are widespread.

12. Population increases in the Sunbelt throughout much of the 1970s were more a function of natural increase than of North-South migration (Jusenius & Ledebur, 1977). Although such labor movements did occur and continue, migration prevailed mostly in the early 1980s, in response to recession. Initial industrial growth in the Sunbelt occurred not as a function of relocation (closing a plant in one location and establishing a facility in another), but as a function of firms creating new facilities and employing local workers.

13. This is consistent with Browne's (1983) analysis, although that work did not concern MIFs specifically.

14. In supply-side, demographic terms, this crowding of relatively unskilled occupations is associated with unprecedented numbers of women, minority youth, and the young elderly in the labor force (Ford Foundation, 1983). From the perspective of production systems, increased demand for skilled workers in restructured operations has effectively reduced demand for unskilled work (Ettlinger, 1990).

15. Angel (1989) examined the labor market for engineers in the semiconductor industry, finding that underemployment was more likely in areas such as Los Angeles than in the Midwest.

16. Henderson (1990) provides some discussion of existing policies, and notes that dislocated defense workers may be better positioned to find work than nondefense workers. Policy formulation requires attention to the general issue of worker displacement in both sectors.

REFERENCES

Adams, G. (1981). *The politics of defense contracting: The iron triangle.* New Brunswick, NJ: Transaction.

Allen, D. N., & Levine, V. (1986). *Nurturing advanced technology enterprises.* New York: Praeger.

Amin, S. (1974). *Accumulation on a world scale: A critique of the theory of underdevelopment*. New York: Monthly Review Press.

Anell, L., & Nygren, B. (1980). *The developing countries and the world economic order*. New York: Methuen.

Angel, D. P. (1989). The labor market for engineers in the U.S. semiconductor industry. *Economic Geography, 65*, 99-112.

Asinof, L. (1990a, April 12). Defense and business, a special report: Tight military budgets make for strange bedfellows. *Wall Street Journal*, p. A1.

Asinof, L. (1990b, April 12). Defense and business, a special report: Wall Street retreats from the defense industry. *Wall Street Journal*, p. A1.

Auty, R. M. (1984). The product life-cycle and the location of the global petrochemical industry after the second oil shock. *Economic Geography, 60*, 325-338.

Aydalot, P. (1981). The regional policy and spatial strategy of large organizations. In A. Kuklinski (Ed.), *Polarized development and regional policies* (pp. 173-185). The Hague: Mouton.

Aydalot, P. (1984). Questions for regional economy. *Tijdschrift voor Economische en Sociale Geografie, 75*, 4-13.

Bahl, R., & Duncombe, W. (1988). State and local government finances: Was there a structural break in the Reagan years? *Growth and Change, 19*, 30-48.

Barff, R. A., & Knight, P. L. (1988). The role of federal military spending in the timing of the New England employment turnaround. *Papers of the Regional Science Association, 65*, 151-166.

Barrett, R. E., & Chin, S. (1987). Export-oriented and industrializing states in the capitalist world system: Similarities and differences. In F. C. Deyo (Ed.), *The political economy of the new Asian industrialism* (pp. 23-43). Ithaca, NY: Cornell University Press.

Berger, R. A. (1986). Private-sector initiatives in the Reagan administration. In P. Davis (Ed.), *Public-private partnerships: Improving urban life* (pp. 14-30). New York: Academy of Political Science, New York City Partnership.

Blackley, P. R. (1985). The demand for industrial sites in a metropolitan area. *Journal of Urban Economics, 17*, 247-261.

Bolton, R. (1966). *Defense purchases and regional growth*. Washington, DC: Brookings Institution.

Borrus, M. G. (1988). *Competing for control: America's stake in microelectronics*. Cambridge, MA: Ballinger.

Bradford, C., & Temali, M. (1986). City venture corporation: Initiatives in U.S. cities. In E. M. Bergman (Ed.), *Local Economies in Transition* (pp. 185-204). Durham, NC: Duke University Press.

Browett, J. (1985). The newly industrializing countries and radical theories of development. *World Development, 13*, 789-803.

Browne, L. E. (1983, November-December). Can high tech save the Great Lakes states? *New England Economic Review*, pp. 19-33.

Browne, L. E. (1988, September-October). Defense spending and high technology development: National and state issues. *New England Economic Review*, pp. 3-22.

Browning, C. E., & Gesler, W. (1979). The Sun Belt-Snow Belt: A case of sloppy regionalizing. *Professional Geographer, 31*, 66-74.

Chandler, A. D. (1962). *Strategy and structure: Chapters in the history of the industrial enterprise*. Cambridge: MIT Press.

Chandler, A. D. (1977). *The visible hand: The managerial revolution in American business.* Cambridge, MA: Belknap.

Clark, G. L. (1981). The employment relation and spatial division of labor: A hypothesis. *Annals of the Association of American Geographers, 71,* 412-424.

Clark, L., & Malabre, A. L. (1990, July 6). Productivity indicates sluggish economy. *Wall Street Journal,* p. A2.

Clayton, J. L. (1967). The impact of the Cold War on the economies of California and Utah, 1946-1965. *Pacific Historical Review, 36,* 449-473.

Coase, R. H. (1937). The nature of the firm. *Economica* (New Series), *4,* 386-405.

Cohen, R. B. (1977). Multinational corporations, international finance, and the Sunbelt. In D. C. Perry & A. J. Watkins (Eds.), *The rise of the Sunbelt cities* (pp. 211-226). Beverly Hills, CA: Sage.

Cohen, S. S., & Zysman, J. (1987). *Manufacturing matters.* New York: Basic Books.

Cooper, A. C. (1971). Spin-offs and technical entrepreneurship. *IEEE Transactions on Engineering Management, EM-18,* 2-6.

DeGrasse, R. W. (1984). The military and semiconductors. In J. Tirman (Ed.), *The militarization of high technology* (pp. 77-104). Cambridge, MA: Ballinger.

Dertouzos, M. L., Lester, R. K., Solow, R. M., & the MIT Commission on Industrial Productivity. (1989). *Made in America: Regaining the productive edge.* Cambridge: MIT Press.

Deyo, F. C. (1987a). Introduction. In F. C. Deyo (Ed.), *The political economy of the new Asian industrialism* (pp. 11-22). Ithaca, NY: Cornell University Press.

Deyo, F. C. (Ed.). (1987b). *The political economy of the new Asian industrialism.* Ithaca, NY: Cornell University Press.

Dorfer, I. (1983). *Arms deal: The selling of the F-16.* New York: Praeger.

Dumas, L. J. (1982a). The conversion of military economy: The United States. In L. J. Dumas (Ed.), *The political economy of arms reduction* (pp. 27-68). Boulder, CO: Westview.

Dumas, L. J. (Ed.). (1982b). *The political economy of arms reduction.* Boulder, CO: Westview.

Erickson, R. A. (1976). The filtering-down process: Industrial location in a non-metropolitan area. *Professional Geographer, 28,* 254-260.

Erickson, R. A. (1977). Sub-regional impact multipliers: Income spread effects from a major installation. *Economic Geography, 53,* 283-294.

Esparza, A. (1989). Defense impact analysis within a social accounting framework. *Growth and Change, 20,* 63-79.

Ettlinger, N. (1984). Comments on the concept of linkages from the perspective of corporate organization in the modern capitalist system. *Tijdschrift voor Economische en Sociale Geographie, 75,* 285-291.

Ettlinger, N. (1990). Worker displacement and corporate restructuring: A policy-conscious appraisal. *Economic Geography, 66,* 67-82.

Ettlinger, N., & Crump, J. R. (1989). The military industrial firm, economic control, and local development. *Environment and Planning C: Government and Policy, 7,* 27-38.

Evans, P. (1987). Class, state, and dependence in East Asia. In F. C. Deyo (Ed.), *The political economy of the new Asian industrialism* (pp. 203-226). Ithaca, NY: Cornell University Press.

Ferguson, T. W. (1990, July 24). An immigrant economy less prone to Pentagon pulverizing. *Wall Street Journal,* p. A15.

Ford Foundation. (1983). *Not working: Unskilled youth and displaced adults* (Working Paper). New York: Author.

Frank, A. G. (1967). *Capitalism and underdevelopment in Latin America.* New York: Monthly Review Press.

Freeman, C. (1989). Technical change and productivity. *Finance and Development, 26,* 46-48.

Frobel, F., Heinrichs, J., & Kreye, O. (1980). *The new international division of labor.* Cambridge: Cambridge University Press.

Fuchsberg, G. (1990, August 3). United Technologies unit to eliminate 4,000 jobs due to military spending cuts. *Wall Street Journal,* p. A2.

Gellen, M. (1971). Whither California? In S. Melman (Ed.), *The war economy of the United States* (pp. 187-200). New York: St. Martin's.

Glickman, N. J., & Wilson, R. A. (1986). National contexts for urban economic policy. In E. M. Bergman (Ed.), *Local economies in transition* (pp. 15-36). Durham, NC: Duke University Press.

Goldsmith, W. W. (1984). Bringing the Third World home: Enterprise zones for America? In L. Sawers & W. K. Tabb (Eds.), *Sunbelt/Snowbelt: Urban development and regional restructuring* (pp. 339-350). New York: Oxford University Press.

Gray, I. (1969). Employment effect of a new industry in a rural area. *Monthly Labor Review, 92,* 26-30.

Griffin, K. (1978). *International inequality and national poverty.* London: Macmillan.

Gupta, U. (1989, July 6). Cleveland's entrepreneurial plan helps offset decline. *Wall Street Journal,* p. B2.

Haggard, S. (1989). The east Asian NICs in comparative perspective. *Annals of the American Academy of Political and Social Science, 505,* 129-141.

Hakanson, L. (1979). Towards a theory of location and corporate growth. In F. E. I. Hamilton & G. J. R. Linge (Eds.), *Spatial analysis, industry and the industrial environment, I* (pp. 115-138). New York: John Wiley.

Harrison, B., & Bluestone, B. (1988). *The great U-turn: Corporate restructuring and the polarization of America.* New York: Basic Books.

Hayes, D. (1989). *Behind the silicon curtain.* Boston: South End.

Henderson, Y. K. (1990, July-August). Defense cutbacks and the New England economy. *New England Economic Review,* pp. 3-24.

Hymer, S. (1977). The multinational corporation and the law of uneven development. In J. Bhagwati (Ed.), *Economics and world order from the 1970s to the 1990s* (pp. 113-140). New York: Macmillan.

James, W. E., Naya, S., & Meier, G. M. (1989). *Asian development: Economic success and policy lessons.* Madison: University of Wisconsin Press.

Johnson, C. (1987). Political institutions and economic performance: The government-business relationship in Japan, South Korea, and Taiwan. In F. C. Deyo (Ed.), *The political economy of the new Asian industrialism* (pp. 136-164). Ithaca, NY: Cornell University Press.

Johnson, C., Tyson, L., & Zysman, J. (Eds.). (1989). *Politics and productivity.* Cambridge, MA: Ballinger.

Jorde, T. M., & Teece, D. J. (1989). Competition and cooperation: Striking the right balance. *California Management Review, 31,* 25-37.

Jusenius, C. L., & Ledebur, L. C. (1977). A myth in the making. In E. B. Liner & L. K. Lynch (Eds.), *The economics of southern growth* (pp. 131-173). Durham, NC: Seeman.

Karr, A. (1990, June 19). Labor letter. *Wall Street Journal,* p. A1.

Kinzer, S. (1979, January 27). The least underdeveloped country. *New Republic*, pp. 18-22.

Klimasewski, T. (1978). Corporate dominance of manufacturing in Appalachia. *Geographical Review, 68*, 94-102.

Krumme, G. (1981). Corporate organization and regional development in the American federal system. In G. W. Hoffman (Ed.), *Federalism and regional development* (pp. 154-192). Austin: University of Texas Press.

Langlois, R. (Ed.). (1986). *Economics as a process: Essays in the new institutional economics*. Cambridge: Cambridge University Press.

Lodge, G., & Walton, R. (1989). The American corporation and its new relationships. *California Management Review, 31*, 9-24.

Lyall, K. C. (1986). Public-private partnerships in the Carter years. In P. Davis (Ed.), *Public-private partnerships: Improving urban life* (pp. 4-13). New York: Academy of Political Science, New York City Partnership.

Malecki, E. J. (1981). Product cycles, innovation cycles, and regional economic change. *Technological Forecasting and Social Change, 19*, 291-306.

Malecki, E. J. (1982). Federal R&D spending in the U.S. *Regional Studies, 16*, 19-35.

Malecki, E. J. (1984). Military spending and the US defense industry: Regional patterns of military contracts and subcontracts. *Environment and Planning C: Government and Policy, 2*, 31-44.

Malecki, E. J. (1986). Research and development and the geography of high-technology complexes. In J. Rees (Ed.), *Technology, regions, and policy* (pp. 51-74). Totowa, NJ: Rowman & Littlefield.

Malecki, E. J., & Stark, L. M. (1988). Regional and industrial variation in defense spending: Some American evidence. In M. J. Breheny (Ed.), *Defence expenditure and regional development* (pp. 67-101). London: Mansell.

Marfels, C. (1978). The structure of the military-industrial complex in the US and its impact on industrial concentration. *Kyklos, 31*, 409-423.

Markusen, A. R. (1985). *Profit cycles, oligopoly, and regional development*. Cambridge: MIT Press.

Markusen, A. R. (1986). Defense spending: A successful industrial policy? *International Journal of Urban and Regional Research, 10*, 105-121.

Markusen, A. R. (1987). *Regions: The economics and politics of territory*. Totowa, NJ: Rowman & Littlefield.

Markusen, A. R. (1988). The military remapping of the United States. In M. J. Breheny (Ed.), *Defence expenditure and regional development* (pp. 17-28). London: Mansell.

Markusen, A. R. (1989). Industrial restructuring and regional politics. In R. A. Beauregard (Ed.), *Economic restructuring and political response* (pp. 115-147). Newbury Park, CA: Sage.

Markusen, A. R., & Bloch, R. (1985). Defensive cities: Military spending, high technology, and human settlements. In M. Castells (Ed.), *High technology, space, and society* (pp. 106-120). Beverly Hills, CA: Sage.

Massey, D. (1979). In what sense a regional problem? *Regional Studies, 13*, 233-243.

Massey, D. (1984). *Spatial divisions of labor*. New York: Methuen.

McGranahan, D. A. (1982). Absentee and local ownership of industry in northwestern Wisconsin. *Growth and Change, 13*, 31-35.

Melman, S. (1986). The limits of military power. *International Security, 11*, 72-87.

Miller, J. G., & Vollmann, T. E. (1985). The hidden factory. *Harvard Business Review, 5*, 142-150.

Mitchell, C. (1987, September 14). A growing shortage of skilled craftsmen troubles some firms. *Wall Street Journal*, pp. 1, 15.

Mowery, D. C., & Rosenberg, N. (1981). Technical change in the commercial aircraft industry, 1925-1975. *Technological Forecasting and Social Change, 20*, 347-358.

Mowery, D. C., & Rosenberg, N. (1989). *Technology and the pursuit of economic growth*. New York: Cambridge University Press.

Naj, A. K. (1990, April 30). GE aerospace unit to cut 4,200 jobs in restructuring. *Wall Street Journal*, p. A6.

National Science Foundation. (1979). *Science indicators: Report of the National Science Board, 1978*. Washington, DC: Government Printing Office.

Oakey, R. (1985). High-technology industries and agglomeration economies. In P. Hall & A. Markusen (Eds.), *Silicon landscapes* (pp. 94-117). Boston: Allen & Unwin.

Pasztor, A., & Wartzman, R. (1990, May 24). Winners and losers: As defense industry shrinks, suppliers face widely varying fates. *Wall Street Journal*, pp. A1, A8.

Peck, M. J., & Scherer, F. M. (1962). *The weapons acquisition process*. Boston: Harvard Business School.

Pred, A. (1976). The interurban transmission of growth in advanced economies. *Regional Studies, 10*, 151-171.

Prestowitz, C. V. (1988). *Trading places*. New York: Basic Books.

Reich, R. B. (1982). Making industrial policy. *Foreign Affairs, 60*, 852-881.

Reich, R. B. (1989). The quiet path to technological preeminence. *Scientific American, 261*, 41-47.

Rundquist, B. S. (1978). On testing a military industrial complex theory. *American Politics Quarterly, 6*, 29-53.

Sauvant, K. P. (1980). From political to economic interdependence: The historical context of the new international economic order. In A. R. Negandhi (Ed.), *Functioning of the multinational corporations* (pp. 13-24). Oxford: Pergamon.

Sayer, R. A. (1985). Industry and space: A sympathetic critique of radical research. *Environment and Planning D: Society and Space, 3*, 3-29.

Scott, A. J. (1985). Location processes, urbanization, and territorial development. *Environment and Planning A, 17*, 479-501.

Selz, M. (1989, October 27). Small contractors scramble to cope with defense cuts. *Wall Street Journal*, pp. B1-B2.

Smilor, R. W., & Gill, M. D. (1986). *The new business incubator*. Lexington, MA: Lexington.

Stohr, W. B. (1982). Structural characteristics of peripheral areas and the relevance of the stock-in-trade variables of regional science. *Papers of the Regional Science Association, 49*, 71-84.

Stohr, W. B., & Taylor, D. R. F. (Eds.). (1981). *Development from above or below?* New York: John Wiley.

Stohr, W., & Todtling. F. (1977). Spatial equity: Some anti-theses to current development doctrine. *Papers of the Regional Science Association, 38*, 33-53.

Storper, M., & Walker, R. (1984). The spatial division of labor: Labor and the location of industries. In L. Sawers & W. K. Tabb (Eds.), *Sunbelt/Snowbelt: Urban development and regional restructuring* (pp. 19-47). New York: Oxford University Press.

Storper, M., & Walker, R. (1989). *The capitalist imperative*. New York: Basil Blackwell.

Vernon, R. (1966). International investment and international trade in the product cycle. *Quarterly Journal of Economics, 60*, 190-207.

Wallerstein, I. (1974). *The modern world-system I*. New York: Academic Press.

Wallerstein, I. (1979). *The capitalist world-economy*. Cambridge: Cambridge University Press.

Wallerstein, I. (1980). *The modern world-system II*. New York: Academic Press.

Warf, B. (1989). Military prime contracts and taxes in the New York metropolitan region: A short-run analysis. *Regional Studies, 23*, 241-251.

Wartzman, R. (1990a, August 7). Defense firm to cut 2,000 in consolidation. *Wall Street Journal*, p. A4.

Wartzman, R. (1990b, November 29). Defense firms gird for end of Cold War. *Wall Street Journal*, p. A4.

Wartzman, R. (1990c, July 17). McDonnell will cut up to 17,000 jobs, many in Long Beach, California, before '91. *Wall Street Journal*, p. A3.

Watts, H. D. (1980). *The large industrial enterprise*. London: Croom Helm.

Wiewel, W., & Mier, R. (1986). Enterprise activities of not-for-profit organizations. In E. M. Bergman (Ed.), *Local economies in transition* (pp. 205-225). Durham, NC: Duke University Press.

Williamson, O. E. (1975). *Markets and hierarchies: Analysis and antitrust implications*. New York: Free Press.

Williamson, O. E. (1981). The modern corporation: Origins, evolution, attributes. *Journal of Economic Literature, 19*, 1537-1568.

Williamson, O. E. (1985). *The economic institutions of capitalism*. New York: Free Press.

Yocum, R. (1990, May 13). As tank plant goes, so goes Lima. *Columbus Dispatch*, pp. 1A, 2A.

Zysman, J., & Tyson, L. (Eds.). (1983). *American industry in international competition*. Ithaca, NY: Cornell University Press.

3

The Pentagon and the Gunbelt

PETER HALL
ANN R. MARKUSEN

THE YEARS SINCE 1945 have seen a profound remapping of industrial America, characterized by the decline of the old industrial heartland, the rise of new industrial regions on the southern and western perimeters of the nation, and the resurgence of New England in the 1980s. The causes of this remapping are complex, but one crucial factor has been the ascendancy of the military-industrial complex. During these years, defense spending became a major determinant of economic prosperity or decay, creating new industrial complexes in California, Texas, and Florida, and—by its relative absence—helping to lay economic waste to cities in the old industrial heartland. The beneficiaries are disposed unevenly around the coastal perimeter, from the state of Washington through California and the southwestern states, Texas and Florida, thence discontinuously up the East Coast to New England. They extend inland only in the West South Central region. In a large-scale research project, a group of us have sought to delineate this remapping, and to try to explain it (Markusen, Hall, Campbell, & Deitrick, 1991). We have titled our study *The Rise of the Gunbelt* because that fairly accurately describes the appearance of the new defense perimeter.

Our main theme is that the rise of the gunbelt has no one single, simple cause. There are some key elements, to be sure: key founding fathers, either born in California or settled there; the skies of America's Sunbelt; the deliberate location of defense plants during World War II, in an interior thought strategically safe; congressional lobbying; a continuing frontier mentality based on urban real estate development, coupled with civic boosterism, in southern and western localities. But, in fact, none of these proved decisive: There were pioneers in the gray Midwest, too; most wartime plants were mothballed; studies have shown that lobbying is like advertising—everyone must participate, but no one really wins.

To unpick the story, the essential basis is that during and especially after World War II, the changing global military mission of the United States powerfully affected the role of the three armed services. During the 1950s, it created a totally new historical phenomenon in the form of the high-technology Cold War, depending on massive and continuing technological advances. This profoundly underlined the fact that military procurement is quite different in nature from commercial production. It also gave a major advantage to the Air Force, which had very different contracting traditions compared with its parent, the Army, and that in turn had complex impacts on U.S. industrial space.

MEASURES OF REMAPPING

There are two main ways of measuring the rise of the gunbelt. One is an *input* measure: the dollar volume of defense contracts that each state or region receives. The other is an *output* measure: the resulting employment impact in these same places. The first is reasonably simple and unambiguous; the second is more complex.

The basic input measure is the volume of prime contracts. In 1952, at the peak of the Korean War, the East North Central division received nearly 31% of prime contracts, with the Middle Atlantic states in second place with 26%. By 1984, that 57% combined share had fallen to 21%. Over that period, the gunbelt—the New England, South Atlantic, East and West South Central, Mountain, and Pacific divisions—increased its share from 38% to nearly 70%. In per capita terms (see Figure 3.1) the shift is even more dramatic: Between 1952 and 1982, New England more than doubled its per capita spending; the East North Central division suffered a loss of more than half its 1952 per capita procurement, and the Middle Atlantic also lost; the Sunbelt divisions all increased their shares, though the Mountain division lost after a spectacular buildup during the 1950s, and the Pacific division remained almost constant.

These geographical shifts reflect underlying trends in weapons procurement and in the share of the three armed services. The Korean War was perhaps the last conventional war fought with conventional equipment. The years that followed were marked by massive buildup

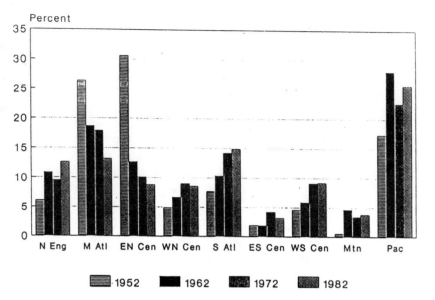

Figure 3.1. Distribution of Prime Contracts by Region

of missile and space systems. The 1980s, the years of the Strategic Defense Initiative (SDI), sanctioned electronic radar-type defensive shields. Since these shifts favored the Air Force, which traditionally had links with the South and West, it was perhaps natural that procurement should show a tilt in those directions (Figure 3.2).

Employment trends followed the same pattern. U.S. Census Bureau figures from 1983 for defense-related employment (almost certainly underestimates) can be compared with estimates of total manufacturing employment to generate location quotients. The resulting map (Figure 3.3) shows that the exceptionally defense-dependent states are New England; New York; the Washington, D.C., area; Florida; the central states from Missouri to Utah; Texas; Arizona; California; and Washington. Table 3.1 shows also that defense job growth was highly concentrated in a few states: California, always the leader, had nearly 17% of new defense jobs between 1967 and 1977 and more than 36% from 1977 to 1983; Massachusetts had more than 5% in the first period, and between 7% and 8% in the second; Florida and Texas had around 7% each in the latter period. In employment terms, as in procurement terms, the gunbelt is real enough.

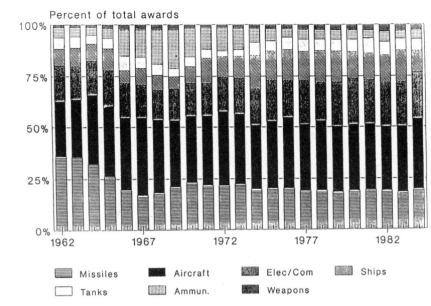

Figure 3.2. Prime Contracts and Categories of Weapons Production

EXPLAINING THE GUNBELT

To explain the rise of the gunbelt, it is necessary to focus on two crucial junctures in U.S. history: World War II, during which small aircraft companies were quite suddenly launched to power and fortune; and the mid-1950s, the time of the Cold War, during which the United States definitively assumed new global responsibilities. To uphold them, it created what came to be called the military-industrial complex: an interwoven system of production comprising the Pentagon, the services, private firms, and political players.

More precisely, the explanation has to be found at a number of different levels of analysis. The starting point is in terms of *key structural forces*. Fundamental here was the country's *strategic mission* as seen by the national leadership. As this vision changed during the 1940s and 1950s, from isolationism to global conflict to Cold War, the notion of strategic response also shifted, from defense of the coasts to strategic bombing, intercontinental missilery, and then SDI. That overarching imperative in turn produced new roles and powers

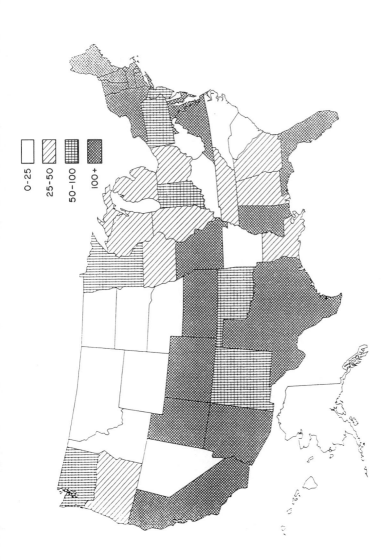

Figure 3.3. Locational Quotients for Military Manufacturing by State, in Comparison With All Manufacturing, 1983 Data

TABLE 3.1

Defense Employment and Manufacturing Employment, 1967, 1977, 1983

	Manufacturing Employment Change		% Defense Employment Change	
	1967-1977	1977-1983	1967-1977	1977-1983
Maine	−0.5	5.5	0.1	2.4
New Hampshire	−3.0	9.6	0.6	4.1
Vermont	0.2	1.3	0.0	0.6
Massachusetts	−27.7	17.6	5.2	7.6
Rhode Island	−1.6	6.1	0.3	2.6
Connecticut	−27.9	−6.6	5.2	−2.8
New York	−57.5	9.7	10.7	4.2
New Jersey	−25.1	4.7	4.7	2.0
Pennsylvania	−36.4	12.2	6.8	5.2
Ohio	−36.0	2.6	6.7	1.1
Indiana	−20.1	4.6	3.7	2.0
Illinois	−29.3	6.8	5.5	2.9
Michigan	−11.9	2.4	2.2	1.0
Wisconsin	−9.2	2.2	1.7	0.9
Minnesota	−15.0	6.4	2.8	2.8
Iowa	−6.1	−2.6	1.1	−1.1
Missouri	−23.6	0.1	4.4	0.0
North Dakota	−0.2	0.0	0.0	0.0
South Dakota	−0.2	0.0	0.0	0.0
Nebraska	−4.2	0.8	0.8	0.3
Kansas	−19.6	13.0	3.7	5.6
Delaware	−0.7	0.0	0.1	0.0
Maryland	−13.1	8.0	2.4	3.4
District of Columbia	0.1	0.0	0.0	0.0
Virginia	−3.8	11.5	0.7	4.9
West Virginia	−3.0	−0.4	0.6	−0.2
North Carolina	−8.0	1.6	1.5	0.7
South Carolina	0.3	0.5	−0.1	0.2
Georgia	−31.6	7.5	5.9	3.2
Florida	−2.8	17.0	0.5	7.3
Kentucky	−0.4	0.2	0.1	0.1
Tennessee	−14.6	4.5	2.7	1.9
Alabama	−2.0	2.1	0.4	0.9
Mississippi	17.7	−14.6	−3.3	−6.3
Arkansas	−2.4	1.0	0.4	0.4
Louisiana	−2.3	1.5	0.4	0.6
Oklahoma	−4.3	5.7	0.8	2.5
Texas	−33.8	15.5	6.3	6.7
Montana	−0.2	−0.1	0.0	0.0
Idaho	0.0	0.1	0.0	0.0
Wyoming	−0.2	−0.1	0.0	0.0
Colorado	−3.6	6.5	0.7	2.8

TABLE 3.1, Continued

	Defense Employment Change		% Defense Employment Change	
	1967-1977	1977-1983	1967-1977	1977-1983
New Mexico	0.5	0.3	−0.1	0.1
Arizona	0.0	4.0	0.0	1.7
Utah	−3.5	3.0	0.7	1.3
Nevada	−0.3	0.0	0.1	0.0
Washington	−3.2	−13.5	0.6	−5.8
Oregon	1.8	−0.2	−0.3	−0.1
California	−89.9	84.9	16.8	36.5
Alaska	0.1	0.0	0.0	0.0
Hawaii	−0.2	0.0	0.0	0.0
United States	−536.5	232.6	100.0	100.0

SOURCE: Data from various publications of the U.S. Bureau of the Census.

of the three armed services, from which stemmed new demands for procurement, thus generating the rise of the military-industrial complex during the 1950s.

The key element was the Cold War. For the first time, weapons were not designed to be used, but to deter the other side from using its arsenal. Increasingly sophisticated weapons—intercontinental missiles, highly sophisticated fighters and reconnaissance planes, a radar shield backed by defensive cruise missiles—became the rule; the process was one of institutionalized innovation. This brought a shift in procurement, causing the industry to face a sudden reorientation to a completely new product requiring new components, new skills, and a commitment to scientific research and development.

The Air Force, very much a junior partner in the defense complex, now became dominant. Its doctrine, well exemplified by General Schriever, chief architect of the ICBM program, was "going to industry and having industry develop and produce for us." By denying itself in-house capacity, it commanded a powerful constituency of scientists, organized labor, and industry; its commitment to free enterprise neatly helped justify the boost in public spending. In sharp contrast, Wernher von Braun and his team, brought to America from Germany with their unequaled experience on the V-2 rocket, worked very much in house at the Army's Redstone Arsenal at Huntsville, Alabama. The Air Force won that battle, though in 1960 von Braun had his triumph when his team became a critical nucleus of the new

National Aeronautics and Space Administration. But they soon found that they could not produce the complex equipment themselves; they had to go to Air Force contractors.

Thus, once the state apparatus began to sponsor innovation—the federal government now underwrites 70% of all R&D, and 70% of this is devoted to military purposes—its nature changed: It became institutionalized and less sensitive to business cycles, and it accelerated. The military-industrial complex, born in the mid-1950s, is literally a new form of continuous industrial innovation. Airframe manufacture became avionics: By the 1960s, electronics constituted 13-20% of an airplane's value, but 50% of that of a missile. The result was the development of a new set of companies. Hughes, McDonnell Douglas, Boeing, Rockwell, Grumman, General Dynamics, United Technologies, TRW, Litton, Lear-Siegler, even if evolved from older industrial firms, represented a new breed of corporation, highly dependent upon defense work, commanding a remarkably high degree of concentrated market power, yet highly dependent on one buyer, the federal government.

By the 1980s, the top 100 companies accounted for 70% of total defense business, the top 25 for 50%, and the top 5 for 20%. And these companies were highly dependent on government orders. But the government does not behave as a textbook private monopsonist would; rather than squeezing the seller, it seeks absolute technical perfection. Further, though cold warfare is extremely capital-intensive, the weaponry is made by very labor-intensive methods. Output is produced not on the assembly line but in small batches, often to unique design specifications. And, because the technologies and the processes and methods of production are quite different from those familiar in consumer goods, production could take place in new locations, outside the traditional industrial heartland. Yet, at the same time, the pressure to innovate has reinforced a tendency toward agglomeration and clustering on the part of the nascent aerospace industry and its suppliers; this is a tendency typical of innovative industry generally, but distinguished here by the fact that products never reach mass production, thus locking the firms in their original locations.

This ensemble of *structural* features—so our analysis runs—then affords spaces to a diverse set of *actors*: generals, university presidents, civic boosters, entrepreneurs, and managers who make decisions based on their preferences and perspectives. Because of the unique market structure of military provisioning, these actors can powerfully influence the selection of sites. On the supply side, they can be described as profit maximizing; on the demand side, their behavior is more complex, encompassing bureaucratic satisficing, strategic concerns, and electioneering goals.

A particular group of (typically male) actors constitute the "founding fathers." These successful innovators require a special kind of environment, a creative milieu; this could be a founder's actual birthplace, or the seat of the university or firm for which he was working when he branched out on his own. But it could also be a place to which he moved because an original environment thwarted ambitions, and to which he was drawn by a variety of factors; since costs of production are generally unimportant, personal preferences or chance may play a crucial role. On the other side lies the state apparatus. Here, no one actor dominates; several exert their influence, including the generals and colonels, the president and advisers, and congressional representatives who review and vote on military appropriations. Military actors, in particular, may be attracted or repelled by certain kinds of places. Collective bargaining, financial incentives, and labor mobility are all foreign to them, causing them to spurn the industrial heartland in favor of remote centers. The role of the congressional actors is more in doubt. There is, of course, a huge literature on pork barreling; however, while individual cases can be cited, there is a notable lack of systematic evidence across time and place. Congress, after all, can generally not initiate a weapons system, and preexisting defense installations account for most defense expenditure; in consequence, the process tends to favor existing centers.

More significant in the context of innovation are the local boosters concerned with expanding the urban tax base, enhancing real estate values, and creating jobs. Such boosters include city officials, real estate developers, and local business interests such as newspapers, banks, sports teams, and even universities. They can be important because they make their efforts at an early, crucial, stage of development.

In turn, there are impacts on the *places*, with their different attributes—some evident, some still latent. Together, actors and places help create the *growth trajectories* of new military-industrial centers: First, new centers emerge, born of the Cold War strategic mission and its major tools; then, these centers develop strong agglomerative growth trajectories; finally, as innovation alters the technology of warfare, new weapons and strategies will themselves favor yet newer centers of activity, tailored to the requirements of the times. These features may give a special role to the preferences and prejudices of individual actors: founders, managers, top military brass, promoters, boosters, and others.

The crucial question is whether places can be said to have inherent advantages or disadvantages for defense production. Many factors—topography, climate, entrepreneurship, labor, government labs, universities, military bases, and local cultural and business climates—have been hypothesized to affect military-industrial location, especially at the high-tech end. Such studies have particularly stressed sun, clear skies, and flat terrain as important for the aircraft and missile industries. But there are always counterinstances: Boeing prospered in rainy Seattle, Grumman in wintry Long Island. More important is human capital, represented by the founder, who started a firm in a hometown, or in one to which a migration occurred. Also important could be retired senior military personnel, who may prove attractive to firms because of their technical or organizational knowledge. Universities, too, may be an important element in the creation of the appropriate creative milieu—and, later on in the growth trajectory, by attracting and holding the right kind of specialized scientific and technological ability. Military RDT&E contracts to educational institutions amounted to $850 million by the early 1980s, and several notable high-technology defense concentrations, like Boston's Route 128 or California's Silicon Valley, have been linked to major research universities.

Much literature has stressed the importance of the amenity factor in this ability of firms to attract and hold professional and technical labor: The notion is that such workers effectively pull firms to the places they prefer. The problem is that no one agrees as to what these amenities might be; some may prefer opera, others the seashore or mountains. There is one general factor that subsumes the contribution of universities and the attraction of amenities. It is that the defense industries, with their special characteristics, are no longer sensitive to cost in the traditional sense that featured so large in traditional textbooks of locational analysis. Rather, the critical factor is the cost of obtaining information.

How then does the military high-tech place embark on its growth trajectory? There must be something to start the process: a founder, a preexisting industrial firm that enters defense production, a local university or research lab, a strategic imperative causing the Pentagon to start a new factory. Once this initial location is established, agglomeration economies begin to build the defense-based local economy. A distinctive labor pool, specialized business service firms, and competitive spin-off firms develop, as in Los Angeles in the 1930s and 1940s, where the airframe industry attracted machining, communications, electronics, software, and services industries. The whole process is rather like a game, where the players start with certain strengths and certain strategies, but nevertheless chance still plays a crucial role.

In our study, we distinguished five distinct paths to the military-industrial city. The first, the *Seedbed Transformed*, begins with an agglomeration of firms, services, and skilled-labor pools, acting as a "seedbed of innovation" for new defense-oriented activity, and offering the advantages of corporate R&D labs, major universities, diversified business services, and extensive skilled-labor markets. The second, the *Upstart Military City*, postulates a single individual or small group starting a firm dedicated to military markets, sometimes with military support, at a site distant from existing major centers. A third, the *Booster-Incubated Military-Industrial Complex*, starts with a local coalition, including congressional representatives, to recruit military facilities and defense contractors, promoting itself vigorously as an ideal site. A fourth, the *Military-Educational Complex*, begins with a university whose faculty and administrators have strong incentives to solicit outside research support, and hence pursue military-funded research; later, some such projects may move off campus into affiliated research institutes or independent firms. Finally, the *Installation-Based Military-Industrial Complex* is initiated by the military itself, which locates key facilities—aircraft testing grounds, defense nerve centers, deployment centers for missiles and spacecraft—that may eventually attract production and/or service facilities. A special case here is the defense services city, such as Washington, D.C.

In our study, we found that some places neatly fit one of these models; others are mixtures, but predominantly one or the other. We traced five different paths in reality. First, we looked at the beginnings of the defense industries in the U.S. heartland, where they grew out of existing industrial traditions—the first model—and their later decline. Second was the rise of Los Angeles during the 1940s and 1950s to be first the airframe and then the aerospace capital of the world—an equally classic case of the second model. Third, we examined the intriguing case of Seattle (another example of the second model, but this time based on a single founding father), which survived apparently despite the odds against it. Fourth, we looked at New England as the model of one industrial region that successfully made the adaptation to high-tech industrial production, partly because its core, Greater Boston, was also a prototype of the fourth case, the Military-Educational Complex. Finally, we examined Washington, D.C., a special case of the fourth model, the defense service complex.

THE RISE AND FALL OF THE HEARTLAND

It is hard to explain why the Midwest, America's industrial heartland, should have virtually disappeared from the defense industrial map. The modern military-industrial complex was born in this region. Powered flight, the technological basis of the entire system, came from here; the early history of the airplane, including its first military adaptation, is basically a history of the heartland—a triangle more than 500 miles wide but only just over 200 miles deep, whose long north side is the Third Coast and whose corners are the great engineering cities of Chicago, Buffalo, and Dayton.

The cities of this triangle embody the early history of American aviation. Dayton, Ohio, was the birthplace of the Wright brothers and housed their first commercial venture, the Wright Company, formed in 1909 to sell the world's first military airplane to the U.S. government in Italy. A little later, Dayton became the permanent center for aircraft procurement for the Air Force, at Wright-Patterson Field. Buffalo, New York, was considered the first aircraft center in the nation; Glenn Curtiss started his Aerial Experimental Association in nearby Hammondsport, New York, in 1908, renamed it the Curtiss Company and moved to Buffalo. Cleveland, in 1917, became the home of the Glenn Martin Company; the Martin Aeroplane Factory was in nearby Elyria, Ohio. The University of Michigan, in the early 1920s, boasted one of five aeronautical engineering programs in the nation. The Detroit Aircraft Corporation was formed in 1929 with ambitions to become the General Motors of the air. Chicago developed a powerful early electronics industry. Down to 1945, this region was a major producer of tanks, airplanes, ordnance, and other military material.

Why, then, did the heartland lose its early lead? Its decline rebuts the hypothesis that early centers of industrial production, the seedbeds of innovation, have a head start because they already house scores of entrepreneurs, sources of money capital, a skilled labor force, and a political structure amenable to change. Both large established companies and smaller engineer-headed firms generate innovations and support services such as accounting, marketing, and legal services. The theory works well enough for the origins: These cities based their early lead on heroic pioneering aerospace attempts by founding-father entrepreneurs who came into the industry from local engineering backgrounds—bicycle manufacture in the case of the Wrights and Curtiss, autos for Ford and Packard's Joy. Yet they lost out, after 1950, to the emerging "gunbelt." Some firms moved (Martin to Baltimore); some opened military-oriented branch plants elsewhere (Motorola in Scottsdale); some lost business to gunbelt competitors and either folded or turned to commercial production. Detailed study shows the reason: Locked into consumer-oriented mass production, and into the business culture it created, these cities and firms found it impossible to adjust to the very different style of defense-related aerospace.

Evidently, then, the seedbed theory does not hold up to the American experience. Empirical studies of the location of innovative activity in the United States confirm that, since the 1970s, it has arisen in new centers (Markusen, Hall, & Glasmeier, 1986). For this there are several possible reasons: New economic developments may emanate not from corporate R&D, but from university and government laboratories (Malecki, 1980); specialized research functions may be separable from headquarters operations, and may constitute large high-tech complexes in their own right; historic accidents, such as the preferences of founders for their hometowns, may explain the birth of new innovative centers (Saxenian, 1985a, 1985b). Equally, existing centers may actually repel new innovative activities: Traditional industries may dominate local resource markets, deterring new investors or entrepreneurs (Checkland, 1975). Large firms may enjoy oligopolistic profits, permitting them to outbid other potential area employers; new industries may find it impossible to assemble resources (Chinitz, 1960; Markusen, 1985); existing well-established companies may be so preoccupied with existing markets that they cannot grasp new market potential. This indeed seems to have been the case with the Midwest: Its major companies, highly successful in producer goods and consumer durables markets, saw no reason to pursue defense markets. It was not that these companies failed to innovate, but that innovation is so different in commercial and in defense markets. Also, the dominant corporate culture appears to have created a political environment—with highly adversarial party politics, a preoccupation with the interests of commercially oriented business and labor, and an indifference to the potential for defense pork barreling.

Finally, then, the Midwest lost out because of a complex set of causes and events. In the 1930s, it lost aircraft production to booster- ist Los Angeles, while the most successful firms, such as Ford, were too busy competing in the relatively depression-resistant auto indus- try. In the 1940s, its leadership in mass producing fighters, bombers, and engines produced only short-lived prosperity. After 1945, West Coast firms pulled ahead while the Midwest concentrated all energies on pent-up consumer demand. Over the entire period, aspirant aircraft entrepreneurs tended to migrate to the perimeter, where local promot- ers were eagerly handing out land and tax breaks and where military facilities offered testing fields and markets. Thus as the military- industrial complex rose with the Cold War, it barely touched the Midwest.

LOS ANGELES:
UPSTART AEROSPACE CAPITAL

The story of Los Angeles is neatly the obverse of that of the Mid- west. At the start of the era of powered flight, almost no one would have bet on its chances. Many places seemed set to do better: Dayton, Detroit, Buffalo, and also New York, home of several pioneer compa- nies. Within California, the San Francisco Bay Area surpassed Los Angeles as an urban industrial center, and showed early promise as an aviation producer. Los Angeles was thus the upstart city at the far southwestern corner of the United States that took on both the heart- land and the older California metropolis and won.

Los Angeles did this, our study concludes, through actions taken by local actors at critical historical junctures, each corresponding to a period in the evolution of American strategic policy and the conse- quent development of the military-industrial complex. First, during the era of isolationism in the 1920s and 1930s, certain founders lo- cated here, including the pioneer aircraft manufacturers—Douglas, the Lockheed brothers, Northrop, Kindelberger and Attwood of North American, Hughes—and the civic boosters who encouraged them, such as Chandler of the *Los Angeles Times*. Second, building on this foundation, there were the beginnings of a military-scientific-indus- trial complex in Los Angeles from the mid-1930s onward, just as the United States emerged from isolationism. Crucial were the establish- ment of a major center of aeronautical research at the California Insti- tute of Technology in Pasadena and its pioneering work on rocket propulsion in the late 1930s, and the active support of General "Hap" Arnold, who was then quartered close by and was in close contact with Caltech's scientific leaders, Millikan and von Kármán. Third, there was the transformation of the pioneer manufacturers into mass producers during World War II. Fourth, after a transitional period during the late 1940s, there was the race into aerospace during the Cold War era of the mid-1950s, which marked the real birth of the military-industrial complex. Each effectively represented a new challenge with a new set of opportunities. Each time, Los Angeles actors responded innovatively and hence successfully to the challenge.

At each juncture in this story, two capacities proved equally important: to found a firm, and later to lead it in new directions. But time, chance, and aging could and often did intervene at both stages, particularly between the stages. Success in the first was no guarantee of success in the second. Almost all the L.A. founders were young engineer-entrepreneurs during the 1920s; they were technical enthusiasts rather than top managers who met many vicissitudes during the Great Depression, remaining small and struggling until the growth of commercial aviation in the mid-1930s, and even until the defense buildup of the late 1930s. Almost all met the challenge of converting to mass production during World War II, but this was small in comparison with the challenge of the 1950s: the need to convert from airplanes to aerospace. That meant a new capacity for innovation, particularly in the marriage of aviation and electronics, at a time when most were already middle-aged (Higham, 1972). Some did brilliantly; some failed completely.

Geography was important here, but not in the conventional sense. Early on, climate was significant for testing and open-air production (Ball, 1962); desert and ocean gave space, isolation, and secrecy. But aerospace could flourish in less propitious climes, and indeed did. The real reason for Los Angeles's triumph was not physical climate but a mental or cultural climate. It was not in the pioneering phase between 1920 and 1940, but in the second period of adaptation between 1950 and 1960 that Los Angeles emerged as overwhelmingly the most successful center. Key individuals and institutions, notably scientists and Air Force officers, contributed to this. Millikan and von Kármán at Caltech supported work on rocket propulsion in the 1930s, when other scientists dismissed it as a "Buck Rogers idea." Arnold encouraged them and later, through the von Kármán committee and the creation of Project RAND, played a key role in steering the Air Force toward long-term technological planning. Key entrepreneurs such as

Kindelberger at North American, and later Ramo and Wooldridge, who broke from Hughes, remained in close contact with their thinking, and in consequence developed a highly innovative, speculative attitude toward R&D.

The conclusion must be that Los Angeles in the 1940s, as in the 1920s, was an innovative milieu, to use the language of Philipe Aydalot (1986; Aydalot & Keeble, 1988). Key individuals built institutions, in both the private and public sectors, dedicated to high-risk research. They then reacted on each other synergistically to create an intellectual climate based on the belief that the impossible could be made possible. There was an atmosphere of optimism, of invention, free of the old industrial and business traditions left behind in the East. These pioneers liked being far away from what they felt to be the cramping, archaic business climate of America's traditional industrial centers. It is surely no accident that Los Angeles, the City of Dreams, should have provided the unique intellectual atmosphere for this process. Of course, places like Dayton and Buffalo and Chicago had it too, but Los Angeles retained it, at least through what proved the crucial decade of the 1950s.

That raises the question: To what extent will Los Angeles retain its lead? Our interviews showed that there are pressures for the industry to disperse away from the crowded, expensive L.A. basin. Yet the industry remains strongly concentrated in its Southern California birthplace. L.A.'s long history of aviation, extending for nearly a century, exerts a huge pull. The regional agglomeration of contractors, suppliers, specialized labor, consultants, universities, research, and government installations is impressive and self-reinforcing. While some peripheral lower-skilled, cost-sensitive activities have moved away, the core of the industry remains. And there is as yet no sign that the region has lost the creativity, the innovative capacity, that was the basis of its meteoric industrial rise to become the aerospace capital of the world.

SEATTLE: SOLITARY SURVIVOR

At first sight, Seattle looks like the last place in the United States to build planes; it is climatically far from Southern California, and it is totally isolated from other aerospace complexes and activities, including procurement agencies. The question to ask must be, How did Boeing make it, and how in turn did it make Seattle, against all the odds? How could the nation's—indeed, the world's—most successful airplane manufacturer develop here, overcoming the massive disadvantage of isolation and lack of local business networks?

The fact is that in aerospace terms, Seattle is unique: not a "company town" but a "company city," the only major American city so clearly dependent on one contractor. Boeing dominates Seattle's economy: It is the only major defense contractor and by far the largest manufacturing employer, military or civilian, in the entire region; it is also the largest employer, public or private. The story of why Boeing is in Seattle is itself fairly simple. It involves no complex corporate and geographic histories such as those of TRW or Litton Industries, nor does it need any elaborate theory of industrial location. What is interesting is why William Boeing stayed in Seattle after producing his first seaplane there in 1916, rather than moving south or east, why he had such success, and whether Boeing's location in Seattle played a role.

The answers seem to lie in long-run company strategy. On the defense side, Boeing has had consistently bad luck in gaining "big-ticket" and "follow-on" contracts; it has an impressively long list of failed bids in the last two decades. But it is the only military airplane maker that has had equal or greater success in the commercial market. The price has been a boom-bust cycle. Periods of euphoria, such as World War II, the Cold War, the golden age of jet travel, the *Apollo* program, and the Reagan defense buildup, have been followed by sharp downturns; during one such, 1968-1971, a banner exhibited the famous exhortation, Would the last person to leave Seattle please turn off the lights?

Boeing's dominance of the Seattle economy has other effects. As the largest employer in the area, it shapes the local labor market, particularly the specialized high-tech labor market, as no single defense contractor in New England or Southern California ever could. The Seattle high-tech labor pool is the Boeing labor pool. Boeing's dominance also means that Seattle differs dramatically from Los Angeles or Boston: It does not have the same complexity of supplier networks, industrial linkages, and service support. In other words, Seattle does not depend to the same degree on agglomeration economies. It is the solitary survivor.

NEW ENGLAND: SUCCESSFUL TRANSITION?

New England is the quintessential old industrial region that made a successful transition to high-technology manufacturing and services.

It thus reversed a long-run deindustrialization trend: From 1968 to 1975 it lost 252,000 manufacturing jobs; from 1975 to 1980 it created 225,000 new ones. This remarkable rate of job creation, far more rapid than in the United States as a whole, was dominated by high-technology sectors (Frankel & Howell, 1988). This much is generally known; less appreciated is the fact that this industrial recovery was actually a double one, the first in the 1950s, the second in the late 1970s and early 1980s that has been overwhelmingly defense based. Avionics in Massachusetts, helicopters and aero engines in Connecticut, and airplanes and missiles and control equipment on Long Island (outside the region in a strict sense, very much part of it in a wider functional sense) have become the region's basic industries. And this reflects the fact that Massachusetts, in particular, was during World War II one of the places where the military-scientific complex was born (Warsh, 1988).

But this is not a single industrial area. The urban-industrial parts of the region are still essentially islands against a background of rural America. This physical separateness emphasizes the fact that each subregion has a distinct urban-industrial character: There is no one dominant industrial tradition that has progressively swallowed the others. Rather, there are at least three New England economies, with different origins, industrial traditions, and growth trajectories. As the complex has grown since 1950, these three industrial complexes have become more functionally interrelated, but they remain physically and economically distinct, with their own industrial traditions and their own economic specializations.

Greater Boston, the first, archetypically represents what could be called the commodification of knowledge. It is home to a vast array of information technology industries, dependent upon electronics, that came out of scientific research in the region's cluster of universities, especially the Massachusetts Institute of Technology (Hall & Preston, 1988). The second, the line of industrial cities along the Connecticut Valley—Springfield, Hartford, Meriden-Middletown, New Haven—had quite different origins. These first rose into industrial prominence in the mid-nineteenth century, the result of what can be called the second American industrial revolution, which generated mass production of precision-engineered products such as guns, sewing machines, typewriters, and small machines. For one of these firms, Pratt & Whitney, airplane engine manufacture was a natural twentieth-century outgrowth of the precision-engineering tradition. The third area, on both sides of Long Island Sound in what are now the outer suburbs of New York, developed a tradition of early aircraft and component manufacture associated with such pioneers as Sikorsky, Chance-Vought, Republic, Grumman, and Sperry, who began operations in New York City but early moved out in search of space and, in some cases where seaplane manufacture was involved, access to water. Three (Sikorsky, Chance-Vought, and Standard) were swallowed by the giant United Aircraft Corporation in the 1920s and were moved out to Connecticut. On the Connecticut side of the Long Island Sound, therefore, this complex merges with the Hartford complex, which has in effect absorbed it. But on Long Island itself, there are three huge survivals: Republic and Sperry, at Farmingdale on Long Island, and Grumman, at Bethpage next door, some 25 miles east of Manhattan. Separate, both geographically and historically, but emerging from the same New York seedbed, is the submarine-making complex of General Dynamics, formerly Electric Boat, at Groton on Thames at the far end of Connecticut.

So this is a very diverse region. Its subdivisions belong to quite distinct industrial traditions that have deep historical roots and that still powerfully condition the way firms perceive their operating action spaces. Nevertheless, to some extent two of these traditions have fused. Aircraft engines in Hartford and airframe manufacture on the shores of Long Island Sound started from quite different origins, the first emerging through diversification from an older precision-engineering tradition, the second through early entrepreneurial activity in a new industry at the edge of the great city, related to contacts with the local navy yard. This, in retrospect, offers obvious parallels with Los Angeles. But from the late 1920s onward they came together, both because of their geographical proximity and because they came in part under the ownership of United Technologies. Whether part of UT or outside it, the typical firm here is large, corporately managed, under pressure to cut costs, and open to political influence. It has been headquartered here for a half century or more, but is finding constraints on its operations, more acutely so if it is close to New York City. It does not feel tied to its traditional location by agglomeration economies; it depends on the skills of its craft engineering workers, but does not draw on a pool of scientific and technical labor out of local universities, recruiting instead all over the nation. It thinks that its present location has some attractions for such scarce technical talent, but also perhaps some disadvantages, especially if close to New York. Therefore, it tends to decentralize operations to the Southeast states, leaving only principal functions, such as headquarters, R&D, and key assembly operations, on Long Island or in Connecticut.

The electronics of Greater Boston, which spill over the Massachusetts line into neighboring New Hampshire, are quite different. They sprang from entrepreneurial agility that married itself to scientific advance, an agility that manifested itself at critical historic turning points: the beginning of World War II and the defense buildup of the 1950s. Individuals, whether university researchers or garage manufacturers, caught critical waves and used them to generate new industries. But those waves, the timing and amplitude of which were determined by the changing strategic role of the United States in the 1940s and 1950s, were crucial to the whole process.

Many of the resulting firms are still small, but for all of them Boston and Cambridge represent the center of an intellectual universe on which they feel their lives depend. Over and over in our interviews we heard the same phrases: the nearness of MIT; the ability to drop in there, to use the scientific facilities, to attend seminars; the sense that here and only here could one keep abreast of the state of the art; the general cultural ambience of Boston; the crucial importance of all these factors in attracting new graduates. These firms left us in no doubt that they labor under considerable disadvantages, including the escalating costs of housing and congealing traffic on the expressways. But despite this, there is no chance that they will ever leave. The interesting point is that though all of these firms are now middle-aged and some are quite large, they essentially retain the attitudes of small startup companies: They seek agglomeration economies in a single specialized industrial quarter, in the same way that similar companies do in Greater Los Angeles.

As media reports have clearly shown, the New England high-tech economy is still dangerously defense dependent. In particular, its remarkable economic turnaround in the 1980s was triggered by military buildup (Barff & Knight, 1988; see also Chapter 4 of this volume). The region's industries, particularly the electronics firms around Route 128, have not on the whole succeeded in making the diversification to a peacetime market economy, and what one wave can lift, another can cast down on the beach.

WASHINGTON, D.C.: THE TERTIARIZATION OF THE DEFENSE INDUSTRIES

Our last case study, the national capital, represents a dramatic new phase in the evolution of the military-industrial complex, as revolutionary in its way as its creation in the 1950s. Standing at sixth rank in the United States in number of high-tech enterprises, after Los

Angeles, San Francisco-San Jose, New York, Boston, and Chicago, it is particularly strong in telecommunications (telephone, satellites, radar), biotechnology, and military electronics (Boquet, 1986). But two features distinguish this concentration from the others. The first is that it arose relatively recently, since the mid-1960s. The other is that it is not concerned with manufacturing. The firms locate in skyscraper offices or campus office parks. Their product, software, represents encapsulated knowledge that may be used to navigate spacecraft, eavesdrop on distant places and events, anticipate and monitor attacks by hostile powers, and perhaps destroy hostile missiles in space. It will then be incorporated in hardware, but that will occur in other locations. In our study we describe this with an ugly word: the tertiarization of the defense industries.

The critical question is, Why should this transition have resulted in the displacement of the defense industries to a new location? In the first era of the military-industrial complex, procurement followed concentrations of existing expertise, whether in the laboratories of major technical universities, such as MIT or Caltech, or in existing manufacturing companies, such as the airframe manufacturers or the electronics companies, who were willing and able to make the major entrepreneurial jump into aerospace. But more recently, these same companies, or their successors, have relocated these activities to the national capital.

There is no ready explanation for this. Founders, whose birthplaces or original locational choices proved so significant elsewhere, have played little or no role here. University research has played little part in the rise of this region; George Mason and George Washington universities have given priority to their electronics programs, but this has occurred in response to demand, not the other way around (Boquet, 1986).

In our study, we adduce the explanation that the process occurred because of a new relationship between the procurement arm and the producers, in what could be called the civilianization of war: War was no longer actually to be fought between real contestants, but would become a highly esoteric and vastly expensive game, fought in software laboratories and in committee rooms where scientific budgets were argued over and thrashed out. The logical location for that war, we argue, is in the nation's capital. Nearness to the Pentagon, and to the myriad bureaucracies and subbureaucracies within and around it, became crucial. The contractors were tied into ever-closer relationships with the officials, whether uniformed or civilian, who wrote the specifications and argued the case for the cash. Since they were also increasingly specialized, it meant ever more relationships with other firms—the same kinds of contractual relationships that earlier had characterized the emergence of industrial complexes in Orange County or on Route 128. And, insofar as the software would eventually be put into equipment that would be built or installed elsewhere, it also implied highly efficient communications with the rest of the United States and the world, through the region's airports. The result has been the establishment of an information complex similar, in many ways, to the cluster of financial institutions on Wall Street or the concentration of industrial headquarters offices in midtown Manhattan.

The Washington complex received a massive boost in the 1980s through the Strategic Defense Initiative. It is likely to receive an equally massive shock in the 1990s from the termination or reduction of the program. Yet, in one form or another, the tertiarization of defense is a very long-term tendency that began with the development of the first electronic information technologies around World War II and has continued apace ever since.

CONCLUSIONS

Why, then, did the gunbelt develop where it did, and why does it continue to be rooted there? If the rise of a military-industrial perimeter is a uniquely American phenomenon, what is it about the American experience that might explain it? One answer lies in what could be called the urban frontier: the existence of cities, often in remote regions, that generated huge capital surpluses available as a supply of local venture capital seeking new speculative outlets. These emerging frontier cities developed aggressive traditions of civic boosterism. During the New Deal and World War II, they were ready to exploit expanding federal spending (Gottlieb & Wolt, 1977; Mollenkopf, 1983; Nash, 1985).

There is a special relationship between the military and this frontier. The long but successful struggle of the Army Air Corps, western in its orientation from birth, to divorce itself from the Army enhanced the attractiveness of the West and created a preference among its leaders for western locations. And because the Air Force, with its preference for outsourcing, won over the Army's preferred arsenal system, the West became the locus for a new private empire selling to a generous public customer.

Thus, so we argue, the origins of the military-oriented western segment of modern U.S. industry lay early in the century. The new aerospace firms that formed the core of the complex—nurtured by government contracts, promoted to large-scale corporate status by World War II, further boosted by the Cold War—clustered in new centers such as Los Angeles and Seattle. There they created an innovative milieu that become progressively embedded in a permanent defense-dependent, research-intensive infrastructure.

REFERENCES

Aydalot, P. (Ed.). (1986). *Milieux innovateurs en Europe*. Paris: GREMI.

Aydalot, P., & Keeble, D. (Eds.). (1988). *High technology industry and innovative environments: The European experience*. London: Routledge.

Ball, J. (1962). *Edwards: Flight test center of the U.S.A.F*. New York: Duell, Sloan & Pearce.

Barff, R. A., & Knight, P. L., III. (1988). The role of federal military spending in the timing of the New England employment turnaround. *Papers of the Regional Science Association, 65*, 151-166.

Boquet, Y. (1986). Les entreprises à technologie avancée dans la région de Washington D.C. *Bulletin de l'Association de Geographes Français, 63*, 217-226.

Checkland, S. (1975). *The upas tree*. Glasgow: Glasgow University Press.

Chinitz, B. (1960). Contrasts in agglomeration: New York and Pittsburgh. *American Economic Review, Papers and Proceedings, 51*, 279-289.

Frankel, L. D., & Howell, J. M. (1988). Economic revitalization and job creation in America's oldest industrialized region. In D. L. Lampe (Ed.), *The Massachusetts miracle: High technology and economic revitalization* (pp. 295-313). Cambridge: MIT Press.

Gottlieb, R., & Wolt, I. (1977). *Thinking big: The story of the* Los Angeles Times, *its publishers, and their influence on Southern California*. New York: Putnam.

Hall, P., & Markusen, A. R. (Eds.). (1985). *Silicon landscapes*. Boston: Allen & Unwin.

Hall, P., & Preston, P. (1988). *The carrier wave: New information technology and the geography of innovation, 1846-2003*. London: Unwin Hyman.

Higham, R. (1972). *Air power: A concise history*. New York: St. Martin's.

Malecki, E. J. (1980). Corporate organization of R and D and the location of technological activities. *Regional Studies, 14*, 219-234.

Markusen, A. R. (1985). *Profit cycles, oligopoly, and regional development*. Cambridge: MIT Press.

Markusen, A. R., Hall, P., Campbell, S., & Deitrick, S. (1991). *The rise of the gunbelt: The military remapping of industrial America*. New York: Oxford University Press.

Markusen, A. R., Hall, P., & Glasmeier, A. (1986). *High-tech America: The what, how, where and why of the sunrise industries*. Boston: Allen & Unwin.

Mollenkopf, J. H. (1983). *The contested city*. Princeton, NJ: Princeton University Press.

Nash, G. A. (1985). *The American West transformed: The impact of the Second World War*. Bloomington: Indiana University Press.

Saxenian, A. (1985a). The genesis of Silicon Valley. In P. Hall & A. R. Markusen (Eds.), *Silicon landscapes* (pp. 20-34). Boston: Allen & Unwin.

Saxenian, A. (1985b). Innovative manufacturing industries: Spatial incidence in the United States. In M. Castells (Ed.), *High technology, space and society* (pp. 55-80). Beverly Hills, CA: Sage.

Warsh, D. L. (1988). War stories: Defense spending and the growth of the Massachusetts economy. In D. L. Lampe (Ed.), *The Massachusetts miracle: High technology and economic revitalization* (pp. 314-330). Cambridge: MIT Press.

4

Living by the Sword and Dying by the Sword? Defense Spending and New England's Economy in Retrospect and Prospect

RICHARD BARFF

AFTER SEVERAL DECADES of relatively sluggish performance, New England's economy was revivified in 1978 and 1979. While several factors contributed to the region's new vitality, such as increased orders for commercial high-technology goods and pent-up housing demand, a major force behind this turnaround was the real increase in federal defense spending that began in 1976. New England was a special beneficiary of Department of Defense (DOD) spending because the composition of the defense budget had changed since previous buildups to include larger shares for high-technology durable goods and R&D industries, which already had an important place in the economies of most of the states in the region. Employment growth was stimulated initially in these sectors—and secondarily in a large proportion of tertiary activities—through the operation of regional multiplier effects; these resulted in regional employment growth rates consistently exceeding those of the nation for the first time since World War II and lasting for most of the 1980s.

Unlike other post-World War II economic downturns, New England weathered the 1981-1982 recession relatively well and recorded vigorous employment growth in 1983 and 1984. By 1985, however, nondurable and durable manufacturing employment began to decline in some states and total employment growth, relative to that of the nation, began to resemble patterns reminiscent of the preturnaround period. By 1988, the situation worsened as the patterns of employment

AUTHOR'S NOTE: Thanks go to Bill Levin for his valuable research assistance.

creation in the region and the nation diverged, with employment nationally continuing to grow, while New England's employment growth rate declined. In prior years, regional decreases in employment were accompanied by similar national patterns, although the region's recessions were frequently deeper and longer. Therefore, for the region to experience a decline in job production as national rates of employment growth increased, as happened in 1988, was unusual and augured a regional recession in stark contrast to the growth period of the early 1980s. In addition, the regional slowdown is becoming perceived as something more than temporary, partly because the combination of a seemingly ever-increasing federal budget deficit and the attenuation of Cold War posturing has resulted in mounting pressure on the U.S. government to reduce the proportion of the budget spent on defense—one of the sectors primarily responsible for New England's prosperity in the 1980s. An important question addressed by this chapter is, If significant reductions in defense spending do occur, will declines in military-related industry and R&D employment in New England exacerbate the weaknesses already apparent in the region's economy?

The discussion of the regional impact of cutbacks in the military budget is placed in the context of the recent history of the relationship between defense spending and employment growth in New England. The first part of the chapter therefore analyzes the nature of employment growth and decline in the region since 1945. This is followed by an examination of the role of federal defense spending in the regional economy, devoting special attention to the timing and structure of New England's recent economic turnaround. The prospects for defense-related employment and the region's economy as a whole are then evaluated in terms of the types of industry concentrated there, the location of such industry, and the strategies that the major employers have adopted to combat expected reductions in orders from the Pentagon.

THE SECTORAL COMPOSITION OF NEW ENGLAND'S EMPLOYMENT GROWTH

The study of the sectoral recomposition of the region's economy builds on and extends the findings of two recent studies (Barff & Knight, 1988b; Knight & Barff, 1987) that reveal that between 1945 and 1979, the annual rate of employment growth in the region tended

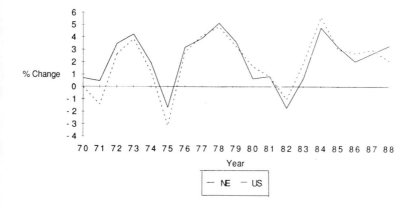

Figure 4.1. Annual Percentage Change in Total Employment, New England and the United States, 1970-1988

to follow the national pattern, but almost always at a lower rate. As Figures 4.1 and 4.2 depict, this condition changed in 1979, when the states in New England began to produce jobs at a consistently faster rate than that of the nation. With the exception of the period between 1984 and 1985, regional job performance outpaced the national economy for the period 1979 to 1987. In terms of the employment history

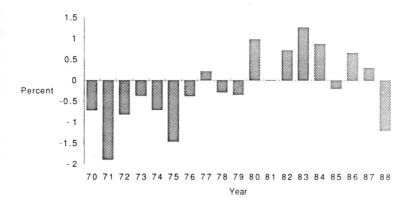

Figure 4.2. Differences in Annual Employment Growth for New England and the United States, 1970-1988

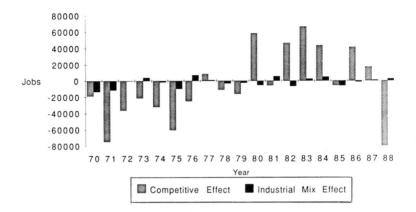

Figure 4.3. Annual Total Competitive Effect and Annual Total Industrial Mix Effect for New England, 1970-1988

of New England, this time span is particularly important, because during the previous 35 years, regional rates of employment growth surpassed those of the nation only during two (nonconsecutive) years. As the papers by Knight and Barff (1987) and Barff and Knight (1988b) note, New England's employment turnaround of the late 1970s was primarily relative. The region did not begin producing jobs at unprecedented rates; rather, the region was better able to maintain higher rates of job creation than the nation as a whole.

Addressing the question of why this switch from a position of inferiority to a position of superiority occurred, previous studies relied in one way or another on a shift-share analysis of New England's economy (Barff & Knight, 1988b; Knight & Barff, 1987; Norton, 1987). These authors concluded that the principal difference between national employment growth and that of the region was attributable to the competitive effect: that is, the actual change in employment in an industrial sector in New England less the hypothetical change in employment assuming the sector had grown at the national rate—a measure of regional competitive advantage. The region's *mix* of industries (the degree to which the region specialized in industries that were growing or declining at the national level) generally had a neutral effect on the region's overall job performance.

Figure 4.3 shows the pivotal role of the total competitive effect and the muted impact of the total industrial mix effect between 1970

TABLE 4.1

New England's Average Annual Shift-Share Competitive Effect by Sector

Sector	1950-1975	1976-1979	1980-1984	1985-1987	1988
Mining/construction	−712	−4,969	+7,553	+25,620	+2,923
Manufacturing	−17,452	+6,945	+17,295	−29,609	−49,701
Transport/public utilities	−931	−2,476	+1,978	+2,935	−3,175
Trade	−3,620	−8,361	+12,937	+12,952	−18,116
Finance, Insurance, Real Estate	−844	−3,397	+3,501	+9,065	+4,523
Services	−1,397	−1,402	+7,026	−6,353	−20,276
Government	−4,103	+2,660	−8,587	+2,882	+4,025
Total	−29,059	−11,000	+41,703	+17,492	−79,797

SOURCE: U.S. Department of Labor, Bureau of Labor Statistics, *Handbook of Labor Statistics*, various years.

and 1988, for seven aggregate employment divisions.[1] The period between 1970 and 1975 is indicative of the whole postwar era, when total job generation lagged behind that of the nation, mainly because of large negative competitive effects. The region drew close to the nation in terms of total job generation between 1976 and 1979, and maintained a position of superiority relative to that of the nation from 1980 until 1987, largely because of a strong competitive effect. The last year for which data are available indicates that the region's slumping economy is due more to the performance of industries in the region vis-à-vis the nation than to the region's industrial mix.

Dissecting the total competitive effect into its component parts uncovers, among other things, the special role of manufacturing in the region's recent economic history. Table 4.1 shows the annual average contributions of the seven broad sectors for five time periods.[2] For each of the periods under scrutiny, manufacturing contributes the most to the total effect. Between 1950 and 1975, while all the seven sectors had negative competitive effects, the value for manufacturing was more than four times as great as the value for the next most negative sector, namely, government. In direct contrast, during the late 1970s manufacturing sharply outperformed all the other major sectors in terms of job creation, relative to the nation as a whole. In the next period, all the sectors of the economy except government registered positive competitive effects and again, the performance of manufacturing was the strongest. From 1985 to 1987, the total annual competitive effect for the region remained positive, despite the switch of manufacturing from a large positive value to a large negative value. The poor performance of manufacturing was, for the most part, offset by the large positive value for construction, with the result that the average total competitive effect for the region as a whole remained positive. In 1988, however, the region's total competitive effect was negative, as manufacturing weakened even more and other sectors in New England—such as services and trade—were outperformed by their national counterparts.

While it is important to remember that shift-share analysis deals with sectoral differences between regional and national employment growth (or decline), rather than actual job growth or decline, manufacturing has clearly had a central role in the lengthy period of stagnation after 1950, the revival of New England's economy in the late 1970s and early 1980s, and the recent slowdown. An understanding of why manufacturing has had such a prominent part in the region's recent economic history centers on two issues: the decline in the region's nondurable goods sector after the reprieve that leather and textiles received during the Second World War and Korean War, and the performance and concentration of the defense-related durable goods sector since the mid-1970s.

THE MILITARY AND MANUFACTURING IN NEW ENGLAND SINCE 1939

1939-1976

During World War II, government orders to industries in New England brought full employment for the first time in several decades. They also had important structural effects. Military contracts for nondurables—primarily uniforms and blankets—temporarily arrested the decline of the region's textile industry between 1940 and 1950. In contrast, Defense Department orders for other products boosted employment in aircraft and shipbuilding, electrical and nonelectrical machinery, and communications equipment, with the result that the region "emerged from the war with a greatly changed industrial structure" (Estall, 1966, p. 35). Military spending during World War II also propelled Draper Lab and Lincoln Lab to national prominence, as these centers enabled important breakthroughs in ballistics and began to establish New England as an important locus of military-related R&D.

From 1950 to the mid-1970s, New England's durable goods sector generally stayed vigorous, in part because of support from federal agencies such as the DOD and NASA (Malecki, 1986). For example, Clark (1972) estimates that during the 1960s, 50% of Boston's firms relied on government contracts for 33% of their sales. The health of durable goods producers, however, was completely overshadowed by the continued long decline of textile employment in the region, one result of which was the inferior "competitive" position of manufacturing captured in the shift-share analysis of the previous section. This was a bleak period for New England. A "hollowing" of the region's economy took place; nonlocal financial conglomerates milked local industry of surplus capital and locally owned producers of leather textiles discontinued direct production as they transformed themselves into importers (Harrison, 1984; Harrison & Kluver, 1989).

The proportion of employment in nondurables declined in the region relative to durables, and as the manufacturing sector became increasingly oriented to high technology, parallel changes occurred in the military budget of the United States. In an effort to enhance military readiness via technological innovation, spending on durable goods and R&D now occupies a much larger proportion of the budget than it did 30 years ago (Galbraith & Wakefield, 1984). These changes in the composition of the defense budget have been pronounced during the most recent buildup, which began in 1977.

1977-1987

Because of the symmetry between the structure of the defense budget and the composition of manufacturing in New England, the region has benefited disproportionately from DOD contracts during the last decade or so. For example, industrial purchases by the DOD between 1978 and 1983 in the region grew by 165%, compared with 122% for the nation as a whole (U.S. Bureau of the Census, 1983). In terms of military prime contracts, the region consistently retained about a 12% share of the total dollar amount awarded between 1977 and 1984—the highest per capita by any census division. Because the total amounts increased substantially over this time, the six New England states experienced a real increase of about 180% in prime contract awards in this seven-year period (U.S. Department of Defense, 1984, 1988). It has been noted that these prime contract awards accounted for more than 7% of Massachusetts's gross state product in 1984.

Such changes in defense spending had a profound impact on employment growth in the New England region. The direct effects of these changes are relatively easy to trace; the indirect effects are more elusive. To investigate the direct association between the DOD and the region's manufacturing, this study adopts Henry and Oliver's (1985) schema of classification, in which subsectors of manufacturing are coded "defense related." According to this schema, an industry is defense related if DOD purchases account for more than 10% of output; the appendix to this chapter contains the full list of manufacturing industries that met these standards in 1985, listed by Standard Industrial Classification (SIC) codes. Table 4.2 contains information on New England and the United States as a whole for total employment, manufacturing employment, and the defense-related subcomponent of manufacturing, for 1977, 1984, and 1987. Table 4.2 also shows the employment totals and associated location quotients. The location quotient (LQ) is a measure of geographic concentration, defined as $LQ = (D_{NE}/D_{US})/(E_{NE}/E_{US})$, where D_{NE} and D_{US} represent defense-related employment for the region and the nation, respectively, and E_{NE} and E_{US} represent total employment. These are presented for the four largest defense-related industries in New England, as well as employment in those same sectors for the nation as a whole.[3]

Table 4.2 shows the concentration of defense-related industry in New England. The location quotient of 1.50 in 1977 for all defense-related industry in the region indicates that New England had 50% more employment in these activities than would be the case if it had the same geographic distribution as total employment. Certain industries within the defense sector are highly concentrated in New England. For example, in 1987 the region had about one-third of the nation's total employment in aircraft and missile engines and parts, and about one-fourth of the nation's employment in shipbuilding and repairing. Related work by Browne (1988) confirms New England as the most defense-oriented census division in the country. Utilizing Henry and Oliver's definition of defense orientation, Browne has shown that all six New England states ranked in the top 12 nationally when defense-related employment was measured as a proportion of total private employment, with Connecticut ranked first, New Hampshire third, and Massachusetts sixth.

The temporal features of the table reveal that between 1977 and 1984, defense-related industry in both the nation and New England expanded employment. New England's rate of growth, however, was

TABLE 4.2

Employment in Manufacturing and Defense-Related Manufacturing:
1977, 1984, and 1987

	1977	1984	1987	% Change, 1977-1984	% Change, 1984-1987
New England					
Total	4,123,095	5,084,265	5,647,026	23.31	11.07
Manufacturing	1,400,130	1,478,399	1,377,933	5.59	−6.80
Defense-related industries	258,276	291,134	282,753	12.72	−2.88
LQ for defense industries	1.50	1.60	1.65		
Radio/TV equipment	34,378	47,246	43,161	37.43	−8.65
LQ	1.63	1.44	1.22		
Electronic components	29,507	54,212	46,656	87.73	−13.94
LQ	2.03	2.30	2.00		
Aircraft missile engines and parts	45,433	50,194	56,000	10.48	11.57
LQ	6.17	4.96	4.82		
Shipbuilding and repairing	33,509	27,113	26,941	−19.09	−0.63
LQ	3.00	3.01	3.46		
United States					
Total	65,004,205	78,021,564	85,483,804	20.02	9.56
Manufacturing	19,638,852	19,325,352	19,002,692	−1.59	−1.67
Defense-related industries	2,707,362	2,794,783	2,542,272	3.23	−9.04
% of total U.S. manufacturing	13.79	14.46	13.38		
Radio/TV equipment	332,647	504,967	534,508	51.8	5.85
Electronic components	229,503	361,296	352,944	57.43	−2.31
Aircraft missile engines and parts	116,086	155,287	175,894	33.77	13.27
Shipbuilding and repairing	176,365	138,120	117,705	−21.69	−14.78

SOURCE: Data from U.S. Bureau of the Census for 1977, 1984, and 1987.

almost four times that of the nation. Because defense-related industry is a relatively large part of total manufacturing in New England, the 12.7% growth in jobs in defense-related industry between 1977 and 1984 resulted in an expansion of employment in overall manufacturing in the region. New England's growth in defense-related industry in this seven-year period is particularly noteworthy because it coincides with the overall changes in manufacturing highlighted by the shift-share analysis. During the same period, total manufacturing in the nation shrank by about 1.6% and defense-related manufacturing employment expanded modestly by 3.2%.

While the period between 1977 and 1984 was a time of job growth in defense-related industry, the period between 1984 and 1987 was marked by job loss. During these years New England lost about 8,400 defense-related jobs, which represents about 3% of the 1984 total. Three of the region's four leading defense-related sectors experienced employment decline, and its manufacturing sector as a whole declined much more sharply, losing more than 100,000 jobs in just three years. Nationally, defense-related employment declined more than 9% in just three years, while manufacturing as a whole recorded more modest losses of about 1.7%.

The post-1977 defense buildup explains the vigor of military-related manufacturing employment growth between 1977 and 1984 in New England. Furthermore, the timing of the defense buildup takes us some way toward understanding the improved performance of New England's manufacturing sector and the fact that manufacturing was the first sector in the regional economy to experience a turnaround in employment growth, relative to job creation nationally. Three important questions about regional economic transformation remain, however. How do we account for the rapid employment growth outside the manufacturing sector? Second, how do we reconcile the employment decline in defense-related manufacturing and manufacturing as a whole in New England between 1984 and 1987 with nonmanufacturing's continued employment growth in this period and in 1988? Third, given the weakness in defense-related activity in the region, and reductions in federal military procurement, what are the prospects in the 1990s for (a) defense-related employment and (b) total employment in the region?

DEFENSE SPENDING AND REGIONAL MULTIPLIERS: 1977-1984

Barff and Knight (1988b) have suggested that the region's strong ties with the military explain, in part, subsequent employment growth in sectors outside of manufacturing. Our argument is as follows. Regional growth theory suggests that employment creation in nonmanufacturing sectors could be related to the expansion of manufacturing via the regional multiplier effect. Capital transferred to the region stimulated employment growth not only in defense-related manufacturing, but, secondarily, in local tertiary and quaternary employment and in those regional manufacturers that supply upstream inputs to the producers of military hardware. In the context of New England in the early 1980s, these multipliers were almost certainly strengthened by the growth in demand for commercial high-technology products, such as computers and related goods, as well as the growth in the region's financial services. Employment in financial services was stimulated by both the region's real estate boom and the growth of national markets for mutual funds and insurance. Barff and Knight (1988b) hypothesized too that the regional multiplier produced by New England's defense linkage would in general be large and, in particular, affect the retailing and housing sectors of the regional economy (Erickson, 1974; Malecki & Stark, 1988).

The logic for these expectations derives from the nature of defense-related industry in New England. Several researchers have noted the association between such industries and high-technology manufacturing: This is a major theme of the edited volumes by Tirman (1984) and Breheny (1988) and a central thesis of O'hUallachain's (1987) analysis of defense spending and regional development in the United States. Browne (1988) has shown that most defense-related industries, as specifically defined by Henry and Oliver (1985), were also high-technology industries. In this vein, it has been illustrated that this was especially the case in New England (Barff & Knight, 1988b). Given this emphasis on commercial and noncommercial high-technology manufacturing, New England's defense-related industries are likely to employ a large proportion of scientists and engineers, relative to manufacturing as a whole. It follows that, for many defense-related manufacturers, labor costs would represent a large proportion of total costs, as raw material costs and capital expenditures would be less important than in more standardized manufacturing (Malecki, 1986; Markusen, 1986; Saxenian, 1985). Therefore, a large portion of the receipts coming into the region from the sale of high-technology goods goes to labor and is thus recirculated *in situ*, which should produce a large multiplier effect. If the latter operates primarily through labor, then the greatest impact should be in those sectors in which household spending is the greatest—that is, retail goods and housing—and this should be especially true in New England, where housing costs are high (Barff & Knight, 1988b, p. 160).

Several fragments of evidence support these arguments. National payroll data for defense-related manufacturing workers from *County Business Patterns* indicate that workers in this sector earned 36% more than the average for all workers in private industry in 1977.[4] This disparity grew between 1977 and 1984, as defense-related manufacturing worker compensation increased 66.5%—compared with 58.8% for total average payroll. These income differences are manifested in the region—a recent study of defense-oriented industries in Massachusetts found average annual wages to be 26% higher than in other manufacturing industries, and 57% higher than in nonmanufacturing industries (Massachusetts Department of Employment and Training, 1989). This suggests that New England's defense sector, with its high salaries and relatively rapid employment growth, has contributed substantially to regional household income since the beginning of the recent military buildup.

Barff and Knight (1988b) also argue that the previous shift-share analyses of New England in the 1980s support this logic, in that the structure of the competitive effects for the period 1980-1984 were consistent with the hypothesis that the manufacturing multiplier would work primarily through the labor sector. For example, with reference to Table 4.1, the three nonmanufacturing sectors with the largest competitive effects between 1980 and 1984 were trade (which is primarily retail trade), construction (strongly influenced by housing demand), and services (which includes a variety of consumer services).

SIGNS OF WEAKNESS

Between 1984 and 1987, New England lost more than 100,000 jobs in manufacturing, and in the same period defense-related manufacturing employment declined about 2.9%. The most recent Bureau of Labor Statistics data indicate that job losses in manufacturing continued between 1987 and 1988, albeit at a lower rate.[5] Even though nonmanufacturing employment continued to grow, job losses in manufacturing and defense-related manufacturing are particularly problematic because they occurred in the very sectors that were instrumental in the region's revival a decade earlier. Several hypotheses to explain these events present themselves. One of the most common is that in the mid-1980s, the region developed a severe labor shortage— particularly in terms of the skilled labor requirements of the high-technology and defense sectors of the economy (Barff, 1989, 1990;

Bradbury, 1985; Harrison & Kluver, 1989; Masnick, 1985). The tight labor market forced regional salaries and wages to rise at rates higher than the national average, so much so that in 1985 the average pay per employee in New England exceeded the national average for the first time in several decades (Browne, 1987). Furthermore, local planners and the local media have for the last five years been reporting the difficulties that New England industry has had recruiting qualified labor. Given these problems, some local manufacturers have reduced employment in the region, begun to curtail plans for expansion in New England, or left entirely (Harrison & Kluver, 1989).

Syron and Browne (1989), however, suggest that the labor shortage of the mid-1980s might have been a blessing in disguise. Other regions that have experienced slowdowns in job creation after a period of rapid growth often experience heightened rates of net in-migration (Ballard & Clark, 1981; Barff, 1990; Plane & Rogerson, 1989). They note, for example, that the downturn in construction employment and the plunge in real estate prices in Texas were exacerbated by the heavy in-migration that preceded the regional recession. In contrast, the migration response to the New England economic turnaround was modest, and will probably not alter dramatically, given the recent signs of regional economic frailty (Barff, 1989, 1990).

As an alternative hypothesis to explain the weaker economy in New England, Harrison and Kluver (1989) suggest that the region may be undergoing a major shift from being a balanced economy toward becoming one based on business and financial services and the redevelopment of the built environment tailored to the needs of these sorts of services. They draw their evidence from a shift-share analysis of the Massachusetts economy, and, given that about 50% of the region's employment base is concentrated in that state, it shows very similar tendencies to those revealed in this investigation (Figure 4.1). That is, between 1984 and 1987, the state (and the region) lost a "competitive" edge in all aspects of manufacturing and that, relative to the nation, the region's competitive advantage became concentrated in trade, finance, insurance, real estate, and, especially, construction. The 1988 employment data for New England as a whole, however, fail to support this trend. As Table 4.1 shows, between 1987 and 1988 the region lost competitive advantage in virtually all major sectors, as the region's economic performance vis-à-vis the nation began to resemble a preturnaround form.

Another hypothesis put forward to explain the weaker regional economy of the late 1980s is that the slowdown in the rate of growth of the federal military budget might have begun to affect New England adversely (Harrison & Kluver, 1989). For any region, we may hypothesize that these effects would occur first in the defense-related sectors of the economy, second in other high-technology sectors of the region's economy, and then in nonmanufacturing sectors. How would this scenario be borne out in New England? The implications of this are important, because of the historic role of federal military spending in the region and continuing direct and indirect dependence on military procurement and prime contract awards. This broad issue occupies the final section of this chapter.

DEFENSE SPENDING AND NEW ENGLAND'S PROSPECTS IN THE 1990s

The contingency of military spending on foreign relations and defense policies often renders many local economies that specialize in military-related activities vulnerable to sudden and often unpredictable shifts in national defense requirements. The recent rapid defense buildup, begun during the Carter administration and accelerated in the first Reagan administration, is testimony to this. New England's economy benefited disproportionately from the increased federal defense spending, and the region's dependency on the military could be a cause for concern. Just as the buildup contributed to the region's resurgence, the slowdown in the rate of growth of defense-spending probably contributed, albeit marginally, to the region's poor job performance relative to the nation as a whole in the later 1980s. In the longer term, a more critical question must be addressed. If the defense budget continues to be trimmed in the 1990s, what will be the effect on New England?

The problem with trying to answer this question is that the future defense budget is unknown and is dependent on unpredictables such as superpower relations and negotiations between Congress and the president. Even if we accept, say, a steady decline in the proportion of GNP devoted to defense, as is the case under the president's proposals in 1990, the *composition* of the defense budget, which may be as important as its overall *size*, remains uncertain.

One scenario of the future defense of the United States has been recently described by the DOD as "flexible," based on a sophisticated quick-response system. In contrast, what prevailed under the Reagan administration entailed not only high-technology projects like the

Stealth bomber and the Strategic Defense Initiative, but also the maintenance of large standing armies and the refurbishment of some World War II warships. It follows that, in the short run at least, while some trimming of expensive projects like the Stealth bomber has already occurred, defense cuts will target primarily personnel and low-technology aspects of defense. As New England has few military bases and an industrial orientation toward high-technology defense-related employment, this logic suggests that such cuts in DOD spending will, in general, affect New England less than other regions of the country. Because some programs are "big-ticket items" in the defense budget, an alternative scenario, which could be associated with relatively large cuts, might involve the deferment or cancellation of expensive defense systems. It follows that procurement and spending on research, development, testing, and evaluation (RDT&E) would be reduced more sharply than spending on personnel and operations. Under these conditions, the employment impacts in New England would be much more severe than if cuts were targeted primarily to operations and personnel.

Assessment of the impact of altered budget priorities in New England is complicated further by the differential effects that such reductions in spending may have within the region. Given the critical importance of technology to overall regional development, one perspective on this problem focuses on the relationship between defense-related industry in a state and high-technology industry in general. If the vitality of the defense-related sector in a state is central to the health of the high-technology sector, then employment losses in defense-related industries would result in job losses in both the commercial and noncommercial high-technology sectors. Browne (1988) has shown that defense-oriented states tend to be places with large concentrations of high-technology industry. Defense orientation (measured as the fraction of defense-related employment relative to all private employment in 1979) is positively and significantly correlated with high-technology industry orientation in 1985, where high-technology industry is defined as it is by Riche, Hecker, and Burgan (1983).[6] Defense orientation is also positively and significantly correlated with employment in high-technology industry, excluding those sectors that are defense oriented.[7]

The New England states generally fit this pattern. Browne has classified the defense-related states into two broad categories: (a) those states with shares of defense-related and high commercial high-technology employment exceeding those in the United States as a whole and the median state, and (b) those states with shares of defense-related employment greater than, and shares of commercial high-technology employment less than, those in the United States as a whole and the median state. In such an analysis, four New England states—Connecticut, Massachusetts, New Hampshire, and Vermont—were numbered among the seven states that formed the high defense/high commercial high-technology industry group. In contrast, Maine was included in the group of six states that constituted the group classified as high defense/low commercial high-technology industry.

Within the four New England states that had above-average defense-related employment and commercial high-technology employment, significant structural differences are evident. In particular, Massachusetts has much more diversity in defense-oriented industries. For example, 70% of the Commonwealth's employment in defense-oriented industries is spread between the communications equipment subsector, electronics, and aircraft and missile parts (U.S. Bureau of the Census, 1987). In contrast, Connecticut and Vermont have large shares of defense-related employment in aircraft. In terms of commercial high-technology employment, Massachusetts and Connecticut (which together account for about 75% of total employment in the region) possess a broad-based industrial mix, whereas New Hampshire and Vermont possess concentrations of employment in computers and semiconductors, respectively (U.S. Bureau of the Census, 1987).

These structural differences are important. The degree to which defense industries are concentrated within a particular state and the types of defense-related industry there regulate to a degree the effects of a reduction in DOD dollars entering the region. For Maine, with about 50% of its defense-related employment in shipbuilding at Bath Iron Works, closure, or even major layoffs, at this facility would result in the state losing between 7% and 10% of its *total* manufacturing employment. Given the size of this work force, the multiplier effects of such a closure would result in further significant job loss beyond manufacturing, but would have little or no effect on high-technology industry within the state.

The concentration of defense-related activity in the aircraft industry in Connecticut around Hartford has different implications. In this state, defense-oriented manufacturing in aircraft production (notably United Technologies and Kaman Aerospace) accounts for more than 50% of all defense-related employment. The defense share of total private employment exceeds 9% and employment in the aircraft industry represents about 5.3% of all private jobs in the state and as much as 19% of the manufacturing sector. The relationship between the aircraft industry and other industry, however, is very different from that between the Maine shipbuilding industry and other industry, because aircraft and related production incorporates sophisticated accessories, often engineered in other high-technology sectors. Such interdependence implies that if significant job loss occurred in the aircraft industry in Connecticut, other regional high-technology production and research jobs in other high-technology industries would also be damaged. Given the size of the aircraft industry in the state and the nature of the multiplier effects associated with high-technology defense manufacturing (discussed above), the direct and indirect effects of cuts in defense spending within manufacturing, and particularly high-technology manufacturing, would be large.

In contrast, although it is geographically concentrated in Greater Boston, the industrial structure in Massachusetts is diverse. Because this diversity occurs in both commercial and defense-related high-technology industry, the eastern Massachusetts economy must be seen as more immune to shifting budgetary priorities than other regions. Indeed, *County Business Patterns* employment data indicate that, unlike the region and the nation as a whole, Massachusetts continued to create jobs in defense-related manufacturing between 1984 and 1987. This is important, because even though the proportion of all jobs in defense-related industry in Massachusetts is less than half that of Connecticut (about 9% in Connecticut and about 4% in Massachusetts), only two states other than Connecticut (California and New Hampshire) have more workers concentrated in defense-oriented industry.

Massachusetts, however, has a different structural problem. Much defense work in the state is concentrated in one company—Raytheon. It is one of the Commonwealth's largest employers and a major national defense contractor, with about 47,000 employees, the majority of whom work in Massachusetts. Most of Raytheon's activity involves R&D on, and the manufacture of, missile and space systems. The structure of New Hampshire's defense industry is even more monopolistic. Lockheed Sanders in Nashua produces advanced electronics and communications equipment, and is responsible for the vast majority of defense-related employment in the state. Given a significantly reduced budget for advanced weapon systems, the prospects for many of these two company's workers would be bleak.

Cuts in defense spending have already begun to take effect in New England's high-technology sectors. For instance, General Electric recently eliminated 900 jobs (out of 4,700) at its Pittsfield, Massachusetts, plant, which makes guidance systems for Trident missiles and parts for the Bradley tank. GE also recently laid off 1,000 employees—50% of the work force—at its Burlington, Vermont, facility, which produces aircraft machine guns. At the GE helicopter engine plant in Lynn, Massachusetts, which currently operates at about 60% capacity, layoffs are imminent after orders were cut in 1989. Orders for Raytheon's Phoenix missile, which arms F-14 fighters, unexpectedly ended in 1990 (Biddle, 1990). Such events have some defense contractors pursuing a diversification strategy, reducing the proportion of total earnings accounted for by defense industries. For example, Raytheon is now owner of Beech Aircraft, D. C. Heath publishing, and GeoQuest, a company supplying software and computer workstations for oil and gas exploration. Raytheon obtained 78% of total earnings from defense contracts in 1989, which is down from 88% just four years earlier. Furthermore, diversification is taking another form—the company is developing new markets overseas, such as the timely half-billion-dollar contract with Saudi Arabia for spare parts and service for Hawk missiles. These efforts, of course, offer no guarantees of future employment. Nonetheless, they are suggestive that major job losses in large defense contracting firms in New England appear unlikely, at least in the short run.

In the longer term, estimates of the effects of a cut in DOD spending vary widely: all, however, predict significant employment losses for the region. Henderson (1990) offers two scenarios. One follows the president's proposal and reduces the FY 1989 defense budget by $50 billion (FY 1989 dollars). The composition of this budget assigns 2.5% of the personnel cuts and 10% of the remaining cuts to the region. A second scenario doubles the reduction, leaving the composition the same. These scenarios reduce the gross regional product of New England by about $4 billion (1.67%) for the moderate reductions and $9.6 billion (3.9%) for the more severe cuts. Henderson anticipates that the consequences for employment are that between 57,000 and 134,000 jobs would be lost in defense-related industries under these conditions. That is, the current nonagricultural work force in New England would be directly reduced between 0.9% and 2.0%. In addition, the indirect effects (from weaker consumer demand) would further reduce the total regional work force. Such multiplier effects, assuming such indirect effects to be between 1.5 and 2 times the direct effects (U.S. Congressional Budget Office, 1983), could produce total employment losses anywhere between 140,000 and 400,000 jobs. These estimates range within those expected in a normal business cycle, but in the context of the present regional recession outside of defense-related industry, the prognosis for the regional economy for the next decade is not bright.

CONCLUSIONS

This chapter has summarized the recent history of the impacts of federal defense spending on New England's economy. Since 1945, the region has benefited disproportionately from military procurement and defense contracts from the DOD. Over the last few years, the spiraling federal budget deficit and shifts in superpower relationships have led to significantly increased pressure for reductions in defense spending. Consequently, the regional economy of New England may be especially vulnerable to shifts in federal budgetary priorities. The study has shown, however, that just as the effects of increased defense spending since 1977 produced complex reactions in the region, the regional economic impacts of reductions in defense spending are difficult to judge fully, not least because the size of the cuts and the future composition of defense budgets are unknown.

Part of this problem is also that the health of the economy is dependent upon factors other than the regional distribution of Pentagon spending. It is important to place New England's defense sector in the context of the regional economy as a whole, because although employment in defense-related manufacturing has had a significant influence on regional economic fortunes, it is not the only dynamic at work in the local economies. For example, many of the region's manufacturers produce for national markets. The recent local downturn has in some ways probably helped this segment of the regional economy, which was noticeably weak in the last half of the 1980s; while revenues have been stable (as national and international demand has been maintained), cost problems have eased, as labor shortages lessen and land costs stabilize or even decline (Syron & Browne, 1989).

The defense cuts come at an inopportune time, however. The regional economy is weaker now than it was five or seven years ago and is in recession, so even if the shocks from reduced spending by the DOD are not significantly different from those we could expect in a normal business cycle, they will certainly exaggerate the extant weaknesses in New England's economy.

APPENDIX:
DEFENSE-DEPENDENT INDUSTRIES

SIC	Industry
2892	Explosives
3131	Boot and Shoe Cut Stock and Findings
3299	Nonmetallic Mineral Products, n.e.c.
3312	Blast Furnaces and Steel Mills
3313	Electro-metallurgical Products
3331	Primary Copper
3332	Primary Lead
3333	Primary Zinc
3334	Primary Aluminum
3351	Copper Rolling and Drawing
3356	Nonferrous Rolling and Drawing, n.e.c.
3369	Nonferrous Castings, n.e.c.
3451	Screw Machine Products
3462	Iron and Steel Forgings
3463	Nonferrous Forgings
3471	Plating and Polishing
3482	Small Arms, Ammunition
3483	Ammunition, Except Small Arms, n.e.c.
3484	Small Arms
3489	Ordnance and Accessories
3511	Turbines and Turbine Generator Sets
3535	Conveyors and Conveying Equipment
3536	Hoists, Cranes, and Monorails
3541	Machine Tools, Metal Cutting Types
3542	Machine Tools, Metal Forming Types
3562	Ball and Roller Bearings
3569	General Industrial Machinery, n.e.c.
3621	Motor and Generators
3622	Industrial Controls
3624	Carbon and Graphite Products
3662	Radio and TV Communication Equipment
3671-3673	Electron Tubes
3675-3679	Electron Components, Except Tubes, Semiconductors

3713	Truck and Bus Bodies
3715	Truck Trailers
3721	Aircraft
3724 & 3764	Aircraft and Missile Engines and Parts
3728 & 3769	Aircraft and Missile Equipment, n.e.c.
3731	Ship Building and Repairing
3761	Guided Missiles and Space Vehicles
3795	Tanks and Tank Components
3811	Engineering and Scientific Instruments
3832	Optical Instruments and Lenses

SOURCE: Henry and Oliver (1985).

NOTES

1. The total effects are the summations over the seven sectors.

2. Table 4.1 updates Exhibit 3 in Knight and Barff (1987). The differences between the third columns in these two tables are attributable to the new benchmarking of the Bureau of Labor Statistics. For details about annualized shift-share analysis, see Barff and Knight (1988a).

3. *County Business Patterns*, on which Table 4.2 is based, sometimes suppresses the publication of employment because of disclosure regulations. These regulations affected this analysis only minimally, but when employment was not disclosed, estimation procedures followed Isserman and Sorenson (1987).

4. Disclosure rules preclude the use of payroll data at the state or regional level. These data probably understate the difference between defense-related employment in New England and the nation as a whole, given the high-technology orientation of defense-related manufacturing industry in the region.

5. The annual average manufacturing job loss in New England between 1984 and 1987 was 38,600. Between 1987 and 1988, the region lost 22,300 jobs in manufacturing.

6. Commercial high-technology employment in 1985 was correlated with defense orientation in 1979 because the defense buildup of the late 1970s and 1980s caused unusual growth in some states' defense-related employment.

7. In Browne's analysis, Delaware featured as a distinct outlier. This state is unusual in that it has virtually no defense-oriented industry and the large commercial high-technology base (almost 15% of all private employment) is concentrated in chemicals. There are two simple ways to deal with outlier problems in correlation analysis. One is to remove that observation; the other is to use rank correlation analysis. Replicating Browne's (1988) correlation analysis with either produces a result quite different from Browne's original finding. Her original analysis produced an insignificant correlation of +0.18; the coefficient is +0.35 with Delaware omitted, and +0.37 as Spearman's rank coefficient using all observations (both significant at $a = .01$). In other words, at the state level, defense activity is positively and significantly associated with commercially oriented high-technology industry, controlling for the unusual industrial mix in Delaware.

REFERENCES

Ballard, K. P., & Clark, G. L. (1981). The short-run dynamics of interstate migration: A space-time economic adjustment model of inmigration to fast growing states. *Regional Studies, 15*, 213-228.

Barff, R. A. (1989). Migration and labour supply in New England. *Geoforum, 20*, 293-301.

Barff, R. A. (1990). The migration response to the New England economic turnaround. *Environment and Planning A, 22*, 1497-1516.

Barff, R. A., & Knight, P. L., III. (1988a). Dynamic shift-share analysis. *Growth and Change, 19*, 1-10.

Barff, R. A., & Knight, P. L., III. (1988b). The role of federal military spending in the timing of the New England employment turnaround. *Papers of the Regional Science Association, 65*, 151-166.

Biddle, F. (1990, January 23). Raytheon's peace plan. *Boston Globe.*

Bradbury, K. (1985, September-October). Prospects for growth in New England: The labor force. *New England Economic Review*, pp. 50-60.

Breheny, M. J. (Ed.). (1988). *Defence expenditure and regional development* London: Mansell.

Browne, L. E. (1987, January-February). Too much of a good thing? Higher wages in New England. *New England Economic Review*, pp. 39-53.

Browne, L. E. (1988, September-October). Defense spending and high technology development: National and state issues. *New England Economic Review*, pp. 3-22.

Clark, N. G. (1972). Science, technology, and regional economic development. *Research Policy, 1*, 296-319.

Erickson, R. A. (1974). Subregional impact multipliers: Income spread effects from a major defense installation. *Economic Geography, 53*, 283-294.

Estall, R. C. (1966). *New England: A study in industrial adjustment.* New York: Praeger.

Galbraith, K. D., & Wakefield, C. J. (1984). National defense spending: A review of appropriations and real purchases. *Survey of Current Business, 64*, 11-16.

Harrison, B. (1984). Regional restructuring and "good business climates": The economic transformation of New England since World War Two. In W. Sawers & W. K. Tabb (Eds.), *Sunbelt/Snowbelt: Urban development and regional restructuring* (pp. 48-96). New York: Oxford University Press.

Harrison, B., & Kluver, J. (1989). Reassessing the "Massachusetts miracle": Reindustrialization and balanced growth, or convergence to "Manhattanization"? *Environment and Planning A, 21*, 771-801.

Henderson, Y. K. (1990, July-August). Defense cutbacks and the New England economy. *New England Economic Review*, pp. 3-24.

Henry, D. K., & Oliver, R. P. (1985, August). The defense buildup, 1977-85: Effects on production and employment. *Monthly Labor Review*, pp. 3-11.

Isserman, A. M., & Sorenson, D. J. (1987, April). *County employment: A description of federal data sources and the construction of a multisource data base.* Paper presented at the annual meeting of the Association of American Geographers, Portland, OR.

Knight, P. L., III, & Barff, R. A. (1987). Employment growth and the turnaround of the New England economy. *Northeast Journal of Business and Economics, 14*, 1-15.

Malecki, E. J. (1986). Research and development and the geography of high technology complexes. In J. Rees (Ed.), *Technology, regions, and policy* (pp. 51-74). Totowa, NJ: Rowman & Littlefield.

Malecki, E. J., & Stark, L. M. (1988). Regional and industrial variation in defense spending: Some American evidence. In M. J. Breheny (Ed.), *Defence expenditure and regional development* (pp. 67-101). London: Mansell.

Markusen, A. R. (1986). The militarized economy. *World Policy Journal, 3*, 495-516.

Masnick, G. S. (1985). The demography of New England: Policy issues for the balance of this century. *New England Journal of Public Policy, 1*, 22-43.

Massachusetts Department of Employment and Training. (1989). *Defense industry profile, Commonwealth of Massachusetts*. Boston: Author.

Norton, R. D. (1987). The role of services and manufacturing in New England's resurgence. *New England Economic Indicators* (2nd quarter), pp. iv-viii.

O'hUallachain, B. (1987). Regional and technological implications of the recent buildup in American defense spending. *Annals of the Association of American Geographers, 77*, 208-233.

Plane, D., & Rogerson, P. (1989). U.S. migration pattern responses to the oil glut and recession of the early 1980s. In P. Condgon & P. Batey (Eds.), *Advances in regional demography* (pp. 257-280). London: Belhaven.

Riche, R. W., Hecker, D. E., & Burgan, J. U. (1983, November). High technology today and tomorrow. *Monthly Labor Review*, pp. 50-58.

Saxenian, A. (1985). Silicon Valley and Route 128: Regional prototypes or historic exceptions? In M. Castells (Ed.), *High technology, space, and society* (pp. 81-105). Beverly Hills, CA: Sage.

Syron, R. F., & Browne, L. E. (1989). One view of what the future holds for New England. *New England Economic Indicators* (4th quarter), pp. iv-xiii.

Tirman, J. (1984). The defense economy debate. In J. Tirman (Ed.), *The militarization of high technology* (pp. 1-30). Cambridge, MA: Ballinger.

U.S. Bureau of the Census. (1983). *Current industrial reports: Shipments to federal government agencies*. Washington, DC: Government Printing Office.

U.S. Bureau of the Census. (1987). *County business patterns*. Washington, DC: Government Printing Office.

U.S. Congressional Budget Office. (1983). *Defense spending and the economy*. Washington, DC: Government Printing Office.

U.S. Department of Defense. (1984). *Military prime contract awards by state, fiscal years 1951-1983*. Washington, DC: Directorate of Information Operations and Reports.

U.S. Department of Defense. (1988). *Prime contract awards by region and state, FY 1986, 1985, 1984*. Washington, DC: Government Printing Office.

5

Military Spending in Free Enterprise Cities:
The Military-Industrial Complex
in Houston and Las Vegas

ROBERT E. PARKER
JOE R. FEAGIN

THIS CHAPTER EXAMINES two Sunbelt cities that metamorphosed into major metropolitan areas using substantial public aid, political rhetoric and conventional wisdom notwithstanding. It concerns frontier towns whose citizens and leaders are strong proponents of a free enterprise ideology. We focus on one part of the subsidy that poured into these two cities—military spending—to explore the influence of public expenditure on the urban environment. Military dollars have made important contributions to Las Vegas and Houston, and wartime spending in particular provided an economic foundation and the physical infrastructure needed for both cities to evolve as major urban areas. A central theme of this chapter is, however, that military spending does not exhibit uniform characteristics in Sunbelt cities. In Las Vegas, the spatial and economic impacts of defense dollars are transparent, whereas in Houston the impacts are difficult to quantify.

In the first part of this chapter we note the emphasis in Houston and Las Vegas on the ideology of free enterprise and the "good business climate." We then document the extent of military-related spending and its different impacts in each city.

AUTHORS' NOTE: We thank Victoria Evans for her research assistance in the preparation of this chapter.

SELLING THE GOOD BUSINESS CLIMATE AND MILITARY SPENDING

Leaders in both Houston and Las Vegas are strongly probusiness in their administrative orientation. Both cities have elite economic actors who stress the connection between a good business climate and economic development, and part of the philosophy shared by those in the two cities is a commitment to low taxes and minimal public expenditures. Yet, the leaders in both cities overlook these commitments when it comes to receiving the public assistance that benefits private economic development. There is perhaps no better way to see this contradiction than through the example of military spending.

HOUSTON

From its inception, the city's founders and business leaders have advertised Houston as the "free enterprise city." Feagin (1988) notes:

An advertisement for Houston by the local business elite in *Fortune* magazine accented the good business climate and the lack of government interference proclaimed from the 1840s to the 1980s: "Houston, by virtue of being in Texas, reaps the benefits of a state that has one of the best business climates in the nation. It is not just lukewarm to business, it is probusiness. It welcomes new ideas and people. There's little in the way of red tape. Free enterprise is still the gospel." (p. 47)

The responsibility for promotion rests heavily with the Houston Economic Development Council (HEDC), a component of the Greater Houston Partnership (GHP). The GHP is a business advocacy organization that was created by, and includes, the Greater Houston Chamber of Commerce. A recent brochure from the group presents some reasons Houston remains known as a city with a good business climate:

Texas is also a right-to-work state, with a labor force unionization rate of only 12.5 percent—the ninth lowest in the country. . . . Approximately 25 to 35 percent of the city's land, office, warehouse and industrial space is available for immediate occupancy—at leasing and purchasing rates that are the most competitive of any metropolitan area . . . housing costs that are 20 percent below the national average. . . . Low Taxes. . . . Your business pays no corporate income taxes—city or state—no unitary tax and no state property tax. Tax abatements which grant reductions of up to 100 percent are available for up to seven years. (HEDC, 1989b, pp. 2-3)

Although Houston's business elite have lately diversified economic development plans, they still rely heavily on aggressive advertising of the city's commitment to the good business climate. And while minimal government interference and intervention are still given lip service, the decades when Houston's economic and political leaders boasted of refusing assistance have passed. No longer is federal urban aid attacked as socialistic by business groups and politicians.

LAS VEGAS

Las Vegas's good business climate is of more recent origin. Nonetheless, the position adopted by business leaders and their allies in Nevada's largest city is quite similar to that used in Houston. And, as in Houston, the list of urban growth proponents in Las Vegas is not exhausted by area businesses. Most citizens (including union members) believe that growth creates more and better jobs, and the local press has a vested interest in boosterism, as a surging population increases circulation and advertising revenues. Everyone in the local urban growth coalition is exalting Las Vegas's boom, as in this excerpt from *Las Vegas Perspective 1989*:

> The word is out. Southern Nevada's secret of prosperity, vitality and promise for the future shines brighter than ever. Pick up the latest issue of any publication forecasting the leaders in income growth, business activity, real estate expansion or quality of life, and there's Las Vegas in the first paragraph. (Las Vegas Review-Journal, Nevada Development Authority, & First Interstate Bank of Nevada, N.A., 1989, p. 5)

Recently, the national business press has begun to amplify the image of southern Nevada as a freewheeling progrowth center. For example, *Inc.* magazine listed Nevada first in its 1989 annual ranking of state economic climates (Brown, 1989, p. 87). The following year the magazine compounded the unbridled imagery by naming Las Vegas the most entrepreneurial city in the United States (Case, 1990, p. 42).

THE LATENT POLITICAL AND ECONOMIC ROLE OF MILITARY SPENDING

In sum, Las Vegas and Houston have long championed the central ingredients of what has become known as a good business climate. In particular, both cities have commitments to low taxation; a large, docile labor force; lax enforcement of environmental and workplace regulations; and generally minimal government interference. However, the leadership of both Sunbelt cities has readily accepted, and at times aggressively sought, government intervention, particularly when it takes a form that benefits privately controlled enterprises. In the late 1980s, Houston's economic development agency listed the receipt of increased military expenditures as an important diversification objective. In Nevada, proposed military cutbacks have been consistently resisted by public and private officials. A central theme of this chapter, then, is that although Las Vegas and Houston have economic leaders who have created and perpetuated a good business climate, both also have elites that have welcomed military spending.

This chapter reveals the direct and indirect effects of military expenditure in the Las Vegas and Houston metropolitan areas. It has been important in both cities, but the form of that spending and its impact have differed. In southern Nevada, military disbursements have had an overt economic impact on the area and its urban form. Major military installations—including the Nevada Test Site, Nellis Air Force Base, and the Tonopah Test Range—have produced substantial economic and spatial effects. In Houston, however, military spending has had more of a clandestine character, hidden in now privately controlled industrial infrastructure and the budget of the Johnson Space Center (JSC), although its impact does not stop there. Military dollars also create a ripple economy that services the men and women engaged in military activities (Burkhart, 1990, p. 1F). Local rental housing, restaurants, bars, dry cleaners, and a variety of other economic enterprises are supported directly by this expenditure.

In the United States, the logic behind the distribution of the military budget is avowedly strategic. "Defense" spending occurs in some areas rather than others because of militaristically sound reasons. Unlike in several European countries, where military sites are sometimes explicitly designed to serve both economic and tactical functions, U.S. defense operations are not allegedly guided by economic or political motivations. Yet, when it serves their purposes, sponsors reveal the additional roles that military spending plays. The U.S. Department of Energy (1986), for example, in highlighting its contribution to the southern Nevada economy, claimed to represent "stability in a one-asset economy that is potentially subject to unanticipated economic fluctuations." Indeed, over the years, officials have appeared anxious to discuss the department's economic role in the region:

> The DOE employs more persons than any hotel/casino complex in Las Vegas by a wide margin. The impact of DOE on southern Nevada is

larger than any other single entity, except for state and local governments. (DOE, 1989)

Similarly, in Houston, local growth boosters have aggressively sought defense dollars and boast of the economic impact of a publicly financed, military-related government project—NASA's Johnson Space Center:

> In total, JSC . . . purchases about $475 million a year in goods and services. . . . Its staff of more than 10,000 government, aerospace engineering, and technical personnel outnumbers that of any other NASA facility. An additional 80,000 people work in related businesses that keep Houston at the forefront of today's space-related technology. (HEDC, 1989a, p. 28)

There are other indications that military spending continues to serve more than a national security function in these communities. In Nevada, cutbacks at the Tonopah Test Range, Nellis AFB, the National Guard, and the Nevada Test Site are being resisted by Nevada's public officials at all levels. In Houston, the city's economic leadership aggressively sought a Navy home port for Galveston. And, as noted, the HEDC has made the receipt of a greater share of military spending one component of its development agenda.

The impact of military spending has been overlooked as a significant economic and social force in the past half century of Las Vegas's and Houston's history. Throughout, the presence of military spending can be seen in the physical infrastructure of the two cities, and this chapter demonstrates that military expenditures have had an impact on the spatial form of urban growth in these metropolises. Additionally, military spending has served as a consistent prop for the local economy, particularly in the case of southern Nevada.

MILITARY SPENDING IN LAS VEGAS: HISTORICAL OVERVIEW

Defense spending has had an uneven impact on Las Vegas's economy, at times providing a stimulus and at others a dampening effect by withdrawing an important economic resource. The expansion of Nellis AFB is a good example of the former, while the transfer of the Stealth Fighter fleet from the Tonopah Test Range to New Mexico exemplifies the latter.

MILITARY SPENDING DURING WORLD WAR II

Southern Nevada received a major economic boost during the Depression when construction of Hoover Dam began in 1931. The Boulder Canyon project represented the first significant civilian federal intervention in Las Vegas. But after 1939, a growing segment of the economic activity generated by government spending came from military expenditures. Soldiers and employees of defense contractors stabilized the early Las Vegas gaming and tourist-based economy when it could have been devastated by wartime mobilization. Las Vegas benefited from a steady stream of military spending in the early 1940s, when it had "an air base, a magnesium plant, and a new suburb to house defense workers. In just over 10 years, Las Vegas was transformed from a sleepy whistle-stop to a city with prospects" (Moehring, 1989, p. 14). War also laid the groundwork for future defense-related expansion. The military site that evolved into Nellis AFB carved out a niche for itself as the "home of the fighter pilot" and more than 600 B-17 gunners and 215 copilots were graduated from the school every five weeks (U.S. Air Force, 1989a). By 1989, more than 12,000 military and civilian employees worked at Nellis (U.S. Air Force, 1989b), and annual payroll at the base had reached $325 million (Williams, 1988). Other significant military spending activities exist: In 1985, "an additional $33 million went to civilian workers and a whopping $98.7 million to Nellis retirees living in the Las Vegas area. The local economy benefited further from the fact that over 80% of all Nellis airmen owned or rented housing off base" (Moehring, 1989, p. 113).

In January 1951, atomic bomb testing was inaugurated at the Nevada Test Site. The preparation for the first detonation generated a significant economic stimulus as some 1,500 workers from Las Vegas erected the physical infrastructure for the site. The testing conducted at the site required a large, albeit fluctuating, supply of workers— more than 3,000 scientists, technicians, and other specialists were working at the test site at times. Huge contingents of military personnel from various branches descended upon the site at other times. Moehring (1989) writes: "The labor force fluctuated from year to year, but, throughout the 1950s, the test site payroll exceeded $176 million—two thirds of which found its way into the Las Vegas economy" (p. 99). Between 1952 and 1962, there were 84 weapons tests, and since then there have been more than 700 publicly announced nuclear detonations at the site. Physically, the facility sits on 814,528 acres of DOE-directed, controlled-access land, an area larger than Rhode Island.

In short, for the last 50 years the city's physical form and economy have been affected by military spending. The next section examines some of the central actors involved in this spending in greater detail.

MAJOR SOURCES OF MILITARY SPENDING

A small number of sites are responsible for the vast bulk of military spending in Nevada, notably Nellis AFB, the Nevada Test Site, and the Tonopah Test Range. No public information is available on the extent of military spending for "black" budget programs, such as the Stealth bomber. Work on the Strategic Defense Initiative is similarly protected from public inspection. In short, even the most consistent information on military spending is likely to be considerably understated.

The Department of Energy

At the end of the 1980s, the annual Department of Energy payroll in Nevada was roughly $320 million, a figure that is expected to remain constant in 1990 (DOE, 1990). The department has approximately 9,500 federal and privately contracted workers in the area. Nearly 5,000 are employed at the Nevada Test Site, 3,400 work in Las Vegas, and 1,200 work at the Tonopah Test Range. According to a DOE report in the late 1980s, more than 20,000 local workers are directly or indirectly employed as a result of its programs. At that level, it is estimated that DOE-related employment supports more than 48,000 southern Nevadans directly or indirectly, some 8% of the work force. DOE programs tend to be professional, technical, and science oriented, and the department employs 15% of all engineers working in Nevada.

In fiscal year 1988, the department's major expenditures totaled $130 million, including about $12 million for health care and related costs. Including payroll expenses, DOE's programs provided an economic stimulus of approximately $570 million to the Las Vegas area (DOE, 1990, p. 2). When the multiplier effect is calculated, the overall contribution of DOE to the southern Nevada economy was approximately $860 million in 1988. Based on personal income estimates, DOE is directly or indirectly responsible for 7.5% of the total personal income for southern Nevada (DOE, 1989, p. 1). Only because of rapid urban growth in southern Nevada did the proportion of the local population tied to DOE activities slip from 9% of the total in 1985 to a little more than 7% in 1988 (DOE, 1986, 1990).

Nellis Air Force Base

Nellis is the largest base in the Tactical Air Command and one of the Air Force's busiest. It has been utilized for flight operations since 1929. In 1940, Las Vegas purchased and improved the field for use in training civilian pilots, and President Roosevelt established the Las Vegas Bombing and Gunnery Range, now officially known as the Nellis Air Force Range (NAFR) (see Figure 5.1). For nearly 20 years the range was used by the Air Force, cattle ranchers, and miners, but these last two uses have now been eliminated by military activity.

Events of the 1950s greatly expanded the role of Nellis AFB. Early in the decade, population pressures connected with the Korean conflict rippled through the community in several ways. The Air Force moved rapidly on several major construction projects to augment its newly inflated role. The projects had both economic and spatial impacts on the city. In addition to creating jobs, the Air Force benefited as public officials in Las Vegas turned over nearly 2,000 acres of municipal land when Nellis officials decided to build a housing project for 400 airmen and their families. Shortly thereafter came the construction of the Nellis grammar school and Nellis Hospital. In addition to these central facilities, $3.4 million was spent on miscellaneous construction projects in one year alone (Moehring, 1989, p. 96).

With each succeeding international conflict, Nellis's strategic importance grew. A year after the truce that ended hostilities in Korea, more than 5,000 personnel were stationed there. Indeed, the Air Force significantly expanded its operations when the Tactical Air Command replaced the Air Training Command in 1958. More important, the growing awareness of Las Vegas's strategic role led President Truman to designate the Las Vegas Valley as a "critical defense area." This executive action became central to the local economy and altered the physical makeup of the city. It meant significant funds for an array of infrastructural projects, including housing, schools, sewers, streets, and fire stations (Moehring, 1989, p. 99).

The 1960s saw the United States become involved in another war, and activity at Nellis surged in concert. During the Vietnam conflict, the installation became the nation's main tactical weapons training center. By decade's end, Nellis had more than 9,000 personnel and an

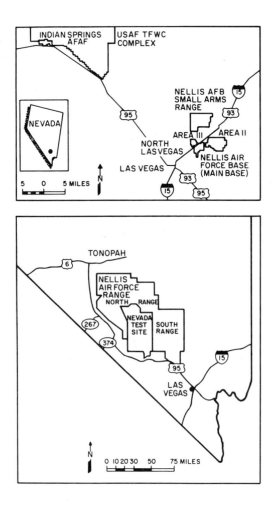

Figure 5.1. Distribution of Military Facilities in Southern Nevada

annual payroll of more than $60 million. The cost of operating the base also rose steadily, to more than $90 million in 1970. These figures largely represent expenditures that went to surrounding businesses from which the Air Force purchased supplies.

Nellis's main base covers more than 11,000 acres just a few miles northeast of Las Vegas. Nearly 5 million acres (7,700 square miles) of airspace north and east of the restricted ranges are also available for military flight operations. In early 1989, Nellis was southern Nevada's largest employer, directly supporting more than 12,000 military and civilian personnel (down from approximately 15,000 in 1985). In 1988, nearly 4% of total employment in Clark County was a result of direct employment at Nellis.

When secondary employees and their dependents are considered, approximately 10% of the Clark County population is tied to activity at Nellis. In addition to an on-base population of 12,000, there are 34,000 family members and 10,000 retired military personnel using the base. As the Air Force has noted, if it were a city unto itself, the Nellis base would be the state's third largest urban area.

Most of Nellis's Air Force workers are assigned to one of the major military activities at the base. Many additional employees provide support services (including workers operating the base exchange and on-base private business services). In early 1989, direct payroll expenditure by Nellis AFB amounted to $270 million (down from $440 million in 1986). The annual wages of military personnel averaged a little more than $24,000 in 1987. Off base, which is where more than 90% of all officers reside, the average pay in 1987 was more than $28,000.

In 1988, Nellis activities generated more than $500 million in personal disposable income, or 5.6% of the total in Clark County. In addition, military personnel have their life-style subsidized by the availability of inexpensive food, medical care, housing, and base exchange privileges. Although these subsidies free up more discretionary income, which is spent in Las Vegas, little attention has been paid to the distribution of such spending (Williams, 1988). In addition to these economic effects, more than 10,000 retirees received an average of $11,553 in annual retirement pay in 1987. The DOE also paid out nearly $120 million in pensions to military retirees living in southern Nevada. Most of the military personnel live off base, where, as of 1986, they resided in 2,500 rental units and 400 owner-occupied homes. In the same year, an additional $1.4 million was paid in hotel room rentals stemming from the 30,000 official visitors to Nellis. Purchases connected with Nellis activities contributed more than $800 million to the gross regional product of Clark County in 1988 (this figure is slightly less than 6% of Clark's total), and of the more than $400 million in total county and city government resources in Clark County, about $39 million can be attributed to Nellis AFB activities.

The total economic effect of Nellis on southern Nevada was slightly less significant in 1989 than in 1986: $711 million compared with $750 million (including payroll, construction, operating expenses and contracts, and multiplier effects). Over Nellis's roughly 50-year existence, American taxpayers have poured more than $3 billion into its physical infrastructure projects alone. In 1987, Nellis spent $176 million for construction and service contracts. This total includes $53 million for social services (commissary, base exchange, health, and miscellaneous expenses), $49 million for utility services, and an equivalent sum for major and minor construction (Williams, 1988, p. 7). The significance of these figures is their omission of the largest expenditures—for aircraft, aircraft fuel, and ordnance—which are manufactured out of state and about which no public information is available.

In 1989, the Air Force deactivated the 474th Tactical Fighter Wing. The 474th's military mission had been to "mobilize and deploy combat-ready squadrons." It had been one of four major military components at Nellis, and in 1987, 1,387 military and 26 civilian employees had been assigned to the unit. The Air Force moved Nellis's F-16 fighter planes to Air National Guard and Air Force reserve units in other states, resulting in the loss of nearly 1,500 jobs.

The Nevada Test Site

The Nevada Test Site (NTS) is a 1,350-square-mile area located within the Nellis complex. It was selected as a site for nuclear weapons testing due to the area's low population density, favorable weather, geology, safety, security, and easy access to labor. Military land for the NTS was first withdrawn in 1952, and additional land was acquired through other withdrawals in 1958, 1961, and 1964, as well as an agreement with the Department of Defense (DOD) in 1967.

The NTS is responsible for more than 2% of total employment in Clark County, directly or indirectly. In 1988, the facility accounted for 2.2% of all personal disposable income, and 2% of the county's population is attributable to direct and secondary employment generated by NTS activities. Of the $400 million in general fund resources for Clark County in 1989, about $9.2 million can be attributed directly to NTS activities.

Since 1950, the year Nevada was selected as a continental nuclear site, DOE and its precursors have spent more than $650 million for capital equipment and approximately $426 million for buildings, roads, power lines, and related testing activities at the site—a significant proportion of the $8 billion spent by all of DOE's Nevada operations over the last four decades (DOE, 1990, p. 2).

TABLE 5.1

Major DOE Contractors in Las Vegas Area

DOE Major Contractors	*Number of Employees*[a]
Reynolds Electrical & Engineering Co.	4,300
EG&G Energy Measurements Group	1,500
Holmes & Narver, Inc.	575
Wackenhut Services, Inc.	425
Science Applications International, Inc.	385
Fenix and Scisson	260

Data abstracted from Las Vegas Review-Journal, Nevada Development Authority, and First Interstate Bank of Nevada, N.A. (1990).
a. At Nevada Test Site or in Las Vegas.

In 1947, Harold Edgerton, Kenneth Germeshausen, and Herbert Grier, three graduates of MIT, formed the engineering firm of EG&G. Three EG&G companies now employ a majority of the workers at the Nevada Test Site. Together, more than 8,000 workers are employed by EG&G Energy Measurements, Inc., EG&G Special Projects, and Reynolds Electrical and Engineering Company (REECO) ("Scientist Edgerton Dies," 1990). Spokespersons for southern Nevada military contractors (including REECO and EG&G Energy Measurements) have expressed skepticism that spending cutbacks will have a negative impact on their operations (Schumacher, 1989, p. 1A). Table 5.1 displays the DOE's major contractors at the Nevada Test Site and in Las Vegas generally.

The Tonopah Test Range

A substantial amount of economic activity in southern Nevada is generated by the Tonopah Test Range (TTR), located in a small town of 4,500 that underwent an economic upheaval in the mid-1980s when Anaconda Copper suddenly ceased operations (see Figure 5.1). With 300 jobs lost as a result of the plant closing, spending on the Stealth project sustained the local economy, and the proposed military transfer of the Stealth from Tonopah would likely have far-reaching economic consequences. Each week, 2,500 Air Force personnel are shuttled in from Nellis. In addition, about 900 REECO employees provide support to the Air Force at the test range.

For the past decade, the TTR has served as the preoperational development site for the Air Force's 54 F-117A Stealth fighters. The military site, created on 369,000 acres in November 1956, is currently a source of friction—between residents and businesspeople in Tonopah and the Air Force, and between public officials in New Mexico and Nevada. At stake are 2,500 direct jobs, 9,000 residents, and other economic effects. The Air Force plans to move the 37th Tactical Fighter Wing from the TTR to Holloman Air Force Base in New Mexico. When Air Force officials held meetings in Tonopah and Las Vegas in March 1990, they were unable to tell residents how many jobs would be removed or what the larger economic impact would be to their communities. They did, however, emphasize that Americans would be saving tax dollars, as operating costs are expected to be reduced by more than $100 million annually as a result of the transfer (Hynes, 1990c, p. 1B).

The potential disruption precipitated by a withdrawn military project illustrates the uneven development impact that military spending can create. Many residents have reacted to the relocation plans with concern and anger; several businesspeople, particularly from Tonopah, have said that they invested money in the community believing the test-range employment would continue to stimulate the economy. One businesswoman asked the officials if they were going to "trash" the town, allow it to dry up and blow away. Others expressed more immediate worries. The Nye County School District superintendent noted that the county just passed a $30 million bond issue to build schools, but now there are going to be 250 fewer students, and the county manager observed that not a whole lot of people would have voted for it if they knew they were not going to have jobs in a few years (Hynes, 1990d, p. 1B).

Other local politicians openly expressed anxiety about the loss of the planes. For example, the Las Vegas city manager asserted that it appears to be okay for Nevada to be used as a testing or a dump area, but when a government project becomes legitimate it is time to move it somewhere else (Hill, 1990b, p. 6A). And Assemblywoman Jane Wisdom called it another case of "doing Nevada in" (Hynes, 1990b, p. 1B).

Governor Miller also criticized the planned move, asserting that the military should not build up an economic base in a community and then leave without justification ("Miller Will Talk," 1990). Nevada's two senators, both Democrats, issued a joint statement in response to the Air Force's plans, arguing that American taxpayers had recently invested hundreds of millions of dollars at the Tonopah facility (Adams, 1990, p. 1A). And Nye County officials expressed their disappointment and their intention to fight the plan (Hynes,

1990a, p. 4A). In the short term, the move is expected to cost the Air Force about $115 million in construction costs at Holloman. But Senator Pete Domenici, who announced the Pentagon's plan, said he expects the move to add 1,800 jobs to New Mexico's economy.

In addition to the proposed cuts at the Nellis and Tonopah sites, southern Nevada is expected to lose other immediate sources of military spending. For example, National Guard units are scheduled to be pruned as part of the DOD's plans to restructure the military. In southern Nevada, the plan is to cut the Guard by one-half. The battalion's absence will have an impact—it spent nearly $5 million in 1989 on payroll and operating expenses. As with other proposed cuts, the Guard is using political pressure to resist the changes. According to a spokesperson for Senator Harry Reid, both Nevada senators plan to work to retain the personnel (Hill, 1990a, p. 1A). This is an excellent illustration of the economic and political roles played by military spending coming out into view. Public officials at all levels are resisting the cuts because they fear the changes may slow local economic growth or damage their own political fortunes. Strategically, however, Nevada's senators appear to be on shaky ground in protesting the cuts, since the National Guard's mission is to provide additional troops for Europe during wartime.

MILITARY SPENDING IN HOUSTON

One theme of this chapter is that military spending patterns in Sunbelt cities do not exhibit uniform characteristics. In the Las Vegas area, the spatial and economic impacts of defense dollars are difficult to overlook, whereas in Houston, the major impact lies in the kind of subsidy that is difficult to quantify. Military spending has been important mainly in providing and accelerating the development of physical infrastructure needed by postwar industries. Since the early 1960s, there have been additional military dollars going to the region through the Johnson Space Center budget, but in neither case is military spending leaving visible traces in the city. In short, in Las Vegas the impact is relatively transparent, while in Houston it remains hidden from view.

Houston's history has involved a virtually uninterrupted series of business elites running and shaping the local government and the growth of the city. Business leaders have been involved with national politics and the federal government since before World War I. One area where this interconnection can be seen is in military spending. Federal capital expenditures have taken the form of assistance for military-industrial ventures, such as the NASA spacecraft facility and space-related contracts for many private corporations. Unlike Las Vegas, Houston was a sizable city with a mature economy prior to 1941; but, like the former, officials in Houston used military spending associated with the Second World War to lay the foundation for a postwar acceleration of its economic growth.

THE HIDDEN CHARACTER
OF MILITARY SPENDING IN HOUSTON

In Las Vegas military spending has taken an overt form, with an active Air Force presence and DOE-managed weapons testing. But in Houston, military spending has been concealed and is far harder to delimit precisely. Military spending is hidden both in NASA budgets and in the city's publicly and privately owned infrastructure. The impact in Houston cannot be seen in the same way that the effects of Nellis AFB can be seen on southern Nevada.

Since 1945, military-related spending in Houston has had a relatively small and dwindling influence on the city compared with other economic sectors. Because of its low profile, many business leaders, public officials, and academic observers deny that the military has played any noteworthy function in Houston's economy.

Consider some representative views recently obtained in telephone interviews with observers in Houston. Skip Kasdorf, spokesperson for the Greater Houston Partnership, said that there was little defense money in the city and that the Reserve Officers Training Corps at the University of Houston (UH) probably represented the biggest single expenditure (personal communication, July 17, 1990). Al Ballanger, of the UH Center for Public Policy, presented a similar description, arguing that with the exception of perhaps a little jet fuel, there is no defense spending in the Houston community (personal communication, July 1990). Lou Stern, a UH economist, also pointed to the lack of military spending in Houston but did acknowledge the connections among defense dollars, the JSC, and the community of Clear Lake, which grew up around it (personal communication, July 17, 1990). Perhaps the most adamant voice came from James Poteet, a UH historian, who claimed that while the aerospace industry is important in Houston, it did not have military underpinnings (personal communication, July 27, 1990). He suggested Seattle as a place where an analysis of space-related military activity could be undertaken (see

Chapter 3 of this volume) and asserted that it was inappropriate to make a connection between the growth of the petrochemical industry in Houston and military spending during World War II. At best, he conceded, the war accelerated the development of petrochemicals, but the development would have taken place anyway. Poteet believes that you need to have military bases, such as the one in San Antonio, before you can talk about any kind of meaningful military impact in a southwestern city.

Jim Poindexter, a spokesperson for NASA in Houston, emphasized that NASA is a *civilian* agency (personal communication, July 23, 1990). In contrast to figures provided by the Houston Economic Development Council, Poindexter drew a conservative approximation of the JSC's economic impact on the city, and argued that if you want to get "real tricky," you can identify some Air Force money that went into the development of the space shuttle. Poindexter added that there was no military aerospace manufacturing anywhere near Houston.

Yet it is clear that Houston's business elites have long understood the benefit of publicly supplied military dollars. As noted, one economic development goal of the business leadership in the late 1980s was to secure a larger portion of the national defense budget for Houston (Feagin, 1988, pp. 94-95).

THE MILITARY'S IMPACT
ON HOUSTON'S PETROCHEMICAL INDUSTRY

We believe the views presented above are typical—and inaccurate. The prevailing wisdom neglects the contribution that military spending has already had on the city and treats the JSC as an entirely civilian agency. This section presents some of the connections between military spending and Houston's economy and form.

In the 1940s oil production and oil-related industries expanded rapidly. Within a radius of 150 miles of Houston, there were 185 productive oil fields. In the greater Houston area, 14 major refineries were operating. Further, much of the world's oil tool and services business was centered there. The growing concentration and power of the industry (half of all U.S. oil flowed through the metropolitan economy) was aided by the inaction of the Roosevelt administration. In the late 1930s, the administration began an antitrust suit against 22 oil companies, but dropped it as war broke out.

There are several reasons Houston became a petrochemical production center. The ship channel, a major transport avenue for oil and gas products, was a natural site for production. Another key reason was the concentration of refinery capacity in the Houston area. But for our purposes, of greater interest is the role of federal aid in concentrating the petrochemical industry in Houston, for it took major subsidies for the petrochemical industry to evolve into its modern form. By the 1940s, the federal government had become a leading source of investment capital for U.S. industry, including the oil and petrochemical industries.

Direct federal investment in the Houston area can be illustrated by examining three specific instances of government-financed petrochemical plants in the 1940s; this material is adapted from Riddell and Feagin (1986). These cases demonstrate the role of government war agencies in generating new, and expanding already existing, privately owned plants. The pivotal agencies involved in these examples are the Defense Plant Corporation (DPC), the Rubber Reserve Company (RRC), and, indirectly, the War Production Board and Reconstruction Finance Corporation. The establishment of the DPC and the RRC was made possible by an amendment to the legislation that created the Reconstruction Finance Corporation (RFC). The facilities involved are the synthetic rubber plants of Dow, Monsanto, and Sinclair, and Dow's magnesium plant.

Dow was the primary producer of magnesium in the country prior to, and during, World War II. The company began magnesium production in Michigan through a process involving the extraction of brine from water. The site in the Houston area (Freeport) was chosen because of its accessibility to salt water, allowing brine to be extracted from the ocean. Magnesium was considered a critical priority material during the war, and to meet the demand the government contracted with Dow to expand its plant in Freeport. Dow also received a major government contract to produce styrene at its nearby factory in Velasco. (Styrene is a chemical derived from petroleum that was combined with butadiene to produce synthetic rubber.) In all, the DPC invested nearly $18 million in the styrene plant at Velasco. Dow did not produce synthetic rubber, just the raw material. Thus the government substantially boosted the industry through its contracts with Dow: to expand its magnesium plant at Freeport, to build a new styrene plant at Velasco, and to expand its styrene plant at Freeport.

One important impact of the government's involvement in the financing of war production was the development of new towns in the region. For example, Camp Chemical and Lake Jackson, both near Freeport, are examples of communities that emerged in the early 1940s. Camp Chemical was a housing development built by the government for the use of Dow employees, in just three months in 1942. After construction adjacent to the Dow plants was complete, the town was larger than Freeport itself.

Camp Chemical was erected as a stopgap measure to provide housing for temporary laborers at Dow. These consisted mainly of construction workers hired to build the new plant and to expand Dow's facilities. Lake Jackson, in contrast, was intended to be a permanent town for Dow's regular work force. By late 1942, Lake Jackson was widely seen as a fully modern city with a population of nearly 3,000. Camp Chemical no longer exists, but Lake Jackson remains a thriving suburban area where most of Dow's employees at the Freeport and Velasco plants reside.

The Defense Plant Corporation's government-owned plants were built through a process of open, competitive bidding among construction companies. All bids had to be approved by both the government and the private company involved. The plants became the property of, and agents for, the Rubber Reserve Company. Since there was no centrally coordinated magnesium program similar to the rubber program, that plant remained the property of the DPC; magnesium was a critical and scarce material, but it did not have the same priority status as synthetic rubber.

Similar arrangements existed between the Rubber Reserve and DPC and Monsanto at Texas City, and Sinclair Rubber, Inc., at Houston. Both of these companies ran government-owned synthetic rubber plants. Monsanto at Texas City produced styrene, and Sinclair Rubber produced butadiene. The DPC financed the construction of these two facilities, which, after completion, became the property of the RRC. The government invested nearly $31 million in the Sinclair plant and $18 million in the one run by Monsanto. Employee salaries and wages at these three plants were paid by the RRC, and, technically, Dow, Monsanto, and Sinclair were agents of the RRC, representing the interests of the government rather than their private investments. The Rubber Reserve Company was the third largest sponsor of DPC expenditures, behind the WPB and the War Department. Among the 48 states, Texas received the third largest amount of DPC investment, including 108 plants, costing $650 million.

Through the Synthetic Rubber Facilities Disposal Act of 1953, the government-owned rubber plants were sold through a competitive bidding process. Dow's bid of $35 million in 1947 was the most competitive offer for the styrene plant it operated in Velasco. Similarly, Monsanto was the highest bidder for its styrene plant in Texas City.

Monsanto's offer for the Texas City plant was $9.5 million in 1946. From most accounts, it was very rare that the so-called operating companies of the Rubber Reserve plants did not make the highest bid and, thus, acquire ownership. Monsanto and Sinclair appear to have purchased their plants cheaply. Evidence suggests that this was the norm during the country's reconversion period.

U.S. government involvement affected the development of the petrochemical industry in three ways. First, technical knowledge was made available to all privately and publicly owned plants, and innovations funded by the government were made available through patent pools. For example, Phillips Petroleum held the patent for extractive distillation, which was made available to synthetic rubber companies for a very small fee. Second, entirely new industries evolved in order to meet the demand quotas set by the armed services. The synthetic rubber industry is a case in point. Several products that required the same type of facilities necessary for synthetic rubber production also emerged during the war. Included here would be plastics, synthetic fibers, building materials, metal-to-metal and metal-to-wood adhesives, soaps and detergents, and silicons. Third, the government's reconversion policy allowed the private sector to attain industrial equipment and plants, in most cases for less than cost. This does not include their appreciated values after 1945. As a result, the growth and profitability of the petrochemical industry increased significantly.

OTHER WARTIME INVESTMENT

In the 1940s, when Houston was not yet a major metropolis, it ranked sixth nationally in the amount of federal capital invested in new manufacturing facilities. Jesse Jones, a central member of Houston's longest-lasting business elite organization—the Suite 8F crowd—played a role in channeling a large amount of New Deal public capital during this time. Approximately $450 million in federal capital expenditures went to private and joint private-public manufacturing enterprises in the Houston area for war-related efforts. Much of the capital was directed toward facilities producing high-octane aviation fuel, synthetic rubber, and toluene, which is used in explosives.

In August 1940, a $500,000 toluene plant was announced for Houston, to be built near a Shell Oil refinery, for national defense purposes. Five oil companies with refineries in southeast Texas created a nonprofit corporation to produce butylene for synthetic rubber. A private corporation ran the plant, but the federal government paid for it, thus providing major capital for petrochemical development. Texas moved from tenth to sixth in the percentage of total U.S. chemical production in this brief wartime period. The area not only received public investment but also benefited from substantial private capital flowing into the local petrochemical industry. Between 1939 and 1950, no less than $1 billion was invested in area chemical plants. Federal recapitalization of U.S. industry during World War II was disproportionately channeled into selected cities, with midsized Houston ranking sixth nationally and first regionally in the total level of federal plant investment (Mollenkopf, 1983).

In 1945 there were major cutbacks in most chemical production areas in the United States, but the impact on Gulf Coast output was minimal. The industry surrounding Houston was sustained because there was a substantial regional demand, once met by imported plastics and similar products, but now met by local petrochemical plants. The federal capital flowing to the area laid the foundation for dramatic postwar economic growth. But these capital flows formed just one prong of a three-pronged federal subsidy to Houston. The government also purchased and consumed the products of these companies and was generally crucial to their long-run profitability and prosperity. Military requirements assured a military-industrial complex long beyond 1945.

Important companies were stimulated by military spending during wartime in the steel, metal fabrication, oil tools, and construction industries. The first major steel plant in the Southwest was built by the American Rolling Mill Company (Armco) on the Houston ship channel. This facility was constructed with a federal (RFC) loan of $12 million. Under the guidance of RFC executive Jesse Jones, it soon became a $40 million facility. Because of the war-generated expansion, the Gulf Coast was no longer dependent on importing metals necessary for oil and petrochemical production, for other manufacturing enterprises, and for the local construction industry.

Federal government investment during World War II also took the form of subsidies for the distribution of gas and oil. In the early 1940s, the Roosevelt administration built two major oil pipelines from Texas to the East Coast, at a cost of $142 million. Known as the "Big Inch" and the "Little Inch," the pipelines were sold at a "fair market" price to Texas Eastern, a new Houston-based gas company created by Brown and Root. The firm used the purchase to become a large multinational corporation, and several others, such as Tenneco and Transco, also became gas giants as the industry became a cornerstone of Houston's economy after 1945.

By the early 1950s, the Houston economy was well into a long postwar boom, stimulated in part by the rising demand for petroleum products such as asphalt and plastics. Much of the demand came from consumers eager to improve their standard of living after years of war-enforced austerity measures. At least as important to this burgeoning demand was the growing military-industrial complex and its ravenous demand for oil-related products.

SPENDING AT HOUSTON'S MILITARY SITES

eginning in the 1930s, Houston and other Texas cities had many influential friends in Washington, D.C. John Nance Garner represented Texas for decades as a member of the House of Representatives and as vice president. At different points, Texans chaired Senate committees on military affairs, the judiciary, agriculture, and rivers and harbors. Between the 1930s and the 1960s, there were many direct links between Houston's business leadership and the federal government, and among the many important politicians to emerge during this time were House Majority Leader and Speaker of the House Sam Rayburn and President Lyndon Johnson.

During World War II, Houston-based firms benefited greatly from the investment of federal capital for the construction of many military installations. In 1941, a member of the Texas Highway Commission noted that the state had the nation's major military complex, with 41 Army, Navy, and Air Corps posts, forts, training bases, fields, and camps. He argued that gasoline taxes should be used to expand the Texas highway system linking these military installations. The commission member was allied with the secretary of war, who supported substantial federal appropriations for improving highways for military purposes. Texas was a major beneficiary of this program—many highways were paved permanently during this period, including major roads to Houston (Feagin, 1988, p. 183).

George and Herman Brown, cofounders of the major construction firm Brown and Root, were key figures involved in the economic restructuring of Houston during wartime. New Deal contracts in the 1930s and 1940s, which saved Brown and Root from bankruptcy, included dam projects, naval air stations, and warships. As noted above, Brown and Root created Texas Eastern Co. to operate war surplus pipelines they had purchased from the government; it is now a *Fortune* 500 firm (Feagin, 1988, pp. 138-139).

The close interaction between local business leaders and the federal government brought other war projects to Houston. Records show regular correspondence between Chamber of Commerce officials and federal officials. In 1940, W. N. Blanton, general manager of Houston's Chamber, wrote to prominent House member Albert Thomas, outlining the city's case for a major airplane plant. Thomas sent the brief to the War Department and got a quick reply from the assistant secretary of war. In coming years, the secretary of the Chamber of Commerce's military affairs committee lobbied the commanding general of the Army, the Air Force, the secretary of war, Thomas, and the entire Texas delegation in Congress in an attempt to keep Ellington AFB in south Houston and to maintain the Army air field in Galveston. Houston's other installations included a National Guard encampment and a major POW camp.

Shortly after the war began, executives of industries connected with the ship channel also expressed concerns about what they saw as an inadequate share of federal wartime contracts. With the help of the local congressional delegation, an intensive lobbying campaign was initiated aimed at convincing Washington to funnel more contracts to the Houston area. The effort resulted in massive federal outlays for the purchase of cargo vessels and tankers, fuels and explosives, and a variety of other products from channel industries. Further, provisions for new plants to be constructed along the channel were made. By 1943, 45 companies located on or near the channel had received $265 million in contracts from the federal government. According to one study, "War contracts alone . . . increased by five times the number of industrial employees, the industrial payroll to ten times its normal size, and the production of manufactured products in the city and county to a sum slightly less than four times its 1940 total" (cited in Shelton, Rodriguez, Feagin, Bullard, & Thomas, 1989, p. 44). By the end of the war, more than a billion federal dollars had filtered into the area's private economy.

For purposes of this volume, it is crucial to recognize that federal wartime contracts laid the foundation for the multibillion-dollar industrial complex that now exists along the Houston ship channel. The petrochemical complex known as the Golden Triangle—Houston, Freeport, and Port Arthur—evolved out of wartime industries. Today, the ship channel looks completely privatized and autonomous, but in fact it has close federal connections. It illustrates the idea that military spending in Houston has taken a hidden form.

TABLE 5.2

Johnson Space Center Economic Indicators, 1987-1989

Fiscal Year	1987	1988	1989
Local economic impact (millions of dollars)	787.7	859.9	972.7
Impact per day (millions of dollars)	3.0	3.3	3.7
Salaries since 1962 (billions of dollars)	2.3	2.4	2.6
Work force equivalents	12,332	13,492	14,728
Average JSC salary (dollars)	40,825	42,007	43,450

SOURCE: Data from Lyndon B. Johnson Space Center (1990b).

THE SPACE-INDUSTRIAL COMPLEX: NASA AND THE JSC

The LBJ Space Center has also had a significant impact on the Houston economy since 1962. During recent economic contraction (1982-1986), the military/space-industrial complex near the NASA facility in south Houston and the continuing expansion of the Texas Medical Center were rare bright spots. The NASA Manned Spacecraft Center provides an insight into the close ties between Houston's local business elite and national politicians. In 1961, NASA was seeking a site for its new Manned Spacecraft Center; Vice President Lyndon Johnson was head of the National Aeronautics and Space Council. Working together with the Suite 8F crowd and Houston Representative Albert Thomas (who headed the key House committee), Johnson pressed vigorously for the Houston location. In 1938, Humble Oil Company (now Exxon) had bought 30,000 acres southeast of Houston for oil exploration. In the early 1960s, Humble Oil's president gave 1,000 acres of this land to Rice University. In turn, Rice gave it to NASA for the Space Center.

This federal facility was won in competition with other cities by Houston's aggressive growth-oriented and business-dominated political elite, and the economic activity generated by the JSC has sustained Houston's free enterprise economy for many years. By the 1980s, the JSC complex employed 10,000 people and was spending more than a half billion in federal dollars annually in the Houston area, or the equivalent of nearly $4 million per day (see Table 5.2).

Today, the Johnson Space Center has 3,250 federal employees on the payroll, with another 9,650 contracted personnel working at the center or supporting its operations. The center also spent $16.1 million

TABLE 5.3
Distribution of JSC Procurements in Texas

Company	Amount (millions of dollars)	% of Total
Rockwell	256	31
All other companies	202	24
Lockheed	133	16
McDonnell Douglas	104	13
IBM	69	8
Boeing	68	8

SOURCE: Data from Lyndon B. Johnson Space Center (1990a).

last fiscal year on public utilities alone (Bolt, 1990, p. 1D). Officially, it is estimated that $40 billion has been pumped into the Houston economy via the space center. The Greater Houston Partnership's president speculates that the impact of the JSC might be 10 to 20 times that much, for large aerospace firms are central to the military/space-industrial complex in Houston. Included among the top 10 companies operating in the city (by employee count) are Boeing Aerospace & Electronics, Ford Aerospace, IBM, Lockheed, McDonnell Douglas, Rockwell International, and UNISYS. Some of these same companies are closely linked to activity at the JSC. Table 5.3 is based on the 50 largest contractors for fiscal year 1988, when JSC procurements reached $832 million.

The above data are useful in identifying key actors in Houston, but they tell us little about what portion of the JSC represents purely civilian activity. Some see the greatest impact of the Johnson Space Center in symbolic terms—according to economist Robert Hodgin, the center served as a ray of optimism during the recent downturn, as an attraction for related endeavors, and as a public relations vehicle for the city (Bolt, 1990, p. 1D). Even if Hodgin's assessment is accurate, the local business elite have made the promotion of the military/space complex an important diversification goal. In the mid-1980s, the facility was assigned the $8 billion space station project, and the University of Houston branch near NASA beat out Caltech and MIT for a joint contract with NASA to develop a new DOD computer language. These contracts ensure a military-industrial presence in the greater Houston area for the foreseeable future (Feagin, 1988, pp. 94-95).

CONCLUSION

It deserves repeating that the information needed to provide a complete picture of military spending is impossible to obtain. Because of projects such as those undertaken at the Johnson Space Center in Clear Lake or the Stealth fighter in Tonopah, we can never be completely confident about the economic impact military spending may have on a community. This difficulty notwithstanding, we have shown that military spending has played a critical role in sustaining economic development and creating new industries. This effect has been of particular significance in southern Nevada, where, in smaller communities such as Tonopah, defense expenditure remains the central economic pillar. Military spending during wartime was also responsible for creating and accelerating the development of industries. The petrochemical industry in Houston is perhaps the best single exemplar of the industry-generating influence found in these two cities.

Equally clear is the influence military spending has had on the spatial configuration of the two areas. In southern Nevada, Nellis Air Force Base pulled the city in its direction, while the location of the Nevada Test Site led to the development of residential enclaves and new roads to serve them. Similarly, in Houston the establishment of the Johnson Space Center led to the development of Clear Lake, now a major residential community in its own right. Together, these illustrations emphasize how military spending has generated critically important economic and spatial effects in southern Nevada and southeastern Texas for the past half century.

REFERENCES

Adams, S. (1990, January 27). Stealth wing may leave Nevada. *Las Vegas Review-Journal*, p. 1A.

Bolt, J. A. (1990, May 28). NASA saves Houston. *Las Vegas Review-Journal*, pp. 1D-2D.

Brown, P. B. (1989). 1989 report on the states. *Inc., 11*, 85-87.

Burkhart, J. (1990, January 31). Catering to the military: Local businesses woo Nellis personnel. *Las Vegas Review-Journal*, p. 1F.

Case, J. (1990). The most entrepreneurial cities in America. *Inc., 11*, 41-48.

Feagin, J. R. (1988). *Free enterprise city: Houston in political and economic perspective*. New Brunswick, NJ: Rutgers University Press.

Hill, M. (1990a, January 31). Local Guard units face extinction. *Las Vegas Sun*, p. 1A.

Hill, M. (1990b, March 6). LV area residents oppose Stealth move. *Las Vegas Sun*, p. 6A.

Houston Economic Development Council. (1989a). *Houston*. Houston: Author.

Houston Economic Development Council. (1989b). *The Houston business advantage*. Houston: Author.

Hynes, M. (1990a, January 27). Nye County officials raise prospect of fight on Stealth. *Las Vegas Review-Journal*, p. 4A.

Hynes, M. (1990b, March 6). Opinions divided on Stealth wing relocation. *Las Vegas Review-Journal*, p. 1B.

Hynes, M. (1990c, March 7). Residents of Tonopah decry Stealth move. *Las Vegas Review-Journal*, p. 1B.

Hynes, M. (1990d, March 12). Secrets kept; promises broken. *Las Vegas Review-Journal*, p. 1B.

Las Vegas Review-Journal, Nevada Development Authority, & First Interstate Bank of Nevada, N.A. (1989). *Las Vegas Perspective 1989*. Las Vegas: Las Vegas Review-Journal.

Las Vegas Review-Journal, Nevada Development Authority, & First Interstate Bank of Nevada, N.A. (1990). *Las Vegas Perspective 1990*. Las Vegas: Las Vegas Review-Journal.

Lyndon B. Johnson Space Center. (1990a). *Distribution of Texas procurements*. Houston: Author.

Lyndon B. Johnson Space Center. (1990b). *Johnson Space Center overview*. Houston: Author.

Miller will talk to Tonopah residents about Stealth departure job loss. (1990, February 2). *Las Vegas Review-Journal*, p. 5B.

Moehring, E. (1989). *Resort city in the Sunbelt*. Reno: University of Nevada Press.

Mollenkopf, J. H. (1983). *The contested city*. Princeton, NJ: Princeton University Press.

Riddell, K., & Feagin, J. R. (1986, March). *Houston and the War Production Board: The untold story*. Paper presented at the meeting of the Southwestern Sociological Conference, San Antonio, TX.

Schumacher, G. (1989, December 17). Thawing of Cold War no big chill for Southern Nevada contractors. *Las Vegas Sun*, p. 1A.

Scientist Edgerton dies at 86. (1990, January 6). *Las Vegas Review-Journal*, p. 7C.

Shelton, B. A., Rodriguez, N. P., Feagin, J. R., Bullard, R. D., & Thomas, R. D. (1989). *Houston: Growth and decline in a Sunbelt boomtown*. Philadelphia: Temple University Press.

U.S. Air Force. (1989a). *Nellis Air Force Base, Nevada*. Nellis Air Force Base: Author.

U.S. Air Force. (1989b). *Nellis' economic impact on Nevada*. Nellis Air Force Base: Author.

U.S. Department of Energy. (1986). *Economic impact of the U.S. Department of Energy in Southern Nevada*. Washington, DC: Government Printing Office.

U.S. Department of Energy. (1989). *DOE impacts heavily on southern Nevada's economy*. Las Vegas: DOE Nevada Operations Office.

U.S. Department of Energy. (1990, February). *DOE continues to impact heavily on Nevada's economy after nearly four decades* (press release). Las Vegas: DOE Nevada Operations Office.

Williams, J. (1988, May). *Nellis AFB and its contribution to the southern Nevada Economy* (Status Report; draft). Denver: Planning Information Corporation.

6

Indigenous Homelands and the Security Requirements of Western Nation-States: Innu Opposition to Military Flight Training in Eastern Québec and Labrador

PETER ARMITAGE

THE 500th ANNIVERSARY IN 1992 of the arrival of Christopher Columbus in the Americas should give us occasion for reflection on the morality of conquest. More specifically, we should consider the possibility that aboriginal peoples and their lands were not simply conquered 400 or 500 years ago when Columbus, Samuel de Champlain, John Cabot, and other explorers first set foot on their soil; that conquest is an ongoing process of invasion of aboriginal lands, the displacement of aboriginal people into impoverished rural ghettos, and their ensuing cultural and spiritual collapse.[1] Thus conquest of aboriginal peoples and the colonization of their lands continue under various guises throughout the Americas.

From this perspective, military flight training by several North Atlantic Treaty Organization (NATO) air forces in Innu airspace in eastern Québec and Labrador is but a recent manifestation of the conquistador's manifest destiny. It is part of the same process that took Custer to the Little Bighorn valley in 1876, and the Canadian army to Saskatchewan during the so-called Riel Rebellion of 1885, to pacify the resident aboriginal populations and to secure their lands for the orderly settlement of European farmers, miners, and merchants. It is part of the same process that has produced "frontiers" throughout the United States and Canada during their chaotic formation as nation-states.[2]

Whereas Europeans have largely coveted aboriginal lands for their mineral wealth, timber reserves, and hydroelectric and agricultural potential, Innu lands and airspace in eastern Québec and Labrador are now coveted because of their utility to Western militaries. This chapter is about the impact of military flight training on the Innu people as well as their struggle against it. It is about the imposition of negative impacts from military training and testing activities—which are unacceptable to urban majorities—on rural and indigenous peoples. Indeed, there are numerous examples of the imposition of such impacts on rural peoples in other parts of the globe: atomic bomb testing and military flight training in Shoshonee Indian territory in Nevada, low-level flight training in rural West Germany and Great Britain, and French atomic bomb testing in the South Pacific, to name but a few. What they all have in common is that people who are demographically few and politically weak are forced to "pay the price of freedom," to support in a very physical and psychological sense the security requirements of urbanized nation-states.

While the Innu's case may therefore not be unique, what is special about them is the tenacity of their efforts to defend their land, as well as their success in mobilizing the attention and support of the non-aboriginal population across Canada. In what follows, I describe the impacts of military flight training on the Innu, their efforts to stop the training, and the response by the Canadian government to their protest actions. I conclude the chapter by identifying some of the actions that relatively marginalized peoples such as the Innu must take in order to extract political concessions from the state. But first, let me quickly describe the Innu and the context for their opposition to the training.

WHO ARE THE INNU?

The Innu, otherwise known as Montagnais-Naskapi Indians, constitute an indigenous nation of about 10,000 people who live in 13 communities in eastern Québec and Labrador (see Figure 6.1).[3] The westerly Innu were first settled by the Canadian government on reserves in the mid-1800s. The more easterly Innu, however, who are the subjects of this chapter, were not settled in government-built villages until much later.

By the 1940s, the Innu of eastern Québec-Labrador were in a desperate state due to falling fur prices and a major decline in the populations

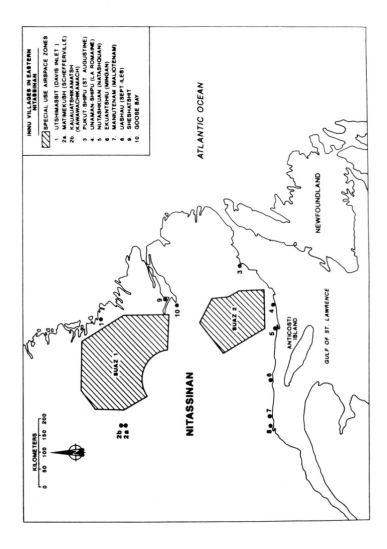

Figure 6.1. Distribution of Innu Settlements and Airspace Used for Flight Training

of local caribou (Brice-Bennett, 1986, p. 39). As a result, many Innu were reluctant to travel far inland for fear of starvation. By their own standards, they were living in extreme poverty. Because of this, they were required to seek increasing levels of relief from the Newfoundland and federal governments in the form of basic foodstuffs. The situation of the Innu from the Sheshatshit band in central Labrador was exacerbated by the presence of Lake Melville settlers, Newfoundlanders, and other non-Innu who progressively pushed them out of some of their best hunting and trapping areas on the Churchill, Traverspine, Naskaupi, Susan, and other rivers that pour into Lake Melville (Budgell, 1959, p. 2; Privy Council, 1927, pp. 3739-3740; Tanner, 1944, p. 585; Zimmerly, 1975, pp. 146-147). The prevalence of tuberculosis and other diseases further weakened the Innu people and their ability to survive on the land free of interference from Euro-Canadian institutions.

After Newfoundland joined the Canadian confederation in 1949, the Labrador Innu were increasingly subjected to policies that promoted their rapid integration into the mainstream of Euro-Canadian society.[4] Their relatives in Québec were subject to similar policies by the federal Department of Indian Affairs. These policies had long-lasting negative consequences for the Innu, in that they promoted culture collapse, and with this a host of social pathologies such as alcohol abuse and family violence.[5] According to the government of Newfoundland at the time, industrial development was the solution to the economic and social problems of Labrador: "Hunting and fishing, along with the social and cultural practices these pursuits entailed, were inconsistent with efforts to modernize Labrador" (Kennedy, 1977, p. 284).

While many of the reasons the Innu settled in government villages can be attributed to coercive policies—such as threats to withhold family allowance and welfare payments from parents who refused to send their children to school—it must be remembered that the Innu had been so weakened by disease, periodic starvation, and other deprivations resulting primarily from contact with Europeans that they were "ready for settlement." As noted, the fur trade had collapsed, and they had lost access to some of their prime hunting territory. These changes resulted in increased dependence on government rations and great effort in transporting flour and other provisions further inland past the hunting and trapping areas that had been usurped by non-Innu trappers (Armitage, 1989, pp. 7-12).

For many Innu, therefore, village life, with improved health care and housing, appeared as an attractive alternative to an increasingly onerous life on the land. In addition, a number of Innu thought their children should receive a Euro-Canadian education and learn English and French in order to be able to deal better with Euro-Canadians and their governments. Many Innu soon recognized, however, that settlement was a tragic mistake, as terrible problems of alcohol abuse, family violence, and other social pathologies became firmly entrenched (Raphael Gregoire, personal communication, July 1987). By the mid-1970s, the complex of omnipresent Euro-Canadian institutions that dominated life in the Innu villages included the school, the Catholic church, the Department of Indian Affairs, the Newfoundland Department of Social Services, the Royal Canadian Mounted Police, the International Grenfell Association, the Hudson's Bay Company, and other stores (see Henriksen, 1973, pp. 91-100; Mailhot & Michaud, 1965, pp. 104-110). In the 1980s, younger Innu labeled the villages "concentration camps" because of the despicable living conditions that prevailed and the domination of village life by Euro-Canadians.

The experience of village life, with its humiliation, despair, and pathological social problems, played a major role in convincing the Innu that something had to be done to revitalize the hunting way of life. In the mid-1970s, the Labrador Innu decided to allocate some of their government funding to "outpost programs" that finance the cost of chartering bush planes to fly men, women, and children out to camps far in the interior of Québec-Labrador each fall and spring. On the Québec north shore, Innu communities used the federally funded "trapping programs" to finance the transportation of men, women, and children to interior hunting camps each fall (Armitage, 1989, pp. 12-20).

The Innu recognize that traveling regularly out to the country to participate in hunting, trapping, fishing, and gathering activities provides a vital lifeline to their culture. They would be a greatly diminished people without the ability to participate in a hunting economy. All age groups take part in harvesting activities of one kind or another. In Sheshatshit, between 120 and 270 people participate in the outpost program each fall and spring, and in La Romaine the number each fall ranges from approximately 150 to 500. In contrast to Sheshatshit, where there are few wildlife resources in the immediate vicinity of the village, La Romaine is blessed with an abundance of migratory waterfowl, fish, lobster, and wild fruits that allow the Innu to harvest throughout the year, even if they choose not to spend the fall at hunting camps further inland.

For Innu throughout eastern Québec and Labrador, the country is one place where relief from the problems and stresses of the villages is possible. The country is also a place where men and women are able to engage in productive activities, where their children respect them for their knowledge and skills and are generally eager to learn from them. The country is permeated with meaning to the Innu; their history as a people is encoded there in geographic features, old campsites, and mythological associations. The forest and the tundra are alive with animal masters and other forest spirits that provide a framework for human behavior and intercourse. Given the importance of the land to the Innu—its historic, mythological, and contemporary value—it is not surprising that many Innu people are prepared to engage in difficult and costly protest actions in defense of their land and the wildlife living there. Their protests against military flight training are not new; they are part of a lengthy struggle for their land and their survival as a distinct people (Armitage, 1989, p. 38).

For many years now, the Innu have protested against actions by non-Innu groups in Québec-Labrador when these actions have threatened their access to the land and wildlife (Mailhot, 1987). They complained bitterly to traders and missionaries, for example, about the incursions made by Newfoundlanders and Québecois into some of their best hunting and trapping grounds. The Churchill Falls hydroelectric development in the early 1970s, which flooded grave sites and prime Innu hunting territory and Michikamau and Ossokmanuan lakes, generated long-lasting resentment and distrust of government among many Sheshatshit Innu (Antane & Kanikuen, 1984, pp. 28-31).

With the lessons of Churchill Falls in mind, the Sheshatshit Innu vigorously opposed the construction of more hydroelectric dams on the lower Churchill River, while their relatives on the Québec north shore fought against plans by Hydro-Québec to build facilities on five major rivers running through their hunting territories.[6] In the late 1970s, the Sheshatshit Innu adamantly opposed a uranium mine proposed for the Kitts Pond and Michelin Lake area northeast of Sheshatshit, citing the possible negative environmental impacts of transporting radioactive "yellow cake" through or near their community as well as through the bush north of it (Government of Newfoundland, 1980). Finally, the Québec and Labrador Innu have consistently resisted the imposition of Newfoundland and federal game regulations, despite heavy penalties in the forms of fines and jail sentences (Armitage, 1989, pp. 21-25).

MILITARY FLIGHT TRAINING IN QUÉBEC-LABRADOR

The military presence in the eastern portion of the Québec-Labrador peninsula dates back to 1941 when the Canadian and U.S. governments first established an airport at Goose Bay to service wartime flights between North America and Europe. After 1945, the Royal Canadian Air Force (RCAF) alone maintained Goose Bay for air-sea rescue and antisubmarine patrols (McGraw, 1987, p. 188).

In 1952, at the start of the Cold War, a 20-year agreement was signed with the United States that transformed Goose Bay into an important support base for the Strategic Air Command (SAC). Early warning stations were constructed on the coast of Labrador at Cartwright and Saglek (part of the "Pine Tree Line") in addition to distant early warning sites in the Arctic (the "DEW Line") and the Ballistic Missile Early Warning Site in Thule, Greenland. A large construction program was undertaken by the U.S. Air Force (USAF) between 1952 and 1960 to develop its support facility at Goose Bay. At its height, the population of Goose Bay and the neighboring community of Happy Valley reached approximately 14,000, of which military personnel accounted for about 6,000. The United States decided to reduce the size of its SAC operation in Goose Bay in 1973. Changes in intercontinental ballistic missile technology, better methods of aerial refueling, and the introduction of longer-range aircraft all reduced the need for the SAC presence at the base. In September 1976, the USAF announced that its 95th Strategic Wing would be completely deactivated (McGraw, 1987, p. 188). Only a small Military Airlift Command (MAC) detachment remained after the SAC withdrawal.

It was not until 1957 that the Innu first experienced the kind of military activity that would in later years become a major source of annoyance and anguish to them. In that year, the Royal Air Force (RAF) began low-level flight training with Vulcan bombers (Canadian Armed Forces, 1987). Vulcan training flights have been sporadic and not less than 170 meters above ground level (AGL). In 1979, a new kind of flight training commenced with the arrival of RAF Buccaneer aircraft—ultra-low flying, as low as 30 meters AGL. In 1980, the German Air Force started low-level flying with F-4 Phantom IIs, and in later years included Alpha jets, Tornado GR1s, and C-160 Transall aircraft in its training syllabus. By 1985, a practice target area (PTA) for bombing with inert bombs (including 1,000-pound concrete and laser-guided bombs) had been constructed and two large areas of special use airspace designated, one north and the other south of Goose Bay. Labeled *low-level training areas* (LLTAs) by the Department of National Defence (DND), the training zones sucked up 100,000 square kilometers of airspace over eastern Québec and Labrador, much of it over productive Innu hunting territory.[7]

A Multinational Memorandum of Understanding (MMOU) was signed on February 13, 1986, by Canada, the United States, the United Kingdom, and West Germany, allowing the air forces of these countries to conduct a variety of training activities with combat and transport aircraft, as well as helicopters. The Netherlands became a party to this agreement in December 1986, and the Canadian government has energetically solicited the participation of the Italian and Belgian air forces. While the current number of low-level training sorties is approximately 7,000 per year, DND hopes the number will increase to 18,000 by 1996, despite the collapse of the Warsaw Treaty Organization (WTO) and progress at the Conventional Forces in Europe talks in Vienna. Under the MMOU, the number of military personnel (mostly male) visiting Goose Bay would increase from approximately 625 every two weeks in 1987 to 1,865 every two weeks in 1996.

It should be noted here that the flight training conducted in Québec-Labrador includes more than low-level flying by combat and transport aircraft. It also includes air combat training (ACT); that is, training in the dogfighting maneuvers that pilots must conduct when attacking or evading other aircraft (see Canadian Public Health Association, 1987, p. 158). In February 1989, two ACT areas were designated, one in each of the two LLTAs. The ACT areas were ostensibly established for practice air-to-air intercepts by the four RCAF CF-18s based in Goose Bay, but the Royal Netherlands Air Force (RNLAF) was also given access to the airspace. DND states that no supersonic flying is permitted in these areas or anywhere else in Québec-Labrador below 30,000 feet above sea level (ASL).[8]

In 1985, the Canadian government announced that it was competing with Turkey for a (US)$500 million NATO tactical fighter and weapons training center (TFWTC). It would see the construction of eight additional bombing ranges (three of them for live weapons), an offshore bombing range, a 2,500-square-nautical-mile air combat maneuvering range instrumented (ACMRI), 60 camera targets, a second runway at Goose Bay, and other facilities.[9] In total, 1,000 square nautical miles of Innu hunting lands would be taken for the bombing ranges. An important part of the training would be "flag-type exercises" involving as many as 90 aircraft in "offensive and defensive maneuvers in an environment that simulates as closely as possible conditions likely to be encountered in the event of war" (Canada, DND, 1989, pp. 3-37).[10] The number of training sorties would be increased to approximately 40,000 per year by 2001, and the number of personnel visiting Goose Bay would increase to 3,365 every two weeks.

In May 1990, NATO announced that, due to the "evolution of the international security environment and . . . pressures on the defense budgets of member states," the TFWTC would not be built (news release from the DND, May 22, 1990). In expressing their disappointment at the news, however, DND representatives said that they hoped the number of training sorties could still be increased under the MMOU. In fact, according to DND, the level of military activity could end up being between the proposed NATO TFWTC and the maximum level envisaged under the MMOU (Canada, DND, 1989, pp. 2-6).

THE IMPACT OF
MILITARY FLIGHT TRAINING ON THE INNU

In October 1987, I was hired by the Naskapi Montagnais Innu Association to prepare its submission to a federal Environmental Assessment Panel studying the impact of military flight training under the MMOU as well as the proposed NATO TFWTC. Innu from the communities of Sheshatshit and Davis Inlet were interviewed that fall and the following winter, concerning the impact of military aircraft on people and wildlife between 1979 and 1987 (Armitage, 1989).[11]

Testimony from male and female informants demonstrated that for most Innu people, direct low-altitude overflights by Tornado GR1, F-4 Phantom II, or F-16 aircraft are a very traumatic experience. The unexpected, and extremely loud, jet noise induces psychological and physiological reactions typical of human response to adverse environmental stimuli. Informants were particularly upset about the negative effects of jet noise on their children. They spoke of children being awakened by jet noise, of children crying and screaming in terror, of children standing paralyzed with fear, while others frantically searched for their parents. Several Innu reported they were so startled by the planes that they fell to the ground. One person stated that he "hit the ground and stayed there." Numerous informants said they would try to cover their ears when jets flew over. According to one person, "We were fishing in the middle of North Pole Lake when two jets flew directly over us. We all ducked down and the young girl was crying and screaming. We all ran to the shore of the lake." Informants reported, furthermore, that the jet noise sounded like a "blowtorch," "something exploding or ripping apart," a "12-gauge shotgun," a "loud, screeching noise." One hunter said the noise "feels like a big smack right in the ears." Another said, "There is no warning or buildup for the arrival of the jet noise. It's like a roar. It seems like it comes out of nowhere. It's deafening. I've never been exposed to any other noise like that."

These statements suggest strongly that the level of jet noise experienced by Innu people while they are in the countryside can be extremely high. The unexpected arrival of such noise is directly responsible for the "startle effect." Failure to appreciate the traumatic nature of Innu emotional reactions to jet noise can lead to erroneous conclusions, such as those reached by Newfoundland Minister of Health Hugh Twomey. After the Canadian Public Health Association released its report on the health effects of subsonic jet noise in May 1987, he attempted to downplay the significance of Innu emotional response by including it in the same category of "stresses" that we would consider to be low level and acceptable in everyday life (Newfoundland House of Assembly, 1987). The stress mentioned by Twomey, however, is not the same as the stress experienced by the Innu when they respond to jet stimuli in the form of noise, bangs (sonic booms or afterburner ignition), slipstream, or exhaust fumes. Innu emotional responses are far more intense and indicate that the adverse stimuli producing them would normally be judged intolerable by most North Americans. The intolerable nature of such aircraft stimuli has been confirmed in numerous statements describing emotional reactions by non-Innu people, including rural Europeans and Americans.

The scientific community has also reached definitive conclusions about the negative impact of aviation noise (see Ando & Hattori, 1977; Cohen, Krantz, Evans, & Stokols, 1980; Grandjean, Graf, Lauber, Meir, & Muller, 1976; Knipschild & Oudschoorn, 1977; Kryter, 1985; Levi, 1979; Spreng, 1990). The literature on this subject is far too extensive and complex to present in any detail in this chapter, but it is useful to consider the conclusions of two prominent researchers in this field, Karl Kryter and Birgitta Berglund. Kryter (1990) has commented on the adequacy of the noise impact section of the Goose Bay Environmental Impact Statement (EIS) and provides his own noise estimates for the LLTAs, transit corridors, and ACMRI. These estimates emphasize that the noise levels in regions subject to military overflights and sonic booms would likely be far above safe exposure standards for humans. The scientific literature referred to by Kryter shows that a number of adverse effects result from exposure to noise at the levels he estimates would be found in Innu hunting territory if maximum levels of training are attained under the MMOU and if the proposed NATO training base had been built (see Figure 6.2). The literature shows that, at such levels, the rate of people admitted to psychiatric hospitals increases dramatically, as does the rate of

RANGE OF COMPONENT 2 EXPOSURE IMPACTS TO SUBSONIC AIRCRAFT NOISE
(IN LOW-LEVEL TRAINING AND CORRIDOR AREAS) AND TO SONIC BOOMS (IN
AIR COMBAT MANOEUVRING RANGE INSTRUMENTED AREA) ACCORDING TO THE
GOOSE BAY ENVIRONMENTAL IMPACT STATEMENT AND AS REVISED IN THIS
CRITIQUE

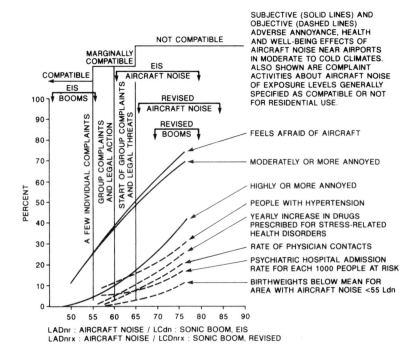

Figure 6.2. Effects of Aircraft Noise on Human Behavior (after Kryter, 1990, p. 14)

NOTE: The studies assume certain forms of home construction and normal levels of outdoor activity; see text for further details.

physician contacts. The numbers of children below mean birth weight start to increase significantly, as do the numbers of people with hypertension and people taking prescription drugs for stress-related health disorders. In terms of annoyance, a high percentage of the population feels highly annoyed or worse (Kryter, 1990).

Berglund (1990), who also has commented on the Goose Bay EIS, notes that a "sudden change in the acoustic surrounding like the one created by a low-level overflight may activate several physiological systems" (p. 5). She points to epidemiological studies by Knipschild, who found that in noisy airport environments "cardiac diseases, doctors' calls, and purchases of medicine are more frequent than in quiet environments" (p. 5). She also notes that certain noise-sensitive groups are more at risk from exposure to high levels of noise than other "normal" groups. High-risk groups include children, shift workers, neurotics, and persons who already have hearing deficits or who suffer from cardiovascular diseases (p. 11).

Since 1979, Innu people from Sheshatshit have seen military aircraft or experienced overflights with varying frequency depending on where their camps were located and the time of year. Overflights ranged from one in a season to as many as 10 direct or near overflights in a day. One hunting group from Davis Inlet reported jet overflights or sightings of military aircraft on 60% of the total number of days spent in the countryside between September 2 and October 12, 1987. Furthermore, since 1979, Innu from Davis Inlet and Sheshatshit have established hunting camps at more than 68 different locations in the interior of Québec-Labrador. Of these, 28 camps were established within the northern LLTA. Innu living at 43 camps saw low-flying aircraft and/or experienced overflights; Innu at 29 camps observed low-flying military aircraft outside the LLTA.

Innu from Sheshatshit and Davis Inlet say they rarely encountered low-flying military aircraft over their hunting territory prior to 1979, but that when training at altitudes as low as 30 meters commenced in 1979, the frequency of such encounters increased dramatically. Innu from La Romaine and Natashquan on the Québec north shore apparently did not encounter any low-flying jets prior to the fall of 1983. No data on the frequency of overflights of Innu from La Romaine and Natashquan are currently available.

As far as the Sheshatshit and Davis Inlet Innu are concerned, the frequency of overflights and sightings of military aircraft in the country appears to have declined since 1987, probably due to the implementation of mitigative measures by DND. DND obtains information on the location of Innu camps from the civilian aviation companies that transport the Innu out of the country each fall and spring. It then instructs military pilots to maintain an avoidance radius of 2.5 nautical miles around each camp. Despite this avoidance strategy, however, the Innu say they are still periodically overflown. They are concerned that DND's apparent vigilance in enforcing overflight restrictions could wane once the public controversy over the training dies down. They are skeptical, moreover, about the long-term viability of the strategy. They argue that no testing has been conducted to see if military pilots really can avoid Innu camps and noise-sensitive wildlife areas once the annual number of sorties reaches maximum levels. Noise-sensitive wildlife areas include breeding, molting, and staging grounds for migratory waterfowl, the home ranges of raptors, and caribou calving grounds. The Innu point to the fact that military pilots do not fly in a haphazard manner throughout the skies of Québec-Labrador; rather, they concentrate their training in river valleys and lake areas where surrounding hills mask them from enemy radar. These are precisely the same areas where wildlife are found and where the Innu focus their harvesting activities.

Throughout eastern Québec and Labrador, the Innu were virtually unanimous in their concern that further expansion of military flight training, the construction of additional bombing ranges and an ACMRI, large-scale supersonic ACT, electronic warfare, frequent flag-type exercises, and other forms of training would render their hunting territory uninhabitable. Their concern focused not only on the potentially negative health effects of the training and on the alienation of hunting territory by bombing range construction, but also on the effect that a greatly expanded population in Happy Valley-Goose Bay would have on the social fabric of central Labrador (e.g., more bars, military culture, and competition for wildlife) and the impact of large numbers of transient military men on Innu women. Most important, the Innu feared that a variety of wildlife species—particularly caribou, migratory waterfowl, and furbearers—would be harmed by fuel dumping, bombing, jet noise, and chemical residues in aircraft exhaust.

THE CAMPAIGN AGAINST
MILITARY FLIGHT TRAINING

The Innu started to present these concerns to the Canadian public in a concerted way in the fall of 1984, when news conferences were held in Toronto, Ottawa, Montreal, and St. John's to announce the "Campaign Against the Militarization of Nitassinan." Protests against military flight training commenced in the context of other grievances over land and industrial resource development. However, the form of Innu opposition to the military differed significantly from opposition to other threats to the integrity of their land and culture. For the first time, the Innu attempted to generate a massive constituency of nonaboriginal supporters to help them put pressure on the Canadian government and its NATO allies.

Three "natural" constituencies were identified from the outset of the campaign from which support could be drawn—the environmental, peace, and aboriginal rights movements. Key individuals and decision-making bodies in each movement were lobbied to educate them about the impacts of military flight training and the strategic implications of military expansion in Québec-Labrador, and to convince them to rearrange their priorities so as to join in protest actions against the training. While the church-affiliated aboriginal rights group Project North rapidly came to the assistance of the Innu, it was not until the summer of 1986 that the peace movement, represented by the Canadian Peace Alliance, took up the issue as a major campaign theme. Peace groups, aboriginal support groups, church groups, and single-issue action groups did most of the hard work in writing pamphlets and fact sheets, organizing demonstrations and vigils, scheduling news conferences and speaking tours, circulating petitions, starting letter-writing campaigns, and lobbying the government, its NATO allies, and the media. The environmental movement, for its part, only belatedly took up the issue when, in 1989, the Canadian Environmental Defence Fund decided to make the military buildup in Québec-Labrador a major campaign theme. The Innu themselves constantly nourished the campaign by participating in the speaking tours, holding news conferences, and occupying the Minipi Lake bombing range and runways at Goose Bay on a regular basis.

The civil disobedience by the Innu, in which more than 200 men, women, and children were repeatedly arrested and jailed, played an extremely important role in providing the drama and sense of crisis required to mobilize and sustain media interest in their plight. Furthermore, their peaceful occupations and protests at Goose Bay became the focal point around which supporters in the above-mentioned constituencies rallied. During the six-year period leading up to the NATO decision not to build the TFWTC on May 22, 1990, the Innu and other participants in the campaign undertook the following activities to protest military flight training in eastern Québec and Labrador:

- In October 1984, four Innu toured Toronto, Ottawa, Montreal, and St. John's, holding public meetings and news conferences at each location.
- In May 1985, the Sheshatshit Innu organized an assembly made up of Innu leaders at North West Point, about four miles from Sheshatshit. National Canadian media attended.
- In April 1986, an "International Joint Action Against Low-level and Supersonic Flight Training" was organized involving rural peoples and aboriginal groups from the United States, Europe, and Canada, where

military flight training was considered an environmental and health hazard by local residents.

- In May 1986, Innu from Sheshatshit and La Romaine toured a number of European countries, meeting with government representatives and holding public meetings and news conferences.
- Québec and Labrador Innu complained to the International Human Rights Federation, which sent a five-person "field mission" to Goose Bay, Sheshatshit, and La Romaine in May 1986.
- At the end of May 1986, Innu representatives from Sheshatshit and La Romaine participated in peace demonstrations and a news conference in Halifax, where NATO foreign ministers were meeting.
- At the beginning of June 1986, an Innu leader from Sheshatshit and a member of Greenpeace locked themselves in a van in front of Parliament in Ottawa and bombarded members of Parliament with loud, tape-recorded jet noise.
- Innu leaders and community members, peace activists, and environmentalists made energetic interventions before the federal Environmental Review Panel when it held meetings in September and October 1986, in La Romaine, Sheshatshit, Schefferville, Davis Inlet, Goose Bay, Montreal, Hull, and St. John's.
- In November 1986 a six-person delegation from the Conseil Attikamek-Montagnais visited France and NATO headquarters in Belgium.
- In April 1987, Innu from Sheshatshit set up five tents at the end of the Goose Bay runway to protest the resumption of low-level flying.
- In the falls of 1987, 1988, and 1989, Innu from Sheshatshit occupied the Minipi Lake bombing range, thereby halting practice bombing by the Luftwaffe and RAF.
- In fall 1988, a massive protest camp was established by Sheshatshit Innu at the end of the runway at Goose Bay, from which a number of occupations of the runway were executed.
- In December 1988, at the behest of the Innu, famous Canadian environmentalist David Suzuki visited the Innu protest camp and an Innu hunting camp near Sheshatshit to express his support for the Innu.
- In the fall of 1989, Innu from La Romaine and Sheshatshit toured a number of European countries as well as major cities across Canada.
- Throughout 1989, members of the Alliance for Non-violent Action staged demonstrations at DND headquarters in Ottawa.
- In April 1989, supporters of the Innu in St. John's, including the CBC Television comedy troupe Codco, held a rally followed by a short occupation of a major city intersection.
- In February 1990, the Canadian Environmental Defence Fund organized a news conference in Toronto for the Innu and their technical advisers to

release a critique of the Goose Bay EIS. Pop music star Bruce Cockburn attended the conference to express his support for the Innu.

- In March and April 1990, the Naskapi Montagnais Innu Association attempted to obtain a court injunction against military flight training. The injunction was not granted.
- In April and May 1990, the Canadian Peace Alliance facilitated a national letter-writing and fax campaign to NATO chiefs of staff and permanent military representatives, heads of government, and opposition parties.
- In the summer of 1990, peace and aboriginal support groups organized the Freedom for Nitassinan Walk from St. John's to Ottawa to educate the public about the plight of the Innu in the face of military expansion.

GOVERNMENT REACTION TO THE CAMPAIGN

Labrador Innu first communicated their opposition to military flight training to the federal government in 1980 when low-level training began. Innu correspondence to the federal ministers of Indian affairs, national defense, and environment outlining their concerns about the impact of training activities on the environment and their culture was "met with perfunctory statements to the effect that government and the military were monitoring the training program on an ongoing basis and had already implemented mitigative measures to avoid negative impacts on human health and wildlife (e.g., reconnaissance flights to determine concentrations of caribou)" (Armitage & Kennedy, 1989, pp. 802-803). It was only in October 1984, when the Innu announced they were starting their international Campaign Against the Militarization of Nitassinan and held news conferences in a number of major Canadian cities, that the federal and Newfoundland governments began to take their opposition seriously. On October 26, 1984, the Newfoundland government held its own news conference to challenge statements made by the Innu. Speaking for the government, Minister of Rural, Agricultural, and Northern Development Goudie stated in a press release on October 24, 1984:

Some spokesmen for the natives have claimed that low-level flying is disturbing their traditional activities and that it is affecting wildlife, specifically caribou and birds. There has also been some suggestion that the military exercises negatively impact on the health of residents as a result of the sound of aircraft overhead and the exhaust fumes. We, as a government, are very sensitive to these concerns, but we do not believe that enough evidence exists at the present time to draw these conclusions. The evidence is simply not available to connect certain events, for example, changes in caribou migration patterns, with low-level flying.

Goudie referred to an "initial environmental evaluation" (IEE) on low-level flight training prepared by Major George Landry in 1981, which "noted that there was no conclusive information available regarding impact on caribou."[12] He announced that the government would conduct studies to assess the effects of low-level flying on caribou. Fred Harrington, a biologist from Mount St. Vincent University, was subsequently awarded a contract to study the impact of the training on caribou (see Harrington & Veitch, 1990).

The following summer, the Newfoundland government asked the Canadian Public Health Association (CPHA) to examine Innu concerns about the impact of military aviation on their health. The CPHA accepted the invitation and formed a three-person task force in the fall of 1985. The task force conducted a literature review and made a few brief trips to Labrador to meet with the Innu, government officials, and other individuals implicated in military flight training, before releasing a final report in May 1987.

Amid continuing public controversy, DND referred low-level flight training under the MMOU and the proposed NATO TFWTC to a formal environmental review process on February 13, 1986. DND acknowledged the role of "public concern" in its decision to refer the project to environmental review, but continued to deny that military flight training caused any negative impacts on people or wildlife. Government representatives went so far as to deny Innu claims that exposure to low-level jet noise is a traumatic emotional experience. For example, federal Minister of Transportation John Crosbie (1986) stated in a televised speech:

There's more noise, by the way, from a snowmobile. There's more danger to you, there's more danger could be caused to you by going around all winter on your posterior on a snowmobile than is likely to be caused to your ears. And look at all the children running through this country with plugs in their ears and the volume turned up listening to the modern music. My God, that does more damage than a hundred low-level flights could do, poor little blighters, to have those things in their ears.

Crosbie's approach here—ridiculing Innu concerns about the health effects of jet noise—appeared to be part of a broader strategy on the part of the government and other proponents of military expansion to destroy the factual basis of the Innu campaign. Innu concerns were not only systematically challenged but also frequently distorted and then ridiculed using classic rhetorical strategies (see Armitage & Kennedy, 1989). They were accused of exaggerating the negative impacts of the training, of embarking on a massive propaganda campaign, and of feeding simplistic and emotional arguments to the media and public.

Attempts were also made to discredit the Innu and their supporters by alleging communist involvement in the campaign. The editor of a Happy Valley-Goose Bay newspaper addressed an editorial to God in which she advanced the communist conspiracy theory:

> Of course, communists and communist sympathizers are quick to pounce on the unrest among Your Innu people. They infiltrate their encampments under the guise of humanitarians, advisors and the like. They are skilled in manipulating the international media and convey the message at home and abroad that the white settlers of Labrador are crucifying the Innu and "stealing their land." (Brett, 1986)

Government representatives generally avoided making such allegations, but in December 1988, Canadian Security and Intelligence Service agents were sent to the Happy Valley-Goose Bay region to interview a prominent Innu supporter and other people about alleged communist involvement.

Besides challenging the Innu statements in news releases and backgrounders, the federal and provincial governments took up a number of additional concrete actions to discredit the Innu and counter their campaign. DND spokespersons addressed meetings of chambers of commerce and Rotary Club chapters in Newfoundland, disseminated promotional videotapes, and funded several junkets to Goose Bay for both domestic and foreign newspaper editors and media correspondents. Most important, the federal and provincial governments sponsored the formation of a promilitary lobby and public relations organization called the Mokami Project Group, made up of representatives from the Happy Valley-Goose Bay Town Council, Mokami Regional Development Association, the Labrador North Chamber of Commerce, and a local of the Public Service Alliance of Canada. The organization, which for most of its existence was headed by a prominent local businessperson and Progressive Conservative party candidate in the last provincial election, received more than

(CDN)$754,000 in funding from the federal and provincial govern-
ments to lobby and conduct media relations in support of low-level
flying and the proposed NATO base. Much of the responsibility for
countering the Innu campaign appears to have been given to the
Mokami Project Group, which also issued news releases, prepared
backgrounders, traveled to Europe to lobby for the military, addressed
meetings of chambers of commerce in Atlantic Canada, and at one
point attempted a provincewide educational tour. The group also conducted research into the impacts of military flight training on wildlife
and on the Labrador economy, and made presentations to the federal
Environmental Assessment Panel.

Of all the tactics used by government and the Mokami Project
Group to counter the Innu and promote military flight training,
DND's EIS was perhaps the most important plank in their public relations strategy. Correspondence with opponents of the training, backgrounders and news releases to the media, and publicity in Europe
made constant reference to the Canadian government's responsible
approach to dealing with the concerns of the Innu, as evidenced by
the work on the EIS and the implementation of a formal environmental review process. When the scientific quality of the Goose Bay EIS
was challenged by technical experts for the Environmental Assessment Panel, the Innu, and other groups in the fall of 1989 and the
winter of 1990, and the credibility of the EIS crumbled, DND's public relations strategy suffered a serious blow (see Armitage, 1990;
Canada, Federal Environmental Assessment Review Office, 1989).

As the NATO Defence Planning Committee meeting approached
(where a final decision on the TFWTC was expected to be made),
DND made a last-ditch effort to sway public and media opinion,
which appeared generally to support the Innu. At the beginning of
May, two DND representatives traveled across Canada to meet with
the editorial boards of major Canadian newspapers. The factual basis
of Innu arguments was again challenged; the Innu were accused of
spreading misinformation to the gullible media and of exaggerating
the impacts of the training (Canada, DND, 1990). The Innu were por-
trayed as political opportunists exploiting the military issue in order
to advance their land claims and other political agendas. A copy of a
Mackenzie Institute report by David Murrell (1990) that accused the
Central Canadian media of biased reporting in favor of the Innu was
disseminated at the same time.[13]

By the time the NATO decision on the TFWTC was made in May,
the Innu and other opponents of military flight training were ready to

announce the success of their campaign. While they believed that the decision not to build the base was made primarily for military and political reasons stemming from the collapse of the WTO, they took some pride in the knowledge that the Canadian government had acknowledged the political pressure exerted upon it. Defence Minister Bill McKnight stated, "Domestically, our government has been under tremendous pressure not to make a NATO training center" (Chepesiuk, 1990). In May, the U.K. House of Commons Defence Committee concluded that the opportunities for export of low-level flying oversees are politically difficult, in reference to the extensive opposition to the training in Canada and other NATO countries (United Kingdom, 1990, p. liv).[14] Federal Minister John Crosbie

> lashed out at Innu residents of the area whose opposition to the training is "extremely unhelpful, unproductive and unfeeling," to the area's economic needs. . . . Even if NATO decides to proceed with a training base at a later date, the 16-member alliance has ruled out Goose Bay and Turkey as sites, Mr. Crosbie said. Goose Bay lost out because of the Innu. . . . "I don't consider their claims to be justified or legitimate," Mr. Crosbie said. (Thomson News Service, 1990, p. 9)

CONCLUSION

The lessons to be learned from the experience of the Innu in opposing military flight training in Québec-Labrador are numerous. The most important are those pertaining to the relative political power of marginalized indigenous peoples such as the Innu vis-à-vis powerful nation-states such as Canada and its NATO allies, and what indigenous peoples must do in order to protect their lands and cultures. The Innu have virtually no political resources at their disposal: They are demographically few, impoverished, and suffering from multiple social pathologies; their rights as a sovereign nation are not recognized by the United Nations; they own no shares in multinational corporations; and they have virtually no military capability. Their only political resource in dealing with the Canadian state and the NATO alliance is public opinion—more specifically, their ability to extract compromises out of the state using the "politics of embarrassment" (Paine, 1985, pp. 190-235).

The Campaign Against the Militarization of Nitassinan evidently succeeded in mobilizing public opinion in defense of the Innu, and in exerting considerable pressure on the Canadian government. The success of the campaign depended on three important variables:

- extensive networking with social action groups across Canada and in Western Europe in order to develop political constituencies that would assist the Innu in lobbying government, obtaining funding, organizing demonstrations and other dramatic newsworthy events, conducting public education work, and orchestrating all the other activities required in an international campaign
- the creation of dramatic "David and Goliath" images that stimulate a sense of crisis, would be newsworthy, and would generate sympathy from the media and the public at large
- the development and maintenance of sound scientific arguments to support the Innu position regarding the negative impacts of military flight training on people and wildlife, including the recruitment of military analysts, social scientists, medical professionals, and other technical experts capable of passing judgment on the scientific merits of the case

On this point, I note that the Innu are engaged in the creation of a "public problem" that they hope will be accepted as valid and serious enough by the public to warrant opposition to the military expansion in their homeland. In order for the Innu to succeed in mobilizing such opposition, however, the public must make two kinds of judgments about the cause of the problem they face: one cognitive, the other moral (Armitage & Kennedy, 1989, p. 808; Dyck, 1986, p. 32). In Gusfield's (1981) view:

> The cognitive side [of a public problem] consists in beliefs about the facticity of the situation and events comprising the problem—our theories and empirical beliefs. . . . The moral side is that which enables the situation to be viewed as painful, ignoble, immoral. It is what makes alteration or eradication desirable. (p. 1)

Social scientists, biologists, and other technical experts obviously have an important role to play in public controversies such as the one discussed in this chapter, because they either support or erode the factual basis of the public problem. In fact, such controversies often become public contests over the "truth" between proponents and opponents, each with their own scientific expertise, each attempting to obtain acceptance of their definition of the "scientific facts." Thus what is eventually established as a "scientific truth" (and a historical one) in the public mind depends on the relative skill and power of the contestants in making effective use of communication media.

The success of the Innu's campaign must be considered in its broader political and economic context. Had the Innu been faced with large resource development (e.g., oil exploration and extraction), major corporate investors in Central Canada and the United States could have mounted an effective public relations offensive against them that, in turn, could have seriously damaged public and media support for their position. Military flight training under the MMOU and the proposed TFWTC appear to have been of interest primarily to DND and elite groups in Newfoundland, which failed to recruit serious allies among other elite groups in the center of the country. Also, had the WTO not collapsed, and Canadians not devalued the usefulness of more military infrastructure and training as a result, the Innu would not have had a "friendly" environment in which to mobilize public support. The Innu benefited, therefore, not only from the apparent lack of interest in the military flight training by Central Canadian elites, but also from the end of the Cold War and the view held by numerous Canadians that the military flight training is completely unnecessary.

It must be remembered, furthermore, that the success of the Innu campaign was limited. While they succeeded in mobilizing a large network of peace, church, aboriginal rights, women's rights, and environmental groups, and in putting considerable pressure on the Canadian government, they did not succeed in forcing the government to abandon its support for military flight training under the MMOU or the proposed NATO TFWTC. Both the federal and provincial governments offered certain "compromises" in response to public pressure, however, in the form of a formal environmental review of the training, the initiation of caribou and health studies, and the implementation of certain "mitigative measures" such as a 2.5-nautical-mile avoidance zone around Innu camps. Nonetheless, military flight training continues and could in fact increase dramatically under the MMOU to more than 18,000 sorties in 1996.

Another important lesson to be learned from the experience of the Innu concerns the nature of their relationships with urban-based majorities and the elite groups resident there. These occupy the most powerful decision-making positions within the nation-state. As mentioned at the beginning of the chapter, Innu opposition to the military is not an isolated incident, but part of a long-term struggle to protect their lands, culture, and identity as a distinct people. The causes of such conflicts are historically based in the relationship between metropoles and hinterlands and in the structure of the Canadian economy, which is heavily dependent on primary resource extraction. The Innu and other aboriginal peoples throughout the north are largely at the mercy of urban majorities that require the iron ore, timber, hydroelectric power, and other resources on aboriginal lands to sustain their lavish levels of commodity consumption. Paradoxically, aboriginal peoples such as the Innu obtain most of their support in urban centers whenever they engage in major struggles over resource exploitation; generally the people who are the most antagonistic to their interests at such times are the nonaboriginal frontierspeople whose job it is to extract the primary resources required by urban consumers.

In Newfoundland, where one of the main sources of employment, the fishery, is in serious crisis due to mismanagement of the fish stocks, nonaboriginal people look increasingly to Innu lands and their resources for economic salvation. Hydroelectric dams, a NATO TFWTC, uranium mines, and pulp and paper industries are supported by many Newfoundlanders, irrespective of their human and environmental impacts, because of the employment opportunities they provide. Thus Labrador—the "one lucky break that nature gave to Newfoundlanders"—is promoted as a frontier where solutions can be found to the unemployment problems resulting from structural defects in the economy of the island portion of the province (Gwyn, 1972). The situation is analogous to that in Brazil, where displaced agricultural workers in the southern part of the country have been encouraged to move north to the Amazon, where they can attempt to wrest a meager income from an unfriendly environment, and where they come into direct conflict with the resident aboriginal population.

The new ingredient in the advance of the frontier in the Canadian north, however, is the growing utility of aboriginal lands for the military. To my knowledge, the only historical precedent in Canada for the kind of military training occurring at Goose Bay is the creation in the 1950s of the bombing-range facilities and airspace at Cold Lake, Alberta, for the RCAF. Cree, Dene, and Metis people lost valued hunting territory as a result. Other military bases and training facilities (including the DEW Line) have in no way involved the amount of airspace and land that military flight training at Cold Lake, and in eastern Québec and Labrador, have involved. It should be noted that the USAF Strategic Air Command has been given approval by the Canadian government to conduct low-level flying along lengthy military training routes in British Columbia, Alberta, and the Northwest Territories. The SAC routes have been strenuously opposed by the aboriginal residents of the region.

Clearly, what has happened here is that the security requirements of the state have taken precedence over the constitutional, human, and aboriginal rights of people living in the hinterlands. Part of the rationale for imposing the negative impacts of military training and testing on such people is that it is somehow acceptable "to do to the few what is unacceptable to do to the many." Aboriginal groups such as the Innu feel that they have already lost large tracts of territory to European industrial developments, and are concerned that new projects will eliminate what little they have left. They are therefore likely to oppose future projects—including military ones—unless a new relationship between themselves and the Euro-Canadian nation-state is defined. The Innu, for their part, will continue to fight against military flight training under the MMOU as well as other government and corporate actions that threaten their land and culture. They will likely employ many of the same methods in the fight against other threats to their land that they have employed in the fight against military flight training.

NOTES

1. Note Francis Jennings's (1975) observation about the first European settlers in the Americas: "Incapable of conquering true wilderness, the Europeans were highly competent in the skill of conquering other people, and that is what they did. They did not settle a virgin land. The invaded and displaced a resident population" (p. 15).

2. I define the *frontier* as a geographic, political, and cultural concept designating the point of contact between an immigrant population or expanding nation-state and an indigenous population. In North America, the frontier has generally appeared wherever the lands of indigenous people have become valued because of their strategic military or agricultural importance, because of the presence of mineral or hydroelectric potential, or because they are considered wastelands suitable for military testing or the dumping of industrial wastes (Armitage & Kennedy, 1989, p. 815).

3. The Innu refer to this territory as *Nitassinan*.

4. When Newfoundland joined the Canadian confederation in 1949, both it and the federal government agreed not to include the Innu in the federal Indian Act. The majority of the Innu are therefore "nonstatus Indians" under Canadian law. In ignoring its constitutional responsibility to the Innu under the British North American Act of 1867 and treating them as full-fledged citizens of Newfoundland, the Canadian government excluded the Innu "from the expanding range of programs and services that were being delivered to native people elsewhere in Canada" (Tompkins, 1988, p. 24; see also Armitage, 1989, p. 8).

5. I define *culture collapse* as a socioeconomic, political, and sociomedical situation resulting from the colonialization of an indigenous people. The result of

this colonial process is that the self-esteem of the indigenous people collapses; the worldview that generates meaning and values in their life disintegrates. Pressured from all sides by an immigrant population and its governments, which totally denigrate his or her culture, the indigenous person sinks into despair and a hopeless sense of power-lessness, which in turn produces a downward spiral of self-hatred, alcohol abuse, fam-ily violence, and other destructive behaviors (Armitage, 1989, p. 40).

6. These include the La Romaine, Sainte-Marguerite, Petit Mécatina, Olomon, and Natashquan rivers.

7. Approximately 50% of this airspace is located over the Québec portion of the peninsula.

8. DND claims either that sonic booms generated at more than 30,000 feet ASL do not reach the ground or else they sound like distant thunder. It should be noted here that a CF-18 flying supersonic at 37,000 feet ASL in the Perth and Buckingham areas, Ontario, March 2, 1990, produced a shock wave that broke numerous windows and in some cases cracked plaster walls in houses (DND, personal communication, Freedom of Information Act responses, June 27, July 5, 1990).

9. An ACMRI is a "weapons range monitored by electronic beacons that receive signals from special pods carried by aircraft taking part in the exercise. The signals are processed through a computer, which displays the mock air battle on huge, four-color video screens that accurately portray the relative positions and flight parameters of all pod-equipped aircraft" (Skinner, 1984, p. viii). Camera targets, otherwise referred to as tactical targets, are prefabricated wooden structures resembling Soviet surface-to-air missiles, tanks, and other targets for simulated bombing strikes by aircraft using video cameras to record the accuracy of their strikes.

10. Flag exercises involve large numbers of aircraft that fly in dedicated roles, often in support of each other. During such exercises, a variety of aircraft fly "mission pack-ages," which are composite strike forces typically consisting of reconnaissance aircraft, electronic countermeasures aircraft (e.g., F-4 Wild Weasel) and their F-15 escorts, the strike (bombing) flights and their fighter cover, followed by more reconnaissance flights, and supported by rescue aircraft, tankers, AWACS, and other electronic warfare aircraft. Flag exercises elsewhere in the world include Red Flag (Nellis AFB in Ne-vada), Cope Thunder (Philippines), and Maple Flag (Cold Lake, Alberta; see Skinner, 1984).

11. While Québec-based Innu from La Romaine, Natashquan, and Schefferville have also experienced the noise of low-flying military jets, they were not included in the study because they are represented by the Conseil Attikamek-Montagnais, which chose to boycott the environmental review process.

12. The IEE is 37 pages in length excluding the title page. The introduction is 2 pages long, the "Project Setting and Description" section 5 pages, the "Environmental Impact" section 7½ pages, the "Major Impacts and Mitigating Measures" section 1¼ pages, the "Residual Impacts" section 1 page, and the bibliography 2½ pages. The total amount of text in the IEE, apart from the bibliography and annexes, is 21 pages. Clearly this is not a scientific document upon which any rational decisions can be based. The IEE states: "It is expected that the opposition voiced by the NMIA, repre-senting about 500 Indians, will continue. They have been unswayed in our previous dis-cussion and remain opposed to any development in Labrador. It is expected that they will maintain their position until the matter of Native land claims and aboriginal rights is resolved. Opposition to the proposed program will likely be used whenever it serves to gain publicity or otherwise further their ends" (Landry, 1981, p. 21).

13. According to Herman and O'Sullivan (1989), the Mackenzie Institute sponsors seminars and conferences and publishes a series called the Mackenzie Papers. Established by Maurice Tugwell in 1986, the institute is registered with Revenue Canada as a charitable organization. "Although the Mackenzie Institute claims to be nonpartisan and concerned to defend the 'Western heritage,' in fact it is a far-right operation in the tradition of its esteemed British predecessor, the CIA-organized ISC. . . . peace movements for [Tugwell] (and the Institute, which he controls) are always witting or unwitting instruments of the KGB. . . . Tugwell has long collaborated with Canadian industrialists in attacking environmentalists as dangerous ideologues and lunatics" (p. 116).

14. The Defence Committee notes that "it would certainly be desirable to reduce the impact of low flying on our own population, but transferring more abroad is not without difficulties. . . . The Innu people who live around Goose Bay, for example, are no keener on low flying than the people of mid-Wales or the Borders. The Innu Resource Centre at Sheshatshit in Labrador has sent us copies of testimonies from a number of Innu people, which testify very clearly to the strength of local opposition to low flying" (United Kingdom, 1990, p. liv).

REFERENCES

Ando, Y., & Hattori, H. (1977). Effects of noise on human placental lactogen (HPL) levels in maternal plasma. *British Journal Obstetrics and Gynecology, 85,* 115-118.

Antane, S., & Kanikuen, P. (1984). The Innut and their struggle against assimilation. *Native Issues, 4,* 25-33.

Armitage, P. (1989). *Homeland or wasteland? Contemporary land use and occupancy among the Innu of Utshimassit and Sheshatshit and the impact of military expansion* (submission to the Federal Environmental Assessment Panel Reviewing Military Flying Activities in Nitassinan). Sheshatshit, Newfoundland: Naskapi Montagnais Innu Association.

Armitage, P. (1990). Critique of the Goose Bay EIS: Human environment and impact sections with special reference to the Innu. In P. Armitage (Ed.), *Compendium of critiques of the Goose Bay EIS.* Sheshatshit, Newfoundland: Naskapi Montagnais Innu Association.

Armitage, P., & Kennedy, J. C. (1989). Redbaiting and racism on our frontier: Military expansion in Labrador and Québec. *Canadian Review of Sociology and Anthropology, 26,* 798-817.

Berglund, B. (1990). Health impact of noise: A review of the Goose Bay EIS on military flying activities in Labrador and Québec. In P. Armitage (Ed.), *Compendium of critiques of the Goose Bay EIS.* Sheshatshit, Newfoundland: Naskapi Montagnais Innu Association.

Brett, I. (1986, August 6). [Editorial]. *Northern Reporter.*

Brice-Bennett, C. (1986). *Renewable resource use and wage employment in the economy of Northern Labrador.* Background report for the Royal Commission on Employment and Unemployment, Newfoundland and Labrador.

Budgell, H. M. (1959). [Letter to J. R. Smallwood].

Canada, Department of National Defence. (1989). *Goose Bay EIS: An environmental impact statement on military flying activities in Labrador and Québec.* Ottawa: Author.

Canada, Department of National Defence. (1990). *Backgrounder: Fallacies and facts about low-level flying at Goose Bay.* Goose Bay, Newfoundland: National Defence Headquarters, Goose Bay Management Office.

Canada, Federal Environmental Assessment Review Office. (1989). *Compilation of comments received from technical experts concerning the Environmental Impact Statement.* Ottawa: Author.

Canadian Armed Forces. (1987). [Promotional videotape on Goose Bay and Canada's bid for the NATO tactical fighter and weapons training center]. Ottawa: Author.

Canadian Public Health Association. (1987). *Final report of the Task Force on the Health Effects of Increased Flying Activity in the Labrador Area.* Ottawa: Author.

Chepesiuk, R. (1990). Interview: The Honorable Bill McKnight, Canada's minister of national defense. *Defense and Diplomacy, 8*(4), 22-23.

Cohen, S., Krantz, D., Evans, G., & Stokols, D. (1980). Physiological, motivational, and cognitive effects of aircraft noise on children: Moving from the laboratory to the field. *American Psychologist, 35*, 231-243.

Crosbie, J. (1986, May 31). [Speech to NATO ambassadors in Goose Bay.] CBC Television.

Dyck, N. (1986). Negotiating the Indian "problem." *Culture, 6*, 31-41.

Government of Newfoundland. (1980). *Report of the Environmental Assessment Board.* St. John's, Newfoundland: Department of Consumer Affairs and Environment, Brinex Kitts-Michelin Uranium Project.

Grandjean, E., Graf, P., Lauber, A., Meir, H. P., & Muller, R. (1976). Survey on the effects of aircraft noise around three civil airports in Switzerland. In R. L. Kerlin (Ed.), *INTER-NOISE '76 Proceedings* (pp. 85-90). Poughkeepsie, NY: Institute of Noise Control Engineering.

Gusfield, J. R. (1981). *The culture of public problems: Drinking-driving and the symbolic order.* Minneapolis: University of Minnesota Press.

Gwyn, R. (1972). *Smallwood: The unlikely revolutionary.* Toronto: McLelland & Stewart.

Harrington, F. H., & Veitch, A. M. (1990). *Impacts of low-level jet fighter training on caribou populations in Labrador and Northern Québec.* Report presented to the Newfoundland-Labrador Wildlife Division, December 1989 (revised May 15, 1990). St. John's, Newfoundland: Department of Environment and Lands.

Henriksen, G. (1973). *Hunters in the barrens: The Naskapi on the edge of the white man's world.* St. John's, Newfoundland: Institute of Social and Economic Research.

Herman, E., & O'Sullivan, G. (1989). *The terrorism industry.* New York: Pantheon.

Jennings, F. (1975). *The invasion of America: Indians, colonialism, and the cant of conquest.* New York: W. W. Norton.

Kennedy, J. C. (1977). Northern Labrador: An ethnohistorical account. In R. Paine (Ed.), *The white Arctic: Anthropological essays on tutelage and ethnicity* (pp. 264-305). St. John's, Newfoundland: Institute of Social and Economic Research.

Knipschild, P., & Oudschoorn N. (1977). Medical effects of aircraft noise: Drug survey. *International Archives of Occupational and Environmental Health, 40*, 197-200.

Kryter, K. (1985). *The effects of noise on man* (2nd ed.). New York: Academic Press.

Kryter, K. (1990). Critique of Goose Bay EIS with respect to the assessment of the effects of aircraft noise and sonic booms on health. In P. Armitage (Ed.), *Compendium of critiques of the Goose Bay EIS.* Sheshatshit, Newfoundland: Naskapi Montagnais Innu Association.

Landry, G. (1981). *An initial environmental evaluation on a proposal to conduct low-level flying training from Goose Bay, Labrador.* Ottawa: National Defence Headquarters, Directorate of Air Plans.

Levi, L. (1979). *Psychosocial factors in preventative medicine* (Report to the surgeon general by the National Academy of Sciences, DHEW [PHS] Publication No. 79-550771A). Washington, DC: Government Printing Office.

Mailhot, J. (1987). Montagnais opposition to the militarization of their land: An historical perspective. *Native Issues, 7,* 47-54.

Mailhot, J., & Michaud A. (1965). *North West River: Étude ethnographique.* Québec: Laval University, Centre d'études nordiques.

McGraw, J. (Ed.). (1987). *On the Goose: The story of Goose Bay.* Happy Valley-Goose Bay, Labrador: Them Days.

Murrell, D. (1990). *A balanced overall view? Media reporting of the Labrador low-flying controversy.* Toronto: Mackenzie Institute.

Newfoundland House of Assembly. (1987, May). [Testimony]. *Hansard, 40,* 2349.

Paine, R. (1985). Ethnodrama and the "Fourth World": The Saami Action Group in Norway, 1979-1981. In N. Dyck (Ed.), *Indigenous peoples and the nation state: "Fourth World" politics in Canada, Australia and Norway* (pp. 190-235). St. John's, Newfoundland: Institute of Social and Economic Research.

Privy Council (Great Britain) Judicial Committee. (1927). *In the matter of the boundary between the Dominion of Canada and the Colony of Newfoundland in the Labrador Peninsula, between the Dominion of Canada of the one part and the Colony of Newfoundland of the other part* (12 vols.). London: W. Clowes & Sons.

Skinner, M. (1984). *Red flag: Air combat for the '80s.* Novato, CA: Presidio.

Spreng, M. (1990). Effects of noise from low-level flights on humans: Part I. In B. Berglund & T. Lindvall (Eds.), *Noise as public health problem: New advances in noise research* (Proceedings, 5th International Congress on Noise as Public Health Problem, Stockholm, August 21-25, 1988) (pp. 293-304). Stockholm: Swedish Council for Building Research.

Tanner, V. (1944). Outlines of the geography, life and customs of Newfoundland-Labrador (the eastern part of the Labrador Peninsula). *Acta Geographica, 8.*

Thomson News Service. (1990, May 26). Crosbie disappointed but not surprised by NATO decision. *Evening Telegram,* p. 9.

Tompkins, E. (1988). *Pencilled out: Newfoundland and Labrador's native people and Canadian Confederation, 1947-1954.* Report prepared for Jack Harris, M.P., on the impact of the exclusion of Newfoundland and Labrador's native people from the Terms of Union in 1949.

United Kingdom, House of Commons Defence Committee. (1990). *Low flying* (Fifth Report, together with the Proceedings of the Committee relating to the Report, Minutes of Evidence and Memoranda, Session 1989-90). London: HMSO.

Zimmerly, D. W. (1975). *Cain's land revisited.* St. John's, Newfoundland: Institute of Social and Economic Research.

7

The Legacy of the Pentagon:
The Myth of the Peace Dividend

GERALD JACOB

THE DIVIDEND FROM THE RETIREMENT of weapons production facilities will not be a budgetary windfall. If there is a significant peace dividend, it is that national security will no longer be tolerated as justification for ignoring the dangerous by-products of a military-industrial economy and its legacy of chemical waste sites, radioactive landfills, and mismanaged nuclear weapons facilities. We are only beginning to address the public health and environmental costs of conventional and nuclear weapons production. It is a legacy found in urban areas throughout the United States; the impact on urban areas in Eastern Europe and the Soviet Union is only beginning to be documented.

The sordid legacy of weapons production at federal facilities near urban areas within this country includes contamination from toxic chemicals and from radioactive materials. The problem of toxic chemical contamination includes careless waste disposal practices and groundwater contamination from solvents and other chemicals used at military bases and facilities producing nuclear weapons. Under authority from the Comprehensive Environmental Response, Compensation and Liability Act (CERCLA, or Superfund), the Environmental Protection Agency (EPA) identifies the most serious toxic waste sites by placing them on its National Priorities List. As of June 1989, 94 military bases were on the Superfund list, along with 13 sites at nuclear weapons production facilities. Some nuclear facilities, such as the Hanford Nuclear Reservation, encompass numerous Superfund sites. Figure 7.1 shows the number of Superfund sites at military bases found in each state and the location of federal facilities involved in the development and production of nuclear weapons.

The problems created by radioactive waste range from leaks in the tanks used to store liquid high-level waste (HLW) to the question of what to do with retired buildings and equipment contaminated with plutonium and other radioactive materials. Environmental problems at weapons facilities have been complicated further by the mixing of toxic chemical and radioactive waste streams. Such problems are found throughout the weapons production complex shown in Figure 7.1. The problem, however, is even more extensive than the map suggests, if one includes the uranium, thorium, and radium mill tailings sites and mines that provided raw materials for nuclear weapons production. In the past few years, the U.S. Department of Energy (DOE) has been spending approximately $100 million a year for environmental activities at these sites.

The geographical distribution and economic impacts of weapons facilities have been documented elsewhere in this book. Here the focus is the impacts that extend far beyond the economic into what the future may hold for local residents and their environments. Haphazard management of radioactive and toxic materials at weapons facilities now leaves plant workers and local residents to live with the threat of serious, long-term health problems. Researchers at a Denver hospital recently linked beryllium, a toxic metal used in the manufacture of triggers for nuclear warheads, to incidents of chronic lung ailments and rare diseases among workers at the Rocky Flats nuclear weapons plant (Schneider, 1990). Residents of suburban housing developments near the plant have expressed their concerns about recent incidents of brain cancers in the community and contamination of a reservoir used to supply drinking water.

TOXIC WASTE AND
CONVENTIONAL WEAPONS FACILITIES

Figure 7.1 shows toxic waste sites at military bases identified by the EPA that are eligible for the Superfund National Priorities List as of July 1989. In California alone, 19 military bases have been identified as Superfund sites. The cost of cleanup is difficult to establish and is subject to final agreements among the Department of Defense (DOD), the EPA, and state agencies. Nevertheless, DOD funding for cleanup of toxic waste sites under the Superfund program increased from $150 million in fiscal year 1984 to $500 million in 1989. By some estimates, $1 billion or more will be required on an annual basis by fiscal year 1994 just to address Superfund sites.

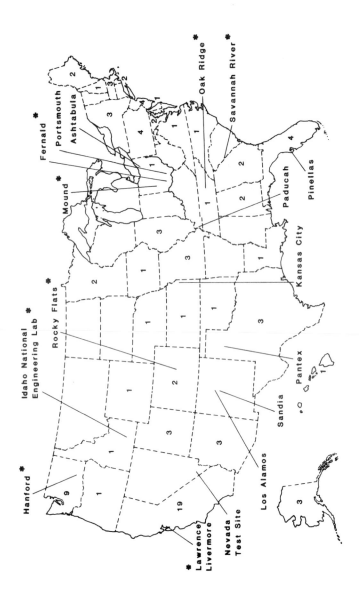

Figure 7.1. Nuclear Weapons Facilities and the Number of Superfund Sites Found at Conventional Military Installations Within Each State

NOTE: This figure includes Superfund sites at conventional military installations, such as army bases and federal munitions plants, as of July 1989.
*Nuclear weapons facilities with Superfund sites as of July 1989.

Table 7.1—by no means a comprehensive description of the hazardous waste problem at military bases and facilities—identifies the very worst sites. Many more will require remediation to take care of lesser toxic waste problems, as well as problems such as the disposal of everything from used oil to chemical weapons. For instance, in 1985 Congress mandated that the U.S. Army dispose of its stockpile of unitary chemical weapons (P.L. 99-145). The Army has decided that it will incinerate the stockpile at eight current storage locations in Maryland, Alabama, Kentucky, Indiana, Arkansas, Colorado, Utah, and Oregon. The Federal Emergency Management Agency (FEMA) has been working with city and state governments to upgrade their capabilities in the event of an accident involving the disposal program.

Also absent from Table 7.1 are numerous private industrial sites found in urban areas where weapons research or production has occurred. Examples of such sites include the Martin-Marietta Plant near Denver and numerous plants in Silicon Valley. Identifying and evaluating toxic waste problems at sites owned by private corporations is beyond the scope of this chapter and would entail detailed assessment of each of the hundreds of corporate sites on the National Priorities List. Nevertheless, pollution from hundreds of private industrial sites that develop and manufacture weapons should be recognized as yet another legacy of the weapons production complex.

OPERATION OF THE
NUCLEAR WEAPONS COMPLEX

The U.S. Department of Energy's Office of Defense Programs oversees nuclear weapons production, responding to demands for weapons production that originate within the decision-making processes of DOD. A total of 17 major installations in 13 states constitute the nuclear weapons production complex (Figure 7.1). These facilities are government owned but are operated by private corporations such as Westinghouse Electric Corporation under contract with DOE. In fiscal year 1990 the total budget for the complex was $10 billion, and some 80,000 people were employed by DOE and its contractors (National Research Council [NRC], 1989).

The production of nuclear weapons is not an activity carried out in isolated rural areas. A significant number of sites are located within major metropolitan areas. To give a few examples: Lawrence Livermore National Laboratory is located in the San Francisco Bay Area.

TABLE 7.1

Military Bases and Conventional Weapons Facilities on the Superfund National
Priorities List as of July 1989

State	Number of Sites	Selected Urban Areas Affected
Alabama	2	Birmingham
Alaska	3	Fairbanks, Anchorage
Arizona	3	Phoenix, Tucson, Yuma
California	19	San Diego, Los Angeles, Sacramento, San Francisco
Colorado	2	Denver
Delaware	1	Dover
Florida	4	Jacksonville, Pensacola
Georgia	2	Albany, Macon
Hawaii	1	Honolulu, Oahu
Idaho	1	—[a]
Illinois	3	Joliet
Iowa	1	—[a]
Kansas	1	—[a]
Louisiana	1	Shreveport
Maine	2	Portland
Maryland	2	Baltimore
Massachusetts	3	Boston
Minnesota	2	Minneapolis-Saint Paul
Missouri	3	Kansas City, St. Louis
Nebraska	1	—[a]
New Hampshire	1	Portsmouth
New Jersey	4	Newark-Paterson, Trenton, New Brunswick, Asbury Park, Camden-Philadelphia
New York	3	Plattsburgh-Burlington (VT), Rome-Utica
North Carolina	1	—[a]
Ohio	1	Dayton
Oklahoma	1	Oklahoma City
Oregon	1	Richland/Tri-Cities (WA)
Pennsylvania	4	Philadelphia, Scranton, Wilkes-Barre
Puerto Rico	1	San Juan
Rhode Island	2	Providence, Newport
Tennessee	1	—[a]
Texas	3	Fort Worth
Utah	3	Salt Lake City-Ogden
Virginia	1	Richmond
Washington	9	Seattle-Tacoma, Bremerton, Spokane
Wyoming	1	Cheyenne

NOTE: This table includes only U.S. Army, Marine, Navy, and Air Force bases, Army depots, and
federal ammunition plants that are final or proposed for the Superfund National Priorities List. Urban
areas affected have sites within 30 miles of the metropolitan area. This sample does not include
national laboratories, nuclear weapons plants, or private industrial sites the operations of which may
include the production of military hardware or weapons components.
a. Nearby town or city of population below 50,000.

Approximately 2 million people live within a 30-mile radius of the Rocky Flats Plant near Denver; residential areas are now within 4 miles of the site boundaries. Sandia National Laboratory is located within the Albuquerque metropolitan area. Within a 50-mile radius, one finds 680,000 people living near nuclear weapons facilities at Oak Ridge, Tennessee, and another 3.4 million living near the Mound Laboratories in the Dayton, Ohio, area. The Nevada Test Site—location of more than 700 nuclear detonations since 1951—lies 70 miles northwest of Las Vegas (see Figure 7.1). Increasingly refined studies have pointed to the link between acute leukemias in children and exposure to radioactive fallout from the Nevada Test Site (Stevens et al., 1990). More than a million people live within a 20-mile radius of the Feed Materials Production Center northwest of Cincinnati. The nuclear weapons complex includes the Kansas City Plant and the Pinellas Plant, located within the St. Petersburg metropolitan area. Environmental problems created by these facilities have the potential to affect millions of people who live in nearby residential areas. One example: Elevated levels of plutonium found in residential areas downwind from the Rocky Flats Plant have been linked to a 1957 explosion and fire at the plant that blew out all 600 industrial filters from the main stack and released a four-year accumulation of plutonium dust into the atmosphere. Some studies have linked this incident to increased cancer rates among residents downwind of the plant, and the issue remains a controversial one. Excessive brain tumors and rare forms of cancer have also been noted among employees of the plant (Johnson, 1981, 1987, 1988).

Even when located in remote areas, facilities such as Hanford, Savannah River, and the Idaho National Engineering Laboratory are a source of concern about surface and groundwater contamination for residents of towns and cities downstream. Contamination can result from radioactive materials as well as from toxic chemicals used and disposed of at these facilities. The Hanford Nuclear Reservation has approximately 1,000 inactive waste sites that include everything from petroleum and chemical waste dumps to facilities storing liquid high-level radioactive waste (U.S. General Accounting Office [GAO], 1988b). Between 670,000 and 900,000 gallons of liquid high-level waste have leaked from storage tanks at Hanford (GAO, 1989). While the significance of the impact is debated, the U.S. General Accounting Office (1988a) found that "groundwater contaminated with radioactive material in excess of drinking water standards is migrating from Hanford into the Columbia River at the plant boundary." The

GAO also concludes that the DOE has not collected sufficient data to trace the migration of this waste or to maintain its long-standing position that impacts of such releases have been insignificant. The Columbia River passes through the Hanford Nuclear Reservation on its way to the Portland metropolitan area.

The Idaho National Engineering Laboratory has at least 232 inactive waste sites. In the past, radioactive waste was discharged into ponds, wells, or directly into the Snake River aquifer located under the site. Groundwater contamination from the lab may be polluting the Snake River, the major source of drinking and irrigation water for towns in southern Idaho. Similar concerns have been voiced about the Rocky Flats Plant, approximately 15 miles northwest of downtown Denver, which has about 100 inactive waste sites. The Los Alamos National Lab has approximately 600 sites. The Savannah River Plant, with 70 waste sites, has spilled radioactive materials into its namesake. In sum, DOE reported 3,276 inactive waste sites at its facilities around the country as of the end of 1988 (GAO, 1988c), although the numbers could go higher as more thorough surveys of these facilities are conducted. The cost of these surveys alone has exceeded $60 million ("Inspector General," 1989).

HEALTH, SAFETY, AND THE ENVIRONMENT

Scaling back the production of nuclear weapons could produce a variety of localized costs in the form of changes and disruptions in local economies, as discussed elsewhere in this book. It should also be noted that cutbacks may produce substantial savings, by retiring aging, costly-to-run facilities and by foregoing the construction of new, expensive replacement facilities.

Much of the nuclear weapons complex was constructed in the 1940s and the 1950s and subsequently suffered from a history of poor maintenance and management that emphasized production goals over health and safety. The GAO and the National Research Council found that the facilities have serious shortcomings in the areas of health, safety, and environmental protection (NRC, 1989). Problems included violations of building, earthquake, and fire protection codes, deteriorated ventilation and filtration systems, marginal piping and electrical systems, antiquated monitoring equipment, and excessive air-polluting emissions (GAO, 1988a). For example, at the Idaho National Engineering Lab, single-walled pipes installed underground in the 1950s carry a mixture of toxic chemicals and high-level radioactive waste to storage tanks—a situation in violation of current federal regulations ("DOE Closes Idaho Plants," 1989). Upgrading existing nuclear weapons facilities to address such problems and to meet existing environmental and safety standards would cost an estimated $20 billion (GAO, 1988a).

DOE has proposed replacing some of its aging facilities and relocating and consolidating other operations. New production reactors to replace those at Hanford and Savannah River would cost $6.8 billion. A $1.2 billion special isotope separation facility would replace old facilities used to separate plutonium from spent reactor fuel. By DOE's accounting, construction of replacement facilities and restructuring of the weapons production complex would require $15-$25 billion (GAO, 1988a). However, the final cost of replacement facilities is likely to exceed DOE estimates. Alternative estimates prepared by the Congressional Budget Office and the GAO found that new production reactors could cost nearly twice what DOE estimated—more than $12 billion versus $6.8 billion ("GAO, CBO Charge," 1989). Permanent closure of outdated, costly-to-run facilities such as plants at Oak Ridge, Hanford, and Savannah River, combined with the elimination of expensive new facilities, could save tens of billions of dollars.

Within the nuclear weapons complex, public health, safety, and environmental quality have repeatedly been sacrificed in the interest of production goals. The absence of a clear commitment on the part of DOE to safety at its production reactors and facilities was belatedly recognized by the secretary of energy and observers such as the National Research Council. As stated in a recent NRC (1987) report:

> The stated *safety objective* for the defense production reactors is the achievement of a level of safety comparable to commercial nuclear power plants. However, the committee found a high degree of confusion both within DOE and among the contractor staff concerning the safety objective. The committee concludes that the Department has not clearly articulated, documented, or implemented any specific safety objective for its reactors. (p. xiv)

DOE management has been criticized repeatedly for its ineffectiveness and reliance on "a loose-knit system of largely self-regulated contractors" (NRC, 1987). Closure of facilities that do not meet the safety standards applied elsewhere in the nuclear industry, along with reduced production of nuclear weapons, would reduce future damage to the environment, public health, and workers at these plants. But still to be confronted are the ongoing costs of the occupational health effects already incurred by workers in nuclear weapons plants and impacts on the health of residents in communities that hosted these facilities.

Consider the dose reconstruction research initiated to determine which residents were exposed to radiation from radioactive materials intentionally released into the atmosphere by the Hanford Nuclear Reservation. In the course of the study it has been determined that 270,000 people in 10 Washington and Oregon counties were exposed to radioactive iodine released by that weapons plant. Studies such as the Hanford Dose Reconstruction Project cost millions of dollars. Compensating the victims may cost much more. A similar situation exists at the Idaho National Engineering Laboratory, where Iodine-131—in quantities thousands of times greater than those released by the Three Mile Island accident—has been intentionally released into the atmosphere.

Along with health impacts on unsuspecting residents, damage to workers' health is another, largely undetermined, cost of nuclear weapons production. Not until 1989, when new Secretary of Energy Admiral James Watkins vowed to reform the department, were non-DOE scientists offered the possibility of reviewing epidemiological data on 600,000 current and past workers at weapons production facilities ("Watkins Announces," 1989). Computerizing health records alone is expected to cost $36 million and take five years to complete. Recently declassified documents suggest the frightful prospects that may be contained therein. Using such documents, workers at the Nevada Test Site have filed a lawsuit in which they allege exposure to dangerous levels of radiation from underground and atmospheric tests that resulted in the premature deaths of at least 200 workers. The Department of Energy has never conducted a comprehensive survey of the health of workers at the Nevada Test Site (Schneider, 1989a). Heretofore classified studies released by the Senate Committee on Governmental Affairs in 1989 indicate that workers and neighbors of federal nuclear sites have developed excessive numbers of cancers and other diseases. While additional research is needed, these studies suggest that the legacy of weapons production may include brain cancer for workers at Rocky Flats, lung cancer among workers at Oak Ridge, and bone cancer among plutonium workers at Los Alamos (Schneider, 1989b). Poor record keeping and lax radiological monitoring by federal agencies and their contractors may prevent scientists from ever knowing the full impact of weapons testing and production on workers' health. Reductions in weapons testing and production may reduce future cases of negligence, but the cost of past negligence—in the form of compensation and medical care for workers and victims of nuclear weapons production—will continue for decades. A reported poll of 332 insurance companies found that 64% believe the number of health claims resulting from exposure to nuclear waste, fallout, and radon radiation will increase by the year 2000 ("Insurers See," 1989).

TOXIC WASTE SITES AT
NUCLEAR WEAPONS FACILITIES

Some of the nation's worst toxic waste sites and the worst offenders of hazardous waste regulations are nuclear weapons facilities managed by DOE. Lawrence Livermore National Laboratory in the San Francisco Bay Area, the Kansas City Plant, and the Rocky Flats Plant near Denver are examples of nuclear weapons facilities in urban areas that now appear on the Superfund list. Groundwater at these facilities has absorbed hazardous contaminants (solvents, acids, lead, mercury, and so on) in concentrations that are hundreds and even thousands of times greater than drinking-water standards. In some cases contamination has migrated off site, and residential wells have had to be closed (GAO, 1988b).

Toxic waste at nuclear weapons facilities is a problem the magnitude of which will take years to determine. For years, DOE maintained that federal agencies and their contractors were immune from state regulations adopted under the Resource Conservation and Recovery Act (RCRA, P.L. 94-580), which governs the handling and disposal of hazardous chemicals. DOE has also maintained that EPA could not force it or its contractors to comply with EPA regulations authorized under RCRA. National security has been used to justify the exemption of DOD and DOE operations from surveillance by independent regulators. In practical terms, this meant that hazardous waste storage and disposal at military and nuclear weapons facilities were governed by "in-house" interpretations of RCRA and CERCLA that allowed otherwise illegal practices to continue. In 1989, the FBI and EPA officials raided DOE's Albuquerque office and Rocky Flats Plant to recover evidence of illegal storage and disposal of hazardous waste, concealment of illegal actions, and falsifying of documents—

charges that could result in criminal prosecutions (Wartzman, 1989). Congress, the courts, and the Justice Department now appear less willing to accept arguments that military and DOE operations cannot be fined or prosecuted for violating federal and state antipollution regulations, including those established under RCRA and CERCLA. Recent agreements between DOE and state governments have resulted in de facto extension of Superfund regulations to nuclear weapons facilities. However, much uncertainty remains about EPA/state oversight and the extension of RCRA to ongoing waste-handling operations at these facilities.

At nuclear weapons facilities, it can be difficult to separate the costs of addressing toxic waste problems from those of radioactive waste. In many cases, radioactive materials have been mixed with a variety of toxic chemicals. Much of the "radioactive waste" destined for burial in the caverns of the Waste Isolation Pilot Plant (WIPP) in New Mexico is actually a mixture of toxic chemical and radioactive waste. WIPP, which will accept only waste from weapons plants such as Rocky Flats, has cost over $700 million to date. Its final cost will be higher by the time the facility is opened.

DOE has estimated that it may take more than $60 billion to address problems at its *inactive* (toxic and radioactive) waste sites. This estimate does not include the cost of decommissioning and cleanup at sites actively being used for the storage of toxic and/or radioactive wastes. The cost of cleaning up inactive toxic waste sites at Los Alamos alone is estimated to be $2 billion; it is expected to exceed $1 billion at Lawrence Livermore (GAO, 1988b). Final costs could be much higher—especially if one considers the technological uncertainties and estimates that environmental restoration at Hanford's inactive toxic waste and radioactive waste sites could exceed $45 billion. These estimates must also be viewed as preliminary, given the incomplete nature of the site surveys conducted to date. For example, the number of inactive waste sites identified at Los Alamos National Laboratory increased from 300 to more than 600 between 1988 and 1989 after more intensive surveys were conducted.

RADIOACTIVE WASTE AT
WEAPONS PRODUCTION FACILITIES

Radioactive waste from the production of nuclear weapons presents an especially difficult and costly problem for communities in the vicinity of these plants. For example, between 400,000 and 552,000 pounds of uranium dust have been intentionally released into the air since 1951 by DOE's Fernald Plant in Ohio. In that time, the water in several off-site wells near the plant has become unsuitable for drinking due to uranium contamination (GAO, 1988a). Residents of Fernald recently received $73 million from DOE to settle a lawsuit alleging that uranium from the facility contaminated air and local water supplies. The money has been earmarked for long-term health monitoring of affected residents and for an epidemiological study of the population near the plant. The settlement does not cover claims related to cancer, genetic abnormalities, or physical injuries caused by releases of radioactive materials.

Similar conflicts have marked nuclear weapons facilities throughout the country. Private wells near the Mound Plant have been contaminated with tritium and at least one spring shows concentrations five times the drinking-water standard. Cesium contamination has been discovered in the Savannah River, and plutonium has been found in soil outside the Rocky Flats Plant. In 1990, approximately 60 pounds of plutonium dust were reportedly discovered in the plant's ventilation system, raising fears about the ineffectiveness of the plant's filtration system and the possibility of unreported releases of plutonium into surrounding communities (Graf, 1990). In 1985, $9 million was paid to five local landowners whose property had been contaminated with plutonium (Day, 1989).

Disposal of the existing inventory of radioactive waste from weapons production sites will be a difficult problem. To this must be added the problem of waste generated when facilities are decommissioned. Much of this waste will be considered low-level waste (LLW) and technically suitable for disposal at facilities being planned under the Low Level Radioactive Waste Policy Act (P.L. 96-573) and its amendments (P.L. 99-240). These facilities, however, are intended for the disposal of commercial low-level waste, making it likely that additional facilities to dispose of military low-level waste will be required.

DOE estimates that treatment and disposal of high-level radioactive waste from its facilities will cost $20 billion (GAO, 1988a). Again, this may be a very optimistic estimate. Consider that a significant portion of this waste is in the form of 95 million gallons of highly radioactive, heat-producing liquids and sludge stored in underground tanks and bins. A planned $1 billion plant will turn liquid high-level radioactive waste stored at Hanford into borosilicate glass—a prerequisite of disposal in an underground repository. Similar facilities will be constructed at the Savannah River Plant and in Idaho. Processing of liquid waste will take 2 to 17 years, at a cost of $13 billion (1988 dollars)—excluding transportation, repository fees, and decontamination and decommissioning costs (GAO, 1990). Final disposal of vitrified waste must await completion of an HLW repository currently being studied by DOE for construction at Yucca Mountain, Nevada. Preliminary studies have already consumed more than a billion dollars, and the repository is unlikely to be completed before 2010. Decontaminating existing nuclear weapons facilities will cost another $15 billion; treatment and disposal of transuranic and low-level waste an additional $10 billion, according to DOE. Taken together, cleanup of inactive DOE waste sites, disposing of radioactive wastes, and decontaminating existing nuclear weapons facilities will require at least $100 billion—if one can assume that existing cost estimates are accurate (GAO, 1988a).

Reliable cost estimates for the activities described in this chapter have been very difficult to produce. The case of commercial high-level waste is instructive, in that DOE repeatedly underestimated the time and costs involved in preparing a repository to receive the HLW generated by commercial nuclear reactors (Jacob, 1990). Considering this experience, DOE's estimated cost of addressing radioactive waste at weapons facilities may prove deceptively optimistic. In the course of addressing environmental problems at weapons production facilities, huge technological uncertainties must also be confronted. Millions of dollars must be dedicated to research, and new processing technologies must be developed. Given such uncertainties, the final economic, environmental, and social costs of decontaminating military sites are enormous and essentially unpredictable.

At some sites environmental restoration may not even be possible, and DOE's cost estimates may reflect only the cost of preparing sites for long-term monitoring. Cost estimates presented in Table 7.2 and Figure 7.2 are intended only to illustrate the scale of the problems still to be addressed. They do not include the Nevada Test Site, nuclear waste dumped in the oceans, decontaminating and decommissioning of smaller facilities, transportation costs, and the final cost of constructing and maintaining at least three different types of waste repositories. Nor does the table include the cost of compensating communities, workers, and local residents injured by toxic and radioactive materials at weapons facilities.

TABLE 7.2

Cost of Addressing Selected Safety and
Environmental Problems at Weapons Facilities

Cost	*Cleanup Activity*
$60 billion	to address environmental problems at *inactive* radioactive, toxic, and mixed waste sites at DOE nuclear facilities
$20 billion	to upgrade nuclear plants to meet current environmental and safety standards
$20 billion	to treat and dispose of high-level radioactive waste from DOE nuclear weapons plants
$25 billion	to construct new facilities to replace aging nuclear facilities and to restructure the weapons production complex
$15 billion	to decontaminate existing nuclear weapons facilities
$10 billion	to treat and dispose of transuranic waste and low-level waste from nuclear weapons facilities
$1 billion	already spent on the Yucca Mountain repository for disposal of commercial spent fuel and military high-level waste
$0.5-1 billion	annual cost of Superfund program at Department of Defense facilities
$700 million	already spent on the Waste Isolation Pilot Plant at Carlsbad, New Mexico
$100 million	annual cost for DOE's environmental activities at uranium mill tailings sites
$73 million	settlement with residents of Fernald, Ohio, for long-term health and environmental monitoring
$60 million	already spent to survey Superfund sites at DOE facilities
$36 million	to computerize health records of employees at DOE's nuclear weapons facilities

NOTE: See text for documentation. Costs of proposed actions are approximations prepared by federal agencies and are not related to specific budget requests or program requirements. Estimates remain controversial and are more indicative of the scale of the problems than of estimates of specific program items.

CONCLUSION

What does all this mean for the urban areas that host this conglomeration of nuclear weapons facilities and military bases? The toxic legacy of weapons production will persist in a variety of forms. Some sites—Rocky Mountain Arsenal and Rocky Flats Plant being two examples—may never be restored and are likely to become sacrifice areas. Portions of some facilities may have to be entombed in concrete and the land set off-limits to human entry. In urban areas, thousands of acres of otherwise high-value real estate may have to be

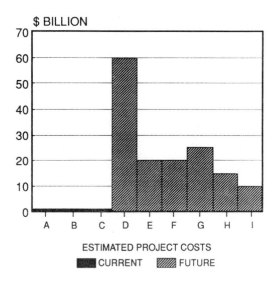

Figure 7.2. Environmental Costs of Weapons Production

NOTE: A = annual cost of DOD Superfund program; B = WIPP; C = Yucca Mountain; D = cleanup of DOE inactive waste sites; E = upgrade of DOE nuclear plants; F = treatment of DOE HLW; G = restructuring DOE weapons complex; H = decontamination of DOE nuclear plants; I = treatment of DOE transuranic and LLW.

abandoned. Perceptions of hazards and concerns about continued exposure to toxic and radioactive materials may result in de facto abandonment, regardless of assurances from government agencies that the land is safe. Local economies and governments will be denied revenue and the possibility of ever putting that land to socially beneficial uses.

Waste from military sites must be handled, processed, packaged, and transported through urban areas before it can be stored in waste repositories such as WIPP in New Mexico. Uncertainties about the health and environmental effects of these activities persist for workers as well as for residents in the vicinity of plants, transportation routes, and disposal facilities.

Intergenerational inequities created by weapons-related pollution are already evident in the form of elevated rates of birth defects, cancer, thyroid conditions, and other as-yet-unidentified health problems. To this we must add the genetic damage wreaked on local food chains and populations of flora and fauna. Such impacts may become evident as epidemiological and other research is conducted on people living near production plants, workers employed by them, and children raised within the shadows of these plants. These intergenerational inequities will persist as future populations must fund environmental cleanups and the care of injured offspring. Current plans foresee cleanup of DOE's nuclear weapons plants extending over the next 25 years. But cleanup may be protracted, as long as a high-level waste repository is unavailable.

At the local level, citizens have been forced to bear the burden of diligence. The health and environmental effects of these sites must be monitored for decades or, in the case of nuclear waste repositories, for thousands of years. An even more difficult impact to quantify is how environmental contamination and purposeful deceit by federal agencies have left many communities with lingering distrust of a government that set the priority of national security above that of protecting the health of its own citizens and environment. How ironic that more deaths should result from government negligence and mismanagement of the nuclear weapons complex than in confrontations with the evil empire those weapons were intended to deter.

Finally, any peace dividend associated with reduced arms production and military facilities pales in comparison to the human health costs and environmental debts incurred over the last 50 years. In short, there is no peace dividend—only, as Secretary of Energy Watkins (1989) has said, a situation in which some very difficult and dirty chickens have finally come home to roost. It is irresponsible to talk in terms of what the peace dividend will buy us in other social goods until we recognize and address this tragic human and environmental legacy of weapons production.

REFERENCES

Day, J. (1989, November 30). Trouble at Rocky Flats/chronology. *Rocky Mountain News*, p. 24.

DOE closes Idaho plants to bring HLW piping up to RCRA standards. (1989, November 9). *Nuclear Waste News*, pp. 411-412.

GAO, CBO charge DOE cost, time estimates on weapons reactors faulty. (1989, May 29). *Inside Energy/with Federal Lands*.

Graf, T. (1990, April 3). Clean up all plutonium at Flats, says Schroeder. *Denver Post*.

Inspector general impunes DOE environmental surveys of facilities. (1989, August 14). *Inside Energy/with Federal Lands*.

Insurers see nuclear exposure health claims increasing. (1989, July 13). *Nuclear Waste News*, p. 251.

Jacob, G. (1990). *Site unseen: The politics of siting a nuclear waste repository*. Pittsburgh: University of Pittsburgh Press.

Johnson, C. (1981). Cancer incidence in an area contaminated with radionuclides near a nuclear installation. *Ambio, 10*, 176-182.

Johnson, C. (1987). Re: Cancer incidence patterns in the Denver metropolitan area in relation to the Rocky Flats Plant [Letter to the editor]. *American Journal of Epidemiology, 126*, 153-155.

Johnson, C. (1988). Re: Mortality among plutonium and other radiation workers at a plutonium weapons facility [Letter to the editor]. *American Journal of Epidemiology, 127*, 1321-1323.

National Research Council, Committee to Assess Safety and Technical Issues at DOE Reactors. (1987). *Safety issues at the defense production reactors: A report to the U.S. Department of Energy.* Washington, DC: National Academy Press.

National Research Council, Committee to Provide Interim Oversight of the DOE Nuclear Weapons Complex. (1989). *The nuclear weapons complex: Management for health, safety, and the environment.* Washington, DC: National Academy Press.

Schneider, K. (1989a, December 14). Nuclear tests' legacy of anger. *New York Times.*

Schneider, K. (1989b, August 3). Senate panel describes data on nuclear risks. *New York Times.*

Schneider, K. (1990, January 17). Energy dept. plans to study effects of beryllium at nuclear plants. *New York Times.*

Stevens, W., Thomas, D., Lyon, J., Till, J., Kerber, R., Simon, S., Lloyd, R., Elghany, N., & Preston-Martin, S. (1990). Leukemia in Utah and radioactive fallout from the Nevada Test Site. *Journal of the American Medical Association, 264*, 585-591.

U.S. General Accounting Office. (1988a). *Nuclear health and safety: Dealing with problems in the nuclear defense complex is expected to cost over $100 billion* (U.S. GAO/RCED-88-197BR). Washington, DC: Government Printing Office.

U.S. General Accounting Office. (1988b). *Nuclear waste: Problems associated with DOE's inactive waste sites* (U.S. GAO/RCED-88-169). Washington, DC: Government Printing Office.

U.S. General Accounting Office. (1988c). *Nuclear waste: Supplementary information on problems at DOE's inactive waste sites* (U.S. GAO/RCED-88-229FS). Washington, DC: Government Printing Office.

U.S. General Accounting Office. (1989). *Nuclear waste: DOE's management of single-shell tanks at Hanford, Washington* (U.S. GAO/RCED-89-157). Washington, DC: Government Printing Office.

U.S. General Accounting Office. (1990). *Nuclear waste: DOE's program to prepare high-level radioactive waste for final disposal* (U.S. GAO/RCED-90-46FS). Washington, DC: Government Printing Office.

Wartzman, R. (1989, August 30). Rockwell bomb plant is repeatedly accused of poor safety record. *Wall Street Journal.*

Watkins announces ten point plan for environmental protection, waste management (R-89-068). (1989, June 27). *DOE News.*

Watkins, J. (1989). [Remarks]. In U.S. Department of Energy Press Release No. R-89-068. Washington, DC: Government Printing Office.

8

Escaping the Conceptual Box:
Ideological and Economic Conversion

MARVIN WATERSTONE
ANDREW KIRBY

MILITARY SPENDING HAS BEEN an accepted, if tacit, industrial policy in the United States for at least five decades (Hooks, 1990). Its perpetuation is due in part to economic exigencies and in part to ideo-logical conceptions of the appropriate role of the modern nation-state. Opportunities for examining the desirability or the effectiveness of this industrial policy have been all too rare. A new orientation toward military spending requires some fundamental adjustments in global geopolitics as well as some redefinition of power. As inconceivable as such changes might have seemed only a year or two ago, recent events in Eastern Europe and the Soviet Union provide an indication that such changes are possible, and that opportunities to rethink our military spending policies are at hand.

However, it is equally the case that as Cold War tensions have begun to recede, members of the military-industrial establishment have been assiduously seeking out acceptable substitutes that will keep military spending at desired levels. By turn, these surrogates have included other potential foreign enemies (Arafat, Ortega, Noriega, Khadafi), the War on Drugs (both at home and abroad), and the protection of oil flows out of the Middle East.

As we observe these machinations, it quickly becomes clear that there is a tremendous concern, in many quarters, about the outbreak of peace and the economic consequences of such an eventuality. Hopes and expectations of a "peace dividend" emerging as a result of diminished Cold War tensions have been quickly dispelled by events. Why does a reduction in military expenditures remain such an elusive

TABLE 8.1

Federal Government Expenditures, Percentage of Total Outlay (1991 estimates)

	1976	*1986*	*1991*
Defense	23.2	26.2	31.2
Social security	19.2	19.7	22.5
Income security	15.7	11.6	11.3
Health	8.2	10.3	11.9
Net interest	6.9	14.0	10.0
Education	4.9	3.0	2.2
Veterans	4.8	2.6	2.3
Transportation	3.6	2.7	2.0
Agriculture	0.8	2.6	1.0
Miscellaneous	12.8	7.3	5.6

SOURCE: Data from the Office of Management and Budget.

prospect? The answer resides in both the historical path that has led to our present position and the current nature of both military spending and contracting, as well as in the institutions that have grown up around these activities. In this chapter, we want to explore these aspects as well as propose a possible escape from our current dilemma.

HISTORICAL OVERVIEW

In the United States, the proportion of the federal budget allocated to military expenditure has continued to increase steadily since the Korean War, and as nuclear technology has increased in sophistication, so have the funds allocated to its development (Table 8.1). We are, in consequence, in a unique, if protracted, period in our nation's evolution, with the existence of what has been called a "permanent war economy" (Melman, 1988). Its origins are to be found in ideological and political as well as economic arguments. The emergence of the present buildup coincided with the onset of the Cold War, a congruence that is not accidental.

Some observers trace the beginnings of the current arms race to the Soviet detonation of a nuclear device in 1950, and the subsequent presidential charge to the secretaries of state and defense to "undertake a re-examination of our objectives in peace and war and of the effect of these objectives on our strategic plans" (U.S. Department of State, 1977; cited by Mosley, 1985). These policy discussions produced

NSC-68, the National Security document that proposed a long-term buildup of U.S. forces. Although there was general agreement on the ideological content of NSC-68, there were fundamental disagreements regarding the ability of the country to fund such a continued arms buildup. Even during the immediate aftermath of World War II, the prevailing economic wisdom had suggested that military expenditures, except for very brief periods of national necessity, hurt rather than helped the general economy. In short, the country could produce either guns or butter, but not both.

The response of NSC-68's proponents was the development of the economic concept now known as "military Keynesianism," in which it is argued that military spending promotes economic growth through the stimulation of aggregate demand. To bolster their arguments, the supporters of this evolving concept pointed to the prosperity generated during World War II, and contrasted this with the developing recession of the postwar period: "The American economy, when it operates at a level approaching full efficiency, can provide enormous resources for purposes other than civilian consumption while simultaneously providing a high standard of living" (U.S. Department of State, 1977). Further, they argued that failure to stimulate the economy with these military expenditures could produce economic stagnation similar to that seen in the interwar period.

These ideological and strategic justifications of a permanent arms buildup, and of the feasibility of military Keynesianism as a way to finance it, were not without their critics. Bureau of the Budget analysts objected to both the foreign policy aspects of NSC-68 (i.e., the "free world" versus "slave world" concept) and its economic analysis. They suggested the basic incommensurability between wartime and peacetime economies, and tried to deny that a massive arms expansion would stimulate the economy to the point where marginal growth of GNP would pay for the buildup. Rather, they argued, such an enterprise would sap the strength of the civilian economy and divert resources and investment capital into nonproductive channels (Mosley, 1985, p. 11).

This debate was ended effectively by the outbreak of the Korean conflict in June 1950; rearmament took place, and at levels far beyond the immediate necessities of the conflict. In fact, the size and scope of the effort closely paralleled the course suggested in NSC-68. The Truman administration accepted the latter's tenets in September 1950, and subsequent administrations have accepted the notions embodied in the document with more or less enthusiasm ever since. As Mosley (1985) notes:

Military Keynesianism thus became, even when Keynesian theory was not yet fully accepted, a de facto policy for shoring up demand in the U.S. economy. It also created the essential institutional preconditions for government intervention in the form of countercyclical demand management through marginal shifts in military expenditure, even when it was not fully acknowledged or ineptly practiced—as during the Eisenhower administration. (p. 14)

Eisenhower was the least enthusiastic of the postwar presidents, stating on many occasions his personal skepticism as to the usefulness of military expenditures to benefit the economy. Military Keynesianism was most explicitly embraced during the Kennedy and Johnson presidencies, when military expenditures were used directly to stimulate the civilian sector. The Nixon, Ford, Carter, Reagan, and Bush administrations all pursued these policies, which have now become entrenched in the formal political discourse of federal spending. The lessons of World War II, Korea, and Vietnam appeared to vindicate this economic tool, although the current period of record federal deficits is beginning to show the fallacies of staying this particular course. The current fiscal situation can, therefore, be traced to the historical development of an economic rationale that underpins a militaristic stand. This means that efforts to evaluate the arms race that focus solely on ideological or security issues are doomed to failure. This is not to suggest that arms buildups are driven solely by economic factors, but rather that such factors play a critical, and underexamined, role. It may appear that debates over the Strategic Defense Initiative or other weapons should take place in the glare of national security, where the issue is clearest, but the reality is a little like the proverbial drunk searching for his keys beneath a street lamp, despite the fact that he lost them somewhere in the darkness. In short, we must avoid the simplicity of studying weapons solely *qua* weapons, and confront their existence as complex components of an equally complex political economy.

THE CONSEQUENCES OF A MILITARY ECONOMY

There are many factors that drive the production of materiel. By the time the initial research and development stages have been completed for new weapons, they begin to take on an economic life of their own. A constituency builds in support of the anticipated contracts and jobs that will be created; the controversial B-1 bomber, for example, is assembled from parts constructed in all 48 of the mainland states. The merits of a particular weapon system get lost in economic issues; currently, defense contracting in the United States is worth approximately $100 billion per year. It is also an extremely stable part of the economy in terms of the firms involved. The top 20 corporations have been in the defense industry for over 30 years and receive more than 50% of federal contracts; the largest 100 get about 75% (Gold, 1991). Many of them do more than half their business each year with the DOD. Moreover, the accounting system of DOD simplifies life for the major contractors. There is relatively little competition. A 1982 study, for example, indicates that in a region consisting of California, Washington, Oregon, Arizona, and Texas, a mere 10 corporations possessed defense contracts worth in excess of $13 billion. Moreover, cost-plus contracts, in which profitability is unrelated to the expenses of production (no matter how high), are highly desirable from the contractors' perspective, but also perpetuate corporate inefficiency.

Any discussion of reductions in military spending therefore invokes counterargument in economic terms. Such moves are seen to be costly in terms of employment—some 7 million jobs are at stake—and in terms of loss of local tax bases. If a search for mechanisms to reduce military spending is to be sustained, at least two things must occur. First, the public must be apprised of the economic and social consequences of the arms race itself (in addition to the consequences of using these arms); second, we must explore the economic alternatives to a military economy.

The tremendous costs of the arms buildup, both in the developed world and, indirectly (through the co-optation of vital resources), in the developing world, exact a massive human toll. Such costs are manifested in a variety of ways. First, it is useful to confront the alternative expenditures that could be undertaken, and some of these are illustrated in Table 8.2. This table is not meant to suggest that all resources diverted from military spending would be committed to social programs; rather, it highlights the ways in which military allocations are traded off against needed infrastructure and social programs in times of austere budgets. The nature of such trade-offs should, of course, be the product of social and political judgments, but their implications must be made clear so that appropriate choices can be made.

A second area of costs is in terms of trained personnel. It has been estimated that somewhere between 30% and 50% of all scientists and

TABLE 8.2

Cuts in Selected Federal Programs, FY 1983

(in millions of dollars)

Program	Amount Cut
Medicaid	680
Child nutrition	280
Supplemental security income	430
Elementary and secondary education	350
Guaranteed student loans	600
Pell grants	120
Energy and conservation	360
Community development block grants	510
Mass transit	500
Economic Development Administration	70
Food stamps	920
AFDC	950
Food program for women and infants	70
Legal services	70
Total	5,970

SOURCE: Data compiled by the Coalition for a New Foreign and Military Policy.

engineers in the United States are engaged currently in military-related work. Furthermore, of the approximately 61,000 engineers trained in the United States annually, one-third enter military-related activities. By comparison, Japan, which trains about 75,000 engineers annually, utilizes almost 98% of these personnel in civilian industrial work (Ullman, 1984, p. 168). Other categories of skilled personnel show similar disparities, and these displacements can be viewed as representing a tremendous opportunity cost. The skewed nature of federal research and development spending in the United States toward military research is summarized in Table 8.3 (see also Gold, 1991).

A third consequence of the arms race is the loss of competitiveness by U.S. firms. Many of these contractors (for the reasons stated above) have been described as "Pentagon junkies." For example, McDonnell Douglas has at times done as much as 80% of its business with DOD (Hartung & Mimroody, 1985, p. 200). As a result of an inherent difference between military and civilian production requirements, the cost of production is a secondary consideration, at best, due to the lack of competition and the cost-plus contracting system. This has led to spectacular failures by military contractors when they

TABLE 8.3

Federal Expenditures on Research and Development, 1986

Department or Agency	Percentage of Total
Defense	61.2
National Institutes of Health	10.4
Energy	10.0
NASA	7.4
NSF	2.8
Agriculture	2.0
Miscellaneous	4.3

SOURCE: Data from the Office of Management and Budget.

have attempted to compete in civilian markets. Examples are legion (DeGrasse, 1984, p. 15; Ullman, 1984, p. 167). Sufficient evidence is accumulating to document inability of these defense-dependent firms to produce competitive products in the civilian sector. In fact, their own recognition of this inability is one of the prime motivations behind their intensive lobbying efforts whenever a DOD contract is threatened, and is also one of the reasons the development of SDI technology has looked so attractive to these firms (Hartung & Mimroody, 1985).

Competitiveness is also decreasing as a result of a lack of reinvestment in traditional infrastructure (the U.S. steel or automobile industries provide two recent examples). As resources continue to be diverted extensively into the military segment of the economy, less is available for revitalizing the basic industries that provided our original economic vigor. These diversions also have clear sectoral and regional implications, as various chapters in this book have indicated (Yudken & Black, 1990).

A fourth economic consequence of the arms race is that the expenditures in the military buildup are dead-ended economically. These expenditures have not, to date, produced any reusable products. Despite all of the arguments to the contrary, these activities are technologically arcane and produce virtually no spin-off products; in fact, the ones that are cited most frequently have come from space-related programs, which, until recent shuttle flights, have been only tangentially military related (Dumas, 1982, pp. 13-14). Furthermore, military expenditures produce limited multiplier effects into the rest of the economy when compared with similar levels of civilian expenditure.

An unpublished 1986 study of regional multipliers undertaken by Employment Research Associates, based on *military* expenditure between 1981 and 1985, indicates that an averaged figure of an additional 0.23 million jobs would have been created via *civilian* spending.

Finally, the arms race produces a number of more subtle, but equally troubling, noneconomic consequences. The increasing militarization of society raises some disturbing questions about the tension between a war-ready posture and democratic freedoms. Attendant on the development of extensive war-fighting capabilities are a defensive mentality (i.e., we are always under siege from some quarter), the perceived need for secrecy, and the loss of public access to information of all types, all of which have been described as elements creating a "garrison state" (Fitch, 1985; Giddens, 1985).

ECONOMIC CONVERSION: THE WAY FORWARD?

Since the end of World War II, a number of analysts (principally economists) have been examining the possibility of converting military production to civilian output. In fact, the United States has undergone such conversions several times in the past. However, it is important to distinguish the types of conversions that occurred before and following World Wars I and II from the type that would be necessary if we are to alter our present course. The primary difference between the previous attempts at conversion and our present situation is that in the former cases we were attempting to reconvert military facilities to their former role of civilian production. Today, that is not the case, for many firms have divisions involved in the armaments industry that have never experienced civilian production or marketing. This presents a very distinctive set of problems.

First of all, what is meant by the term *economic conversion*? In the most general sense, this concept is meant to encompass the physical and economic alteration of a plant or factory from producing one type of good or service to another. It would entail the formulation, planning, and execution of organizational, technical, occupational, and economic changes necessary to convert activities and facilities from their current output to a more socially useful, civilian set of goods and services. The targets for conversion would include basic industries, laboratories, training institutions, bases, and other facilities. Such an enterprise would yield a variety of benefits. First would be

TABLE 8.4

Employment Opportunities

(jobs per billions of dollars spent)[a]

Economic Sector	Number of Jobs
Missile production	29,402
Housing	30,899
Railroads	31,819
Public utility	38,192
Solar energy and conservation	38,650
Mass transit	45,397

SOURCE: Adapted from Council on Economic Priorities (1981), based on data from the U.S. Bureau of Labor Statistics.

a. In constant 1980 dollars.

the diversion of some resources (including fiscal, personnel, and expertise) to socially desirable production. Second, and contrary to widely held beliefs (which fuel many of the armament arguments), would be the creation of more jobs as the result of investment in civilian rather than military production. Table 8.4 illustrates a number of the potential trade-offs in terms of job creation by comparing expenditures in a variety of economic sectors. In addition to the creation of more jobs through investment in civilian activities, the mix of jobs would also be somewhat different. There would tend to be more jobs created for lower-skilled workers, and this could begin to address some of the problems of deskilling and unemployment in an era of complex economic restructuring (Harvey, 1989).

A third advantage of conversion would be an increase in both national and global security. This would occur for several reasons, notably, because the numbers of weapons would be decreased, reliance on weapons technology would be reduced, and, perhaps most important, the underlying causes of conflict would themselves be removed or at least reduced. By freeing up resources to meet human needs, we could begin to alleviate some of the collective suffering that underpins many conflict situations. Beyond this, the effort to take conversion seriously would have to be predicated upon a significant alteration in current thinking about geopolitics, such as that embodied in the garrison state view.

Of course, there are also a number of significant costs and obstacles to economic conversion. First, there would have to be a fundamental reorientation in political and corporate thinking. Many of today's arms contractors have never known, and do not want to know, another type of economic life. As noted above, the relationships among the Pentagon, Congress, and military contractors are still comfortable at present. This relationship, which has been called the "iron triangle," is characterized by revolving doors connecting the three institutions and mutual accommodation (Adams, 1984). Military contractors must be shown not only that civilian production is possible for them, but that it is actually in their long-term economic self-interest. This might be accomplished, at least in part, by a greater analysis of, and emphasis upon, the frequent boom/bust nature of military production. Such an assessment seems particularly timely in light of recent discourse on lowering military expenditures.

A second hurdle to be overcome entails the retraining of military production workers. This will undoubtedly require some federal government assistance during a transition period. In some cases, the retraining necessary will be minimal (e.g., in the conversion from the production of military to civilian aircraft); in others it might be quite extensive. A number of studies have begun to examine these retraining requirements, but much work remains to be done (Dumas, 1982, 1986; Gordon & McFadden, 1984). Retraining managers in military-related firms will also be necessary, and may prove to be much more difficult than retraining workers.

Third, economic conversion will require investment to alter plant and equipment capabilities to meet civilian production needs. Again, the level of needed investment will be highly variable, depending on the degree of congruity between current military activities and the production that supplants it. A fourth necessity is the process of identifying the appropriate civilian goods and services to substitute for current military production. Here several questions need to be addressed: (a) How will these products be identified? (b) Who will identify them? (c) What about the problem of the creation of unfair competition by federal government subsidization of converting industries? However, despite all of these difficulties, the promise of economic conversion and the benefits it offers far outweigh the potential disadvantages.

ECONOMIC CONVERSION IN PRACTICE

As the foregoing discussion has illustrated, the concept of conversion from military to civilian production has been raised many times.

However, the data to support or controvert the feasibility of such schemes have never been adequate to the task. It is true that there have been numerous efforts to collect such data on a macro scale, at highly aggregated levels of generality. It is also true that there have been a few studies that have tried to characterize individual conversions within particular plants. To date there has been no systematic research effort undertaken to inventory the resource base from which a concerted conversion might be launched. In the remainder of this chapter, therefore, we do four things. First, we give a brief outline of the role of federal spending in local economies, using data from Arizona to emphasize the substantial disparities that exist. We contrast the salience of military expenditures versus nonmilitary ones, and begin an analysis of Pima County that explores the recipients of contracts from defense organizations and other federal agencies. This indicates not only the respective *proportions* of spending, but, more important, the *types* of recipients within the civilian and military sectors in terms of corporate employment and the contribution to the local economy. We then use these data as a basis for some speculations on the implications of a reduction of federal spending on military contracts and the possibilities of economic conversion.

FEDERAL EXPENDITURE IN PIMA COUNTY

Pima County has a population of 683,000, approximately 20% of Arizona's total. The county contains the metropolitan area of Tucson, and is, like southern Arizona as a whole, heavily dependent upon tourism, tertiary services, and military activity for its employment. Major employers include the Davis-Monthan Air Force Base (7,767 employees, annual payroll $152 million) and Hughes Aircraft Corporation (6,500 employees, annual payroll $231 million). Although 1990 unemployment is below 4% (and thus below the national average), the economy has been damaged in the past decade by a number of external changes. First, the constant devaluation of the peso has affected retail trade in a community only 60 miles from Mexico. Second, continued falling prices for copper, plus increased environmental controls on copper smelting, have further damaged one of the "Copper State's" traditional economic activities. Third, the imprudent construction financed by the savings and loan industry and the subsequent crash have weakened the construction sector and badly damaged real estate prices.

TABLE 8.5

Defense Agencies and Contract Dollar Amounts,
Pima County, 1987

Agency	Total Contracts Awarded
Department of the Air Force	669,428,000
Department of the Navy	228,689,000
Department of the Army	169,016,000
Defense Logistics Agency	5,725,000
Office of the Secretary of Defense	685,000
Uniformed Service University of Health Sciences	26,000

SOURCE: Calculated by the authors using data obtained from Military Spending Research Services.

All these changes have contributed to public sensitivity to the role of federal spending in the local economy. Announcement of plans to close the Davis-Monthan base in June 1990 resulted in an immediate public meeting and a delegation of elected officials to Washington to plead for the survival of the facility, which is deemed to be worth $687 million annually to the local economy.[1]

The visibility of base closures and attempts to find alternative roles for these facilities (in the "drug war," for example) mask the centrality of other forms of federal spending in local economies. In 1987, for example, 42 different federal agencies had contracts with area businesses and directed more than $1.1 billion to Pima County. The bulk of these contracts (in dollar amounts) were for weapons-related purposes, and we examine these first.

TABLE 8.6

Recipients of Largest Contracts, Pima County, 1987

Contractor	Total Contracts Received
Hughes Aircraft Company	1,002,791,000
Darling Industries, Inc.	3,822,000
Garrett Enterprises	8,238,000
University of Arizona	3,136,000
Burr-Brown Corporation	629,000
IBM General Products Division	389,000
Learjet Corporation	208,000

SOURCE: Calculated by the authors using data obtained from Military Spending Research Services.

WEAPONS AND WEAPONS-RELATED CONTRACTS

The agencies shown in Table 8.5 distributed a total of $1,073.5 million in 1987 within Pima County. There is a skewed distribution in terms of the recipients of these contracts, with only seven contractors accounting for in excess of 94% of the contract value (see Table 8.6). Table 8.6 could in turn be simplified, insofar as the Hughes Aircraft Company alone accounts for 93.4% of weapons-related contracts, a total in excess of $1 billion.

These tables reveal that military spending, on weapons, weapons-related systems, and the maintenance of military facilities, involves significant dollar amounts. This notwithstanding, it is not clear that the multiplier effects of the billion dollars spent in Pima County are large. Hughes, for example, employed only 6,500 persons in 1988, which was 1,000 persons fewer than in 1987; projections for 1992 will reduce that number to 4,000 persons. (The next three ranked firms, Burr-Brown, Garrett, and Darling, which received very much smaller contracts, still contributed significantly to the local economy, with 1,250, 360, and 278 persons employed, respectively.)

These data do not address the existence of subcontractors, who typically receive between 40% and 60% of the dollar amount of any contract; for Hughes, for example, the figure is approximately 50% (personal communication with Hughes personnel, 1990). These companies are frequently small and highly specialized, and are consequently not necessarily close to major corporations. Case studies show, therefore, that while a prime contractor or ordnance plant may be a major employer, the multiplier effects for the immediate locality can be small. A study of the Mare Island shipyard in Vallejo, California, for instance, indicated that skilled personnel were recruited regionally and nationally, rather than locally, with the result that prosperity existed amid high rates of unemployment. Contracts tended to go repeatedly to established suppliers, and procurement practices excluded local corporations, who in this instance made up only 13% of the shipyard's suppliers (Schneider & Patton, 1988).

CIVILIAN CONTRACT EXPENDITURES

As noted above, a large number of nondefense agency contracts were issued in the county in 1987, which summed to $101,138,000. These are summarized in Table 8.7; only contract totals in excess of $100,000 are noted.[2] Two things can be inferred easily from this table. The first is that the spread of contracts is much larger than in

TABLE 8.7

Total Disbursement of Federal Nonweapons Contracts,

Pima County, 1987

Agency	Total Contracts Awarded
Bureau of Reclamation	46,530,000
National Science Foundation	25,072,000
National Aeronautics and Space Administration	4,316,000
Bureau of Prisons	3,786,000
Veterans Administration	3,718,000
Health Services Administration	3,209,000
Agency for International Development	2,894,000
Bureau of Indian Affairs	1,491,000
Social Security Administration	1,457,000
Office of the Assistant Secretary for Health	1,333,000
National Institutes of Health	858,000
Environmental Protection Agency	718,000
Department of Energy	692,000
Health Resources Administration	655,000
Nuclear Regulatory Commission	465,000
National Park Service	437,000
Office of Public Buildings	337,000
Office of Personnel Management	295,000
Forest Service	287,000
Tennessee Valley Authority	280,000
Bureau of Land Management	276,000
Administration for Children, Youth, and Families	260,000
Bureau of the Census	201,000
Foreign Agricultural Service	151,000
Coast Guard	125,000
Internal Revenue Service	105,000

SOURCE: Calculated by the authors using data obtained from Military Spending Research Services.

the defense agency sector; second, the dollar amounts are inevitably much smaller. These factors have a number of important implications for our analysis.

Table 8.7 gives some hints as to the wide range of contracts that are made by nondefense agencies. Although a significant number are related to technological research and development, an equally large number are devoted to very basic activities such as waste removal and treatment and the payment of utilities. It is impossible to estimate the numbers of employees supported, even in part, by these disbursements. It is interesting to note, however, that the total of civilian contracts, as we are characterizing them here, is in fact greater than the total of disbursements made by defense agencies *outside the very narrow category of weapons production*. As we saw in Table 8.6, almost all the defense dollars coming into Pima County are channeled to Hughes Aircraft for missile production, a category that is, at the time of this writing, under scrutiny by the secretary of defense.

In summary, then, we can liken weapons spending to a funnel; a number of agencies generate a large number of contracts, but these become concentrated to a very small number of primary manufacturers, and an unknown number of subcontractors, both in and out of state. In contrast, nonweapons spending involves much smaller amounts but places them much more widely, creating a root network that spreads throughout the local economy. While the cessation of contracts to a manufacturer like Hughes would have repercussions for the Pima economy, we can see that the impacts are identifiable and finite, and the numbers of jobs involved are also relatively small. The cessation of civilian contracts would have wider implications in many more sectors of the economy.

CONVERSION STRATEGIES

Although Pima County classes itself as a defense-oriented locality, we can see that the defense contracting sector is in reality very narrow, a finding that is echoed elsewhere. This notwithstanding, any attempt to switch off the pipeline of DOD funds will meet with great opposition within the locality, as has happened recently in San Diego, which receives about $2.6 billion per annum in contracts. There, local politicians have proposed a "Dollar-for-Dollar Act," which would simply shift all military cuts (including those related to bases and home ports) to civilian purposes, such as drug prevention and public works ("San Diego," 1990).

The likelihood of such legislation is small, for two reasons. First, defense cuts are being predicated, in large measure, on the problems of the federal deficit, for, as noted above, there are always new political versions of "the other" that can be used to justify militarism (Enloe, 1989). Consequently, overall savings will be sought, rather than a blanket redirection of funds. Second, there is an increased groundswell of support for improving the efficacy of social programs, as many American cities are seen to be sliding precipitately toward new crises of health care (notably with respect to AIDS), drug dependency, and drug-related crime. Again, within the context of deficit reduction, such funds will be distributed competitively, and any legislation that automatically directs social spending to relatively prosperous cities such as Tucson or San Diego is unlikely.

This is not to argue conversion out of court. The simplest and most effective argument in its favor remains that a dollar spent on a defense contract can have very limited impacts on the locality. Base closures may be serious in the short term, but long-term studies suggest that civilian jobs reappear, and in higher numbers.[3] Even a simple analysis such as that undertaken here shows that nonweapon spending goes directly to local employers who recruit within the locality, whereas weapons contracts contribute to the corporate profits of transnational firms and their many subcontractors.

Our conclusion is that residents and growth interests in cities such as Tucson should face the shrinkage of the weapons sector with equanimity, and should see the possibility of base closure as a short-term economic problem (President's Economic Adjustment Committee, 1989). The large defense corporations in the locality are responsible for serious air-quality problems, and constant overflights by the military are antithetical to a city trying to develop a tourism industry.[4] In Logan and Molotch's (1987) terms, as far as use values are concerned, the loss of defense spending would be a plus; in terms of exchange values, the picture is not at all bleak.

NOTES

1. Department of Defense estimates are lower, at $386 million; these do not include the expenditures of military retirees, who are assumed to move with the base in the city's calculations.

2. The following agencies had contract disbursements below $100,000 in 1987: Science and Education Administration ($34,000); Food and Drug Administration ($29,000); Geological Survey ($44,000); Immigration and Naturalization Service ($46,000); Employment and Training Administration ($70,000); Customs Service ($48,000); Federal Law Enforcement Training ($87,000); Equal Employment Opportunity Commission ($24,000); U.S. Information Agency ($11,000).

3. A DOD (1989) study of 100 bases closed between 1961 and 1986 showed 131,138 civilian jobs replacing 93,424 DOD or contractor jobs.

4. Hughes Aircraft alone was responsible for more than 611,000 pounds of toxic emissions into the atmosphere in 1989, more than two-thirds the recorded total for the city ("Tucson Firms Emitting," 1990). As Hughes has slowed production, air pollution has dropped proportionately.

REFERENCES

Adams, G. (1984). *The politics of defense contracting: The iron triangle.* New Brunswick, NJ: Transaction.

Council on Economic Priorities. (1981). *Misguided expenditures: An analysis of the proposed MX missile system.* New York: Author.

DeGrasse, R. W., Jr. (1984). The military economy. In S. Gordon & D. McFadden (Eds.), *Economic conversion: Revitalizing America's economy* (pp. 3-18). Cambridge, MA: Ballinger.

Dumas, L. J. (Ed.). (1982). *The political economy of arms reduction: Reversing economic decay.* Boulder, CO: Westview.

Dumas, L. J. (1986). *The overburdened economy: Uncovering the causes of chronic unemployment, inflation and national decline.* Berkeley: University of California Press.

Enloe, C. H. (1989). *Bananas, beaches and bases.* London: Pandora.

Fitch, J. S. (1985). The garrison state in America. *Journal of Peace Research, 22,* 32-45.

Giddens A. (1985). *The nation state and violence.* Cambridge: Polity.

Gold, D. (1991, January-February). Military R&D a poor scapegoat for flagging economy. *Bulletin of Atomic Scientists,* pp. 38-43.

Gordon, S., & McFadden, D. (Eds.). (1984). *Economic conversion: Revitalizing America's economy.* Cambridge, MA: Ballinger.

Hartung, W., & Mimroody, R. (1985). Cutting up the Star Wars pie. *The Nation, 241*(7), 200-202.

Harvey, D. (1989). *The condition of postmodernity.* Oxford: Basil Blackwell.

Hooks, G. (1990, September). *The material foundations of economic planning: Federal investment policies during World War II.* Paper presented at the annual meeting of the American Political Science Association, San Francisco.

Logan, J., & Molotch, H. (1987). *Urban fortunes: The political economy of place.* Berkeley: University of California Press.

Melman, S. (1988). Economic consequences of the arms race: The second rate economy. *Papers and Proceedings of the American Economics Association, 78*(2), 55-59.

Mosley, H. G. (1985). *The arms race: Economic and social consequences.* Lexington, MA: D. C. Heath.

President's Economic Adjustment Committee. (1989). *Diversifying defense dependent communities.* Washington, DC: Pentagon, Office of Economic Adjustment.

San Diego: A city in search of a peace dividend. (1990). *Bulletin of Municipal Foreign Policy 4*(3), 19.

Schneider, J., & Patton, W. (1988). Urban and regional effects of military spending: A case study of Vallejo, California and Mare Island Shipyard. In M. J. Breheny (Ed.), *Defence expenditure and regional development* (pp. 173-188). London: Mansell.

Tucson firms emitting less toxins in air. (1990, September 4). *Arizona Daily Star,* p. 3B.

Ullman, J. E. (1984). Can business become a participant? In S. Gordon & D. McFadden (Eds.), *Economic conversion: Revitalizing America's economy* (pp. 164-174). Cambridge, MA: Ballinger.

U.S. Department of Defense. (1989). *Twenty-five years of civilian reuse.* Washington DC: Pentagon, Office of Economic Adjustment.

U.S. Department of State. (1977). *Foreign relations of the United States, 1950.* Washington, DC: Government Printing Office.

Yudken, J. S., & Black, M. (1990, Spring). Targeting national needs. *World Policy Journal,* pp. 251-288.

9

Epilogue: The Pentagon,
the Cities, and Beyond

MARVIN WATERSTONE

IN THE PRECEDING CHAPTERS, the authors have characterized
the relationships between military spending and its impacts, particularly as applied to urban areas. The scale of these investigations
has varied from the global (Ettlinger) through the national (Hall
& Markusen; Jacob) and regional (Barff) and finally to local,
urban (Parker & Feagin; Waterstone & Kirby), and rural (Armitage)
effects.

In addition to Ettlinger's chapter, which suggests how military
industrial firms might fit into more general development theory,
these chapters provide insightful overviews into the history, magnitude, distribution, and effects of military spending in the United
States. Taken together, the chapters offer a variety of perspectives
on the evolutionary nature of military spending and a sense of both
the structural characteristics of U.S. defense expenditure and its
particular manifestations on several relevant scales.

In this epilogue, I want to accomplish two related purposes.
First, I would like to extend the examination of the impacts of military spending that the other authors have begun, and focus this examination more directly on impacts in urban areas. Second, I
would like to try to situate the role of military spending and militarism in a somewhat broader political-economic framework in order
to make a few predictions about the future shape of military spending and its impacts.

THE IMPACTS OF MILITARY SPENDING
ON URBAN AREAS

In the foregoing chapters, the authors have documented a wide variety of positive and negative effects of military spending in the United States, particularly over the last five decades. These have ranged from infusions of capital and technical support to the legacy of hazardous wastes. In extending these explorations, I examine the nature of such spending in more detail, and, second, I draw out some more explicit linkages between military expenditures and impacts on cities, especially in terms of opportunity costs.

The first distinction to draw is in the nature of military spending per se. In very general terms, it is possible to place these expenditures in two categories: personnel, and goods and services. Understanding the composition of the mix is extremely important for identifying effects on such factors as employment, social services, and municipal multipliers. Over the last 20 years, the mix of military expenditures has been undergoing dramatic restructuring. For example, in 1972 the split between expenditures on personnel and on goods and services was about equal. During the 1980s, however, the former category was receiving only 33% of the military budget, while the latter had increased to account for the remaining two-thirds (Beneria & Blank, 1989, p. 192).

One important effect of the changing mix of expenditures is on the magnitude and composition of resulting employment. Military expenditures can affect employment either through spending on personnel or through the purchase of goods and services through the private sector. The differences are critical for examining employment-related factors (e.g., multipliers in terms of local expenditures).

MILITARY EXPENDITURE FOR PERSONNEL

In this spending category, the numbers and types of workers employed are directly related to current military needs. According to Sivard (1989, p. 50), the United States had just over 2 million military personnel in 1986. However, this figure can vary substantially over time. For example, given recent events in Eastern Europe and the apparent improvement in U.S.-Soviet relations, Secretary of Defense Cheney has proposed troop reductions of 25% by the year 1995. What would this mean for local and regional economies?

Except in times of conflict, many of these personnel are stationed at bases in the United States, often located near, and providing expenditures for, urban areas. Clearly, one implication of lowering direct military employment or shifting military spending from personnel to goods and services would be a change in dollar flow from military personnel into the local economies of which they are a part. Direct expenditures on local goods and services, education, off-base housing, and the like decline substantially as fewer personnel are employed directly by the military. This is not to suggest that such declines cannot be offset or replaced over time. However, it does account for much of the overt concern over potential base closings and downsizing of the military.

Another aspect of interest here is the gender, racial, and ethnic composition of this labor force. Although the number of women in the military is increasing, this employment force is still largely male. Currently, approximately 10% of both enlisted personnel and the officer corps of the U.S. armed forces is female and, disproportionately, minority (Beneria & Blank, 1989, p. 194). The male segment of the armed forces is also disproportionately made up of minorities. In recent years, the all-volunteer army—with its slick advertising, enticing men and women to "be all that you can be"—has been viewed as a source of employment, job training, and financing for education largely unavailable through other mechanisms. For many, especially members of racial or ethnic minorities, the military is the only avenue for attaining such ends.

Military service has also provided a number of other rewards, including low-interest loans, hiring preferences, and health benefits (Beneria & Blank, 1989, p. 195). To the extent that the military has been dominated by males, these additional benefits have been closed to women. For urban areas, these benefits often translate into the provision of goods and services (e.g., health and counseling, housing, education) and additional employment (based on military skills and training) to those leaving military services. The magnitude and nature of such local economic effects will depend to a great extent on the gender, racial, and ethnic mix of those in the armed forces.

One final component of direct military employment merits some discussion. Many individuals have been able to access a wide variety of military-related benefits (including wages, retirement pensions, and health benefits) by serving in reserve or National Guard units. As is often the case with volunteer army personnel, these so-called weekend warriors usually join for additional income, retirement benefits,

or training opportunities. The additional income helps fuel local economies, and the retirement benefits may also be advantageous for pro-
viders of local products and services. However, one underappreciated
aspect of this facet of military spending is the impact on local economies and infrastructures when these units are activated. Again, while
this is an infrequent event, the recent call-ups in connection with the
Desert Shield and Desert Storm operations demonstrate the extreme
dislocation for localities when significant numbers of their service-
aged populations are called to duty.

MILITARY EXPENDITURE FOR GOODS AND SERVICES

Employment stemming from contracting (i.e., the purchase of military goods and services in the private sector via the federal procurement process) takes on very different characteristics (for instance, in
spending on personnel) and therefore produces substantially different
local economic effects. The employment mix depends on the types of
goods and services being purchased. In recent years, as several of the
chapters in this volume indicate, expenditures have increasingly been
focused on weapons and weapon systems, frequently utilizing high-
technology processes. The industrial categories that receive the bulk
of military contracting dollars include guided missiles, aircraft, aircraft parts, shipbuilding, electronics, and radio and other communication equipment. Military expenditures in heavy equipment and
manufacturing (e.g., for the production of tanks and personnel carriers) have declined in both relative and absolute terms.

These types of disbursements have important implications for the
employment mix in terms of skill categories as well as gender, race,
and ethnic composition. Much of the expenditure goes to highly
skilled (and high-wage) professionals: engineers, mathematicians,
physicists, and some technical workers. These professions tend to be
dominated by white males: In the major military-industrial categories,
77% of employees are male. Women and minority workers, therefore,
are underrepresented in this indirect military employment.

Finally, it is important to assess the relative strength of multiplier
effects of military goods versus civilian production (Waterstone &
Kirby address this issue in some detail in Chapter 8). Here, it is important only to note one fundamental difference between military and
civilian goods. The multiplier effects attached to a civilian product
include not only the employment and materials used to manufacture
the good initially, but, frequently, additional labor and income derived

from the prolonged use of that good. This is not the case with most military goods, and is particularly not the case with weapons. This fact should be considered by economic planners when they are considering the relative merits of investment in military versus civilian production activities.

OPPORTUNITY COSTS AND MILITARY SPENDING

As several of the chapters in this book have indicated, U.S. cities are facing a wide variety of crises, including homelessness, widespread poverty and hunger, drug-related violence and crime, health and safety issues (including AIDS), deteriorating infrastructure and transportation networks, air pollution, and a host of others. While it is not clear that these problems could be resolved by throwing money at them, it is fairly evident that a lack of resources is inhibiting their timely resolution. The president, as well as many state and local politicians, have taken up the chant of "no new taxes." The result is a zero-sum game. Increased expenditure in one sector means decreased resources available somewhere else. The massive military budget increases through most of the 1980s translated into reduced spending in other segments of the economy, most notably (and unsurprisingly) for social programs aimed at those who have been least powerful politically (i.e., the poor, women, and minorities). The result is that women and minorities are not only disadvantaged in terms of employment by shifts in military spending as just discussed, they are also harmed by budget cuts in social programs that provide at least a minimal safety net.

SUMMARY

Cities are affected by military spending in three important ways: through direct expenditures for military personnel who may reside in or near a particular locality and participate in the local and regional economy; through expenditures on contracted goods and services, which affect the employment mix in particular local economies and therefore the consequent multiplier stream; and, finally, through the imposition of opportunity costs that affect local abilities to deal with the myriad problems of modern urban life.

It seems increasingly clear that localities that become heavily dependent on military spending are vulnerable to periodic shifts in such spending. This is true for both personnel expenditures and contracted goods and services. Each of these areas undergoes cyclical patterns, as military needs for personnel wax and wane, and as the mix of military products and services changes. This type of vulnerability, and the accompanying economic uncertainty, is highly undesirable from the perspective of economic planning.

Do local-level planners have any alternatives? The 1991 crisis in the Persian Gulf notwithstanding, the military remains an attractive employment and training opportunity for many young people. In fact, for some, particularly minority youth, this is the only legitimate opportunity currently offered by society. As government budgets (at all levels) are constricted, many firms look to military contracts as a stable source of income. So, in a time of economic uncertainty, many individuals and firms (and the local and regional economies of which they are a part) see military spending as the one remaining area of federal government largess. The infrastructure that now constitutes our "military-industrial complex" has shown remarkable growth, persistence, flexibility, and stability since 1945. Why should this be so? Can the durability of this institution be explained simply on economic grounds, or is the explanation more subtle and complex? It is to these issues that I turn in the next section.

THE ROLE OF MILITARISM: WHITHER OR WITHER THE PEACE DIVIDEND?

Prediction is always a dangerous enterprise. In times of rapid social change, it is a particularly precarious undertaking. The chapters in this book offer testimony to this. Together, the authors have presented both a cautionary tale regarding the impacts of military spending and some glimmers of hope about reducing the downside of such effects in the future. Several have pointed to the remarkable series of events that took place at the end of the 1980s, culminating in the symbolic, and then the actual, razing of the Berlin Wall, the end of the Cold War, the dismantling of the Warsaw Pact apparatus, the apparent alliance of the superpowers in attempting to thwart Saddam Hussein, and several others. While many saw (and continue to see) in such events the possibility of reductions in military spending, and a concomitant redirection of resources toward the nonmilitary side of the federal budget—the so-called peace dividend—it is now becoming clear that such a windfall is unlikely to appear.

There are a number of ways in which one might account for the rapid dissipation of optimism. One is that, given the general disarray of the federal budget (including the enormous deficit, the unfolding savings and loan crisis, and the reluctance of the president and public to increase federal revenues), it was simply unrealistic to expect that savings in the military sector would translate into social spending. A second is that such savings would not materialize in any event. Although Cold War tensions between the East and West may have decreased, this does not mean that military activity (or spending) will decline. Rather, such activities are merely transferred to other arenas (the drug war, low-intensity conflicts, counterterrorism, and so forth). A third reason, connected to the second, goes to the heart of the role of militarism in modern society.

In this section I want to examine the issue of whether the military state will one day just wither away. Most of the discussion over military spending can be divided into two main areas: (a) arguments over increased or decreased security, and (b) arguments over economic benefits or disbenefits. In other words, arguments over effectiveness and/or efficiency: Does our military spending buy what it is supposed to buy, and is it worth the cost? The terms of debate for the first type of argument are generally over the kinds of weapons to be purchased and the relative levels of spending on personnel versus weapons. The parameters for the second type usually focus on the "guns or butter" issue (i.e., how much we should spend on the military versus the civilian side of our economy).

The arguments, framed in either of these ways, miss an essential aspect of militarism. Specifically, such arguments do not really consider the essential functions that militarism and military activities play within society. Whose interests and what values are served by the continuation of a strong military force? Aside from the obvious opportunities a strong military presents for foreign projections of power and international coercion (which I do not wish to downplay), what other vital components of state evolution and reproduction are served by a militaristic structure? How are militarism and aggression related to masculinity, and how are these characteristics related, in turn, to foreign imperialism and patriarchal power at home and abroad?

MASCULINITY, AGGRESSION, AND MILITARISM

In *The Parable of the Tribes*, Andrew Schmookler (1984) makes the argument that power and aggression, though not necessarily inherent in human nature, are unavoidably a part of human circumstance. To paraphrase the parable's argument, with the rise of civilization came the ability to transcend the limits placed upon humanity by the natural world. This, in turn, led to conflicts between social units as they sought to escape resource scarcities in a finite world. The new limits were other societies rather than natural ones. As Schmookler puts it, "In such circumstances, a Hobbesian struggle for power among societies becomes inevitable. We see that *what is freedom from the point of view of each single unit is anarchy in an ungoverned system of those units.* . . . civilized people were compelled to enter a struggle for power" (p. 20).

Given the advent of power in this way, Schmookler argues that only four possible options exist for social units faced with aggression: destruction, absorption and transformation, withdrawal, and imitation. He frames the argument in terms of the parable of the tribes: "In an anarchic situation . . . no one can choose that the struggle for power shall cease. . . . *no one is free to choose peace, but anyone can impose upon all the necessity for power.* This is the lesson of the parable of the tribes" (p. 21).

In Schmookler's view, "Power is like a contaminant, a disease, which once introduced will gradually yet inexorably become universal in the system of competing societies. . . . *A selection for power among civilized societies is inevitable.* . . . This is the new evolutionary principle that came into the world with civilization" (p. 22). Yet is this view of the origin of power and social aggression apt? As Schmookler himself states, "The idea is simple" (p. 22). Where, in this view, is the role of human choice, of human responsibility? Schmookler insists that the inevitable progression from egalitarian primitivism through the Hobbesian anarchy brought by the advent of civilization eliminated human volition and replaced it with the four alternatives just articulated. The appeal of this *deus ex machina* is seductive. It absolves us of a need for further examination. It allows us to elide the fundamental questions of who and what are served by aggressive social relations, ultimately resolved through threatened—or actual use of—coercive force.

These latter issues have been confronted in recent years by an expanding literature of feminist critique. For the sake of space, I pursue only one such argument here, and present it as a contrast to the parable of the tribes. My purpose is not to settle the issue, but simply to indicate the kinds of insights that are available if one is willing to shift the orientation of the question. In a recent article, Hartsock (1989) first builds upon the psychoanalytic arguments of Chodorow (1978) and Flax (1978), and then draws upon a variety of historical sources, to identify a series of relationships among masculinity, mortality, heroism, and, finally, militarism. In this argument, she first indicates that

> the key to understanding heroic action and masculine citizenship can be found in masculinity as ideology—a set of cultural institutions and practices that constitutes the norms and standards of masculinity. . . . I will argue that masculinity has been centrally structured by a linked fear of and fascination with the problems of death, mortality, and oblivion. These fears and fascinations have emerged in the West in many areas of social life but nowhere more importantly and dangerously than in politics and war. (p. 135)

In essence, Hartsock argues that men are much more concerned than women with the duality of existence (i.e., humans as both finite and infinite, mortal and immortal) and with issues of finitude, mortality, and the meaninglessness of a life that ends in death. In large part this is because men's lives "come to be structured by different issues than women's and that hierarchical and dualist modes of thought [are] generated by [these different experiences]. . . . the female is associated only with the body, not with godlike transcendence" (p. 137).

One way in which males confront death (and thereby establish their masculinity) is through contest, either ritual or actual. Drawing on the work of Walter Ong (1981) and the earlier work of Robert Stoller (1968), Hartsock (1989) contends that "masculinity is fundamentally defined by agonistic activity, by ritual combat of different sorts. . . . contest and combat are central to masculine identity" (p. 138). This concern with contest is important to the present argument because it can lead to, or become indistinguishable from, war. As Ong (1981) states: "Even war can be a kind of game, perhaps seasonal, in which killing is an objective only halfheartedly or incidentally achieved. The ancient Greeks called off their wars for the Olympic games and resumed them immediately afterward; psychologically, the wars and the games were somewhat equivalent" (p. 62). This statement was eerily echoed in the 1991 Superbowl game, the news media coverage and action of which were likened to—and interspersed with reports of—the war in the Persian Gulf.

A value linked to contest, and ultimately to masculinity and the need to confront meaningless existence, is heroism. As Hartsock argues, "For the last three thousand years of Western history, heroism has been the answer the men who have controlled societies have given to the problems of masculine embodiment; it has been an ideal they put forward as the highest human achievement" (p. 139). Hartsock documents the origins and early construction of heroism through an examination of Homer's *Iliad*. In her assessment, Hartsock indicates that heroism offers a solution to meaningless death through a series of four required steps: (a) the exclusion of women from important action, (b) a "zero-sum competition between the men" for honor (p. 140), (c) heroic action in which death can actually be confronted, and (d) abstraction—of the situation, of one's opponents, and of time. All of this leads to a denial of death (or of death's meaninglessness) through a social rebirth. As Hartsock states, "Whereas the first birth, from the body of a woman, is a death sentence, the second, through the bodily might of the man himself [i.e., through heroism], leads to immortality" (p. 141).

In the final part of the argument, Hartsock applies these Homeric conceptions to present circumstances. Here, she indicates, one may see the contemporary play of these critical elements of heroism in the conduct of foreign policy and military activities. First, women are prohibited (under U.S. law) from engaging in combat (although they may be present in combat areas, and may cheer on the troops from afar). Second, we have certainly developed a zero-sum game over honor. We demonize our enemies to the point where our gain can come only at the expense of their total loss. Further, the persistent chant in the 1991 Persian Gulf crisis of "No more Vietnams" indicates that much of that contest was over honor, and the elimination of the humiliation of previous defeat. Third, our foreign policy has been marked by repeated "brinkmanship" and flirtation with destruction; one need only recall the deadline of January 15, 1991, to put this element into focus. Finally, heroism requires abstraction. Here the language of the 1991 conflict is especially telling. The reports of tank kills, ordnance deliveries, pinpoint targeting, and the like are all aimed at sanitizing the conflict and removing the human consequences—in short, abstracting certain parts (for political and symbolic reasons) from the horrific whole.

Hartsock concludes, for "Achilles and Hektor, there could be no complete manhood without war. . . . [However, given today's capacity for mass destruction] human survival may well depend on breaking the linkage of masculinity with both military capacity and death" (p. 148). Given the historical evolution, breaking this linkage is a difficult task in itself. However, it is further complicated by the fact that militarism serves other vital functions for the modern state, and it is to these issues that I turn in the final section.

MILITARISM, THE STATE, AND SOCIAL RELATIONS

At the beginning, the United States maintained a steadfast opposition to militarism, the formation of large standing armies and military establishments. At the end of the revolutionary war, for example, George Washington disbanded the army and left the country's defense to the state militias. Early on, the Continental Congress expressed its views on militarism as follows: "Standing armies in times of peace are inconsistent with the principles of republican governments, dangerous to the liberties of free people, and generally converted into destructive engines for establishing despotism" (Dupuy, 1961, p. 38). When Washington requested establishment of a standing army several years later, he justified it by its small size.

This antimilitarist stand persisted until 1945. Although the United States engaged in numerous conflicts over this long period, the military contracted whenever hostilities ended. After World War II, this was not the case. As Lens (1987) describes, the country engaged in a tremendous expansion of its military activities, so that by 1961, "at the peak of this development there were 450 major and 2,208 minor bases . . . [and by one generation after 1939] Washington was spending $80 billion a year on its military machine (about 150 times that of 1939), had troops stationed in 119 countries and had formed military alliances with forty-eight nations" (pp. 12-13).

The fear of militarization was reiterated in 1951 by Senator Ralph Landers (a Republican from Vermont), who indicated: "We are being forced to shift the American way of life into a pattern of the garrison state. . . . Our wealth, our standard of living, the lives of our young people and our institutions are under the control of the military" (quoted in Lens, 1987, p. 13). In his farewell address, Eisenhower also tried to warn Americans of the dangers of the "military-industrial complex." How and why did this transformation take place? After 1945, the need for a strong military was justified in part by the incipient Cold War ideology of containment and anticommunism. It was also justified as a necessary adjunct to Roosevelt's notion of a "benign imperialism." With the tremendous increase in U.S. national income during the war, the need for foreign markets was great. As Lens (1987) describes it, Roosevelt

> planned for a postwar world in which the United States would exercise global domination—and he saw nothing sinister in this. In short, Roosevelt envisioned a partnership—the benign imperialism—between the United States and its client states. American business would enjoy a quantum jump in foreign trade and investment, protected by an American navy and army that would guarantee the overseas stability required by such ventures. (p. 21)

It was argued that such a world economic system, with the American military to act as global cop, would create the precondition for a warless world. Capitalism and peace were equivalent in this view. As Lens puts it, "Only the United States had the military might, economic resources—and overriding need—to establish such a system" (p. 22). Of course, the notion of benign imperialism quickly gave way to geopolitical reality. However, the economic imperatives underlying this foreign policy necessitated the creation and maintenance of a vast military machine, a set of secret organizations to carry out the covert operations that were often "required," as well as a domestic mind-set that would accept the new arrangement. Again, according to Lens:

> The American system was soon transformed from government by consent of the governed to government without the consent of the governed. The pernicious feature in all of this was not only the expansion of military influence into civilian areas from which it should have been excluded, but the injection of militarist elan throughout our society. . . . Whereas the nation was built upon the philosophical ideals of liberty, democracy, equality and peace, the basic military principles are authority, hierarchy, obedience, force and war. (p. 22)

Without getting into arguments over the founding values, it is undeniable that the "permanent war" that Lens asserts characterizes life in the modern United States has exacted certain costs in terms of public acceptance of government wrongdoing (e.g., Bay of Pigs, Watergate, Iran-Contra), the proliferation of violence as the first rather than the last resort in resolving conflict, a curtailment of civil rights at home and abroad (e.g., through the FBI's COINTELPRO), and the overthrow of sovereign governments (through either assassination or subversion). Lens asserts that, after four decades of permanent war, Americans have adjusted to a political regime in which government officials can do almost anything under the cover of such code words as national security or executive privilege, without being held legally accountable. Even in the rare instances where they are brought to trial and convicted, they are judged and treated by a different standard. (p. 7)

In essence, a policy that was initiated to advance capitalist economic interests (i.e., the unimpeded access to resources, and the opening and maintenance of foreign markets) has resulted in a militarization of U.S. society. The military now plays a significant role (either directly or indirectly) in almost every aspect of domestic life, and has moved our society in increasingly authoritarian directions.

Finally, it is important to note that one result of this authoritarianism has been the effective reproduction of dominant gender, ethnic, and racial relationships. As Harris and King (1989) state:

The militarization of culture is of particular concern to feminists [and, one could add, to ethnic and racial minorities] who have been challenging the authority of [white, middle/upper-class] men in society and working to reshape social life in ways that respect the full humanity of everyone. Sexual repression and a conscious manipulation of traditional family values by a well-financed, resurgent right-wing fundamentalist movement go hand in hand with increasing authoritarianism in every aspect of daily life. . . . With apparent ease, the U.S. public is accepting a level of disregard for other human beings and a resurgence of a Darwinian social philosophy. Militarized culture establishes itself in the life of citizens as xenophobia, a refusal to recognize the humanity of others within this country, just as soldiering abroad depends on denying the humanity of "alien" peoples. (p. 5)

CONCLUSION

The ways in which military spending (and militarism more generally) affect our lives are many and complex. Simple arguments for the necessity of strong militaries for security purposes have been undercut by early work on the military-industrial complex and iron triangles, and by more recent work on economic conversion. These examinations have demonstrated that military disbursements frequently continue for purely economic gain. In many cases, such spending actually reduces rather than enhances security, as well as weakens a nation's economic potential. More recent work, particularly by feminist scholars, has begun to unmask some of the more subtle effects of militarism on society. The linkages being identified and explicated among masculinity, aggression, and militarism offer new strategies for moving society toward greater real security. This work also provides insights into the ways in which militarism and the resultant authoritarianism reproduce gender, racial, and ethnic relationships that favor the status quo. More research is needed to elucidate some of the other impacts of militarism, which include (a) maintenance of the state's monopoly over coercive power, (b) restrictions on personal and civil liberties in the name of national security, and (c) other state ends that are furthered by a militaristic institution but are as yet underexplicated.

The phenomena that I have examined here are linked in both conceptual and pragmatic ways. Militarism and military spending certainly have impacts on local and regional economies (some positive, some negative). But it is also through institutions of the "local state" (e.g., schools, police forces, local politics and economics) that relations of gender, ethnicity, class, patriarchy, aggression, patriotism, and others are articulated and constructed. The prescription to "think globally and act locally" is apt in this connection. While militarism and the military machine appear to be national or global phenomena, the underpinnings are directly affectable at the local level. The kinds of social relations that lead to militarism (and its adverse impacts) are produced and reproduced in particular places, and must be confronted in these localities as well as in their manifestations on other scales. It is only when these underlying attributes of militarism are challenged effectively that we may begin to think about deriving any sort of peace dividend.

REFERENCES

Beneria, L., & Blank, R. (1989). Women and the economics of military spending. In A. Harris & Y. King (Eds.), *Rocking the ship of state: Toward a feminist peace politics.* Boulder, CO: Westview.

Chodorow, N. (1978). *The reproduction of mothering.* Berkeley: University of California Press.

Dupuy, R. E. (1961). *A compact history of the United States Army.* New York: Hawthorne.

Flax, J. (1978). The conflict between nurturance and autonomy in mother-daughter relations and in feminism. *Feminist Studies, 4*(2), 171-189.

Harris, A., & King, Y. (1989). Introduction. In A. Harris & Y. King (Eds.), *Rocking the ship of state: Toward a feminist peace politics.* Boulder, CO: Westview.

Hartsock, N. C. (1989). Masculinity, heroism, and the making of war. In A. Harris & Y. King (Eds.), *Rocking the ship of state: Toward a feminist peace politics.* Boulder, CO: Westview.

Lens, S. (1987). *Permanent war: The militarization of America.* New York: Schocken.

Ong, W. (1981). *Fighting for life.* Ithaca, NY: Cornell University Press.

Schmookler, A. B. (1984). *The parable of the tribes: The problem of power in social evolution.* Boston: Houghton Mifflin.

Sivard, R. L. (1989). *World military and social expenditures.* Washington, DC: World Priorities.

Stoller, R. (1968). *Sex and gender: On the development of masculinity and femininity.* New York: Science House.

Index

About the Authors

PETER ARMITAGE is an anthropologist based in St. John's, Newfoundland, Canada, and is Research Director for the Innu Nation. As an aboriginal rights activist, he was actively involved in the Innu campaign to halt military flight training. He is currently editing a book on this and similar struggles in Canada.

RICHARD BARFF is Assistant Professor of Geography at Dartmouth College. He received his Ph.D. from Indiana University in 1985. He has published several articles on employment change in New England. His interests in regional development embrace the contemporary and historical geography of the New England economy, and also the occupational structure of interregional labor migration and the transformation of industry to flexible modes of production. His current projects include analysis of labor control in nineteenth-century industrial towns in New England and the impact of immigration on the geography of internal population movements in the United States between 1975 and 1980.

NANCY ETTLINGER is Assistant Professor in the Department of Geography at The Ohio State University in Columbus. Previously, she was an Assistant Professor at the University of Nebraska. She is a graduate of the University of Oklahoma, and her research interests lie in economic geography.

JOE R. FEAGIN is Graduate Research Professor in Sociology at the University of Florida, Gainesville. His research interests include racial and ethnic relations, social problems and public policy, and urban sociology. He is the author or coauthor of more than 75 articles and 20 books, including *Free Enterprise City: Houston in Political and Economic Perspective* (1988). He is currently writing a book with

Mel Sikes, featuring hundreds of in-depth interviews with African-Americans, that demonstrates the continuing significance of race in American society.

PETER HALL was born in 1932 in London, and received his master's and doctoral degrees from the University of Cambridge. He was Lecturer in Geography at Birkbeck College, University of London, from 1957 to 1965, Reader in Geography at the London School of Economics from 1966 to 1967, and Professor of Geography at the University of Reading from 1968 to 1989. In addition, he has held the post of Professor of City and Regional Planning at the University of California at Berkeley since 1980 and has been Director of the Institute of Urban and Regional Development since 1989. His principal works include *London 2000* (1963), *World Cities* (1966), *Urban and Regional Planning* (1975), *Great Planning Disasters* (1980), *Cities of Tomorrow* (1989), and *London 2001* (1990).

GERALD JACOB was Assistant Professor of Geography and Public Planning at Northern Arizona University in 1990-1991. A graduate of the University of Chicago and the University of Colorado, Boulder, he now serves as a policy analyst and consultant to government and industry on a variety of energy and environmental issues. In 1990 his book *Site Unseen: The Politics of Siting a Nuclear Waste Repository* was published by the University of Pittsburgh Press. He is currently working on a second book about risk and public opposition to the transportation of hazardous materials, and is based in Boulder, Colorado.

ANDREW KIRBY is Professor of Geography and Regional Development and a Udall Fellow in Public Policy at the University of Arizona. His interests lie in the social, political, and economic development of places, and his recent publications have appeared in *Policy and Politics, Policy Studies Journal, Government and Policy, Urban Affairs Quarterly, Public Administration Review, Society and Space, Urban Geography, Journal for the Theory of Social Behavior, Critical Studies in Mass Communication,* and *Urban Studies.* He recently edited *Nothing to Fear: Risks and Hazards in American Society* (University of Arizona Press). *A State of Chaos: The Survival of Local Politics in the Modern State* will be published by Indiana University Press in 1992.

ANN R. MARKUSEN is Professor and Director of the Project on Regional and Industrial Economics at Rutgers University in New Jersey. Her teaching and research interests include international growth disparities and urban and regional policy, regions and regionalism, state and local economic development planning, economic analysis and planning for women, and metropolitan public finance. Her books include *The Politics of Regions* (Rowman & Littlefield, 1987), *Profit Cycles, Oligopoly and Regional Development* (MIT Press, 1985), and *Silicon Landscapes* (with Peter Hall; Allen & Unwin, 1985). She has also coauthored, with Peter Hall, Scott Campbell, and Sabina Deitrick, *The Rise of the Gunbelt*, published by Oxford University Press (1991).

ROBERT E. PARKER is Assistant Professor of Sociology at the University of Nevada, Las Vegas. His research interests include urban sociology, the sociology of work, and race and ethnic relations. He is coauthor, with Joe R. Feagin, of *Building American Cities* (1990). He has authored several other chapters on Houston, dealing with such aspects as political change and economic restructuring. He is currently engaged in an analysis of the rapid urban growth being experienced in southern Nevada.

MARVIN WATERSTONE is Associate Professor of Geography and Regional Development at the University of Arizona, where he has also been Associate Director of the Water Resources Center. A graduate of the University of Colorado, Boulder, and Rutgers University, he has published widely in the fields of policy and risk analysis. His edited collection, *Risk and Society*, was published by Kluwer in 1991.